D1314598

PREJUDICED COMMUNICATION

Prejudiced Communication

*A Social Psychological
Perspective*

~

JANET B. RUSCHER

THE GUILFORD PRESS
New York London

© 2001 The Guilford Press
A Division of Guilford Publications, Inc.
72 Spring Street, New York, NY 10012
www.guilford.com

Printed in the United States of America

This book is printed on acid-free paper.

Last digit is print number: 9 8 7 6 5 4 3 2 1

Library of Congress Cataloging-in-Publication Data

Ruscher, Janet B.
    Prejudiced communication : a social psychological perspective /
Janet B. Ruscher.
        p.   cm.
    Includes bibliographical references and index.
        ISBN: 978-1-57230-638-7

        1. Prejudices. 2. Interpersonal communication. I. Title.

BF575.P9 R87 2001
303.3′85—dc21   00-054356

For my teachers: Colleen, Eileen, David, and Susan

About the Author

Janet B. Ruscher, PhD, is an Associate Professor in the Department of Psychology at Tulane University. She earned both an MS degree and a PhD in social psychology at the University of Massachusetts–Amherst, where she also received the student publication award from Division 8 of the American Psychological Association. Her work at the University of Massachusetts, with Susan Fiske, initially focused on the relation between stereotyping and competitive interdependence, while later work focused on stigma and decisions about discontinuing interdependence. Her current research interests primarily are in stereotyping and prejudice in everyday communication, and her recent empirical work has been published in the *Journal of Personality and Social Psychology, Personality and Social Psychology Bulletin,* and the *Journal of Language and Social Psychology.* An integrative review of her research on prejudiced communication appeared in the 1998 volume of *Advances in Experimental Social Psychology.*

Preface

People communicate prejudice through a variety of means, including nonverbal behavior, particular words selected to describe outgroups, visual portrayals, and general disdain for outgroup communication patterns. Explicitly or implicitly, the prejudiced communication that results conveys stereotypic beliefs, prejudiced attitudes, or discriminatory intentions. Chapter 1 introduces several functions that prejudiced communication may serve, including the protection of ingroup dominance and status, ingroup enhancement, and sheer economy of expression. The potential roles of these functions reemerge in subsequent chapters, weaving a common thread among the various social science disciplines that speak to prejudiced communication.

Although the correspondence between language and thought admittedly is imperfect, language can provide insight into how outgroup members are cognitively represented. Taking this linguistic perspective, Chapter 2 examines how outgroups are described (and perceived) in noncomplex, negative, and stereotypic ways, as well as in ways that enhance the ingroup. These descriptions include group epithets and the linguistic intergroup bias. Through conversations that emphasize noncomplex, negative, and stereotypic views of outgroups, ingroup members develop shared stereotypes of outgroups and of individual outgroup members. Chapter 3 focuses on how these shared understandings develop and are transmitted among ingroup members.

Whereas Chapters 2 and 3 focus on communication *about* outgroup members in interpersonal settings, Chapter 4 examines prejudiced communication directed *toward* outgroup members. Drawing on social psychology and communication literatures, the chapter distinguishes between speech directed toward outgroup members who are lower in status versus speech directed toward members who are of equal status (or aspire to equal status); the former tends to be patronizing, whereas the latter tends to be controlling. Chapter 4 also explores the domain of performance feedback, primarily in organizational and school settings, as other contexts in which people may talk down to outgroup members. Continuing with the focus on outgroups as recipients of prejudiced communication, Chapter 5 explores nonverbal forms of communication, such as the facial expressions, immediacy behaviors, and status displays directed toward outgroup members. The nonverbal communication styles of outgroup members—nonstandard accents, paralinguistic qualities, and peripheral nonverbal patterns—that elicit discrimination and disdain from individuals who use standard—and purportedly superior—communication patterns are explored as well.

Moving beyond interpersonal communication into mass communication, Chapter 6 examines the role of the news media in prejudiced communication. Along with sociology and social psychology, the communication and journalism literatures provide insight into how traditionally disadvantaged groups are portrayed by the news media. Issues important to such groups may receive little or less prominent coverage, while stereotypic photographic and video images appear regularly. The first part of Chapter 7 revisits these themes in the advertising and entertainment industries, showing how prejudiced communication permeates the larger culture in which people live, while the latter part of this chapter examines two types of prejudiced speech that are extant cultural phenomena: prejudiced humor and hate speech. Whether a television sketch, advertisement, or joke transmitted over electronic mail, recipients "get" prejudiced humor precisely because stereotypes are familiar. The indirectness of prejudiced humor is then contrasted with hate speech, which involves unambiguous derogation of an individual or group; work by First Amendment scholars provides the backdrop for the discussion of hate speech, as it is studied empirically by social scientists.

Finally, Chapter 8 revisits some major themes that cut across the earlier chapters, such as the relation between prejudiced communication and status, and how stereotypic representations of minorities and women consistently emerge irrespective of whether communication is directed to them or about them in interpersonal or mass communication settings. The book concludes by commenting on empirical and theoretical gaps that the next generation of researchers who study prejudiced communication may wish to address.

Acknowledgments

This book benefited greatly from my former and current graduate students, Elizabeth Hammer, Elliott Hammer, Laura Duval, Sherry Schnake, Elizabeth Cralley, Daniel Beal, Anh Thu Burks, Kimberly O'Farrell, Alecia Santuzzi, and Christy McLendon. I am grateful for their contributions to the research, their influence on my thinking about research traditions both within and beyond social psychology, and their infinite patience while I was writing. I also thank several anonymous reviewers for their comments, as well as Seymour Weingarten, Editor-in-Chief at The Guilford Press, and the staff at Guilford for their welcome assistance with my first book. Finally, I thank my friends, colleagues, and family for astutely recognizing when I needed a break . . . and for just as astutely recognizing when I needed to remain on task.

Contents

PREJUDICED COMMUNICATION

ONE

Introduction:
The What and Why
of Prejudiced Communication

A European American interviewer interrupts a Mexican American interviewee, then leans back in his chair and folds his arms.

A jilted woman and her sister embark on a rousing session of male bashing.

A radio personality comments to his African American sidekick that he wishes all blacks would be as well behaved and well dressed as Boyz II Men.

A company's written health insurance policy extends coverage to employee spouses, but orally the company argues that the term "employee spouse" implies an opposite gender individual.

A white professor comments to her black student that the test was hard, but emphasizes that he should have studied more.

Yet another movie starring a white protagonist and his comic black sidekick hits it big in the theaters.

WHAT IS PREJUDICED COMMUNICATION?

Communication involves the transmission and reception of ideas, feelings, and expectations among individuals. The prototypic communication scenario involves one person orally transmitting a message to an-

1

other individual or a group of persons. For example, a political leader delivers a speech that blames an ethnic outgroup for various social problems. But verbal communications need not be oral, nor even originate with the witnessed communicator. For example, a bored employee may e-mail a recently received hetero-sexist joke to members of her recipient list; the message is written and, although she has chosen to transmit the message, someone else purportedly generated the prejudiced content. Communication also may be nonverbal, including the conveyance of feelings and emotions. For instance, a middle-aged woman may frown and wrinkle her nose in disgust at a young adult's pierced eyebrow. Alternatively, nonverbal behavior may communicate expectations, such as when an instructor encourages a seemingly bright student to elaborate on an orally expressed point in class. Communication even may rely heavily upon images, such as works in the plastic or performing arts, documentary films and televised news, photographs, and situation comedies on television.

On the receiving end, the prototypical receiver hears and is affected by the communicators' message. For example, the political leader who blames a particular ethnic group for troubles may incite a riot among a few like-minded extremists. He also may attract critics to condemn the message, or he may encourage supporters of less extreme positions to construct less extreme versions of the message that can sway a wider range of people. Less prototypically, recipients of electronically transmitted humor may send the message along to other residents of cyberspace or may delete the offending message in disgust. Lastly, the receiver of images learns how the world should be or seems to be—at least to some subset of the population. The receiver need not agree with a message to be affected by it.

Communication that is prejudiced or stereotypic specifically involves the explicit or implicit conveyance of stereotypic beliefs, prejudiced attitudes, or discriminatory intentions. Although prejudiced communication includes blatant forms such as hate speech, written discriminatory policies, and extreme symbolism (e.g., swastikas), a good portion of prejudiced communication is subtle. In the contemporary "politically correct" climate, many individuals recognize social and legal sanctions against blatantly prejudiced communication, so many types of prejudiced communication are less obvious than hate speech and explicit discriminatory policies. For example, when talking to outgroup members, people may close their postures, interrupt, or talk down to outgroup members more than they do when talking to ingroup members. Communicators may not always be consciously aware that these behaviors transmit beliefs that the outgroup is unworthy of greater consideration or is simply inferior, or even that they are conveying feelings of disdain or distrust. Indeed, without a direct comparison between how individuals treat ingroup and outgroup members, onlookers may fail to recognize subtle behaviors as reflecting prejudice. Similarly, verbal communication about outgroup members may not be blatantly prejudiced or discriminatory but still may convey negative thoughts and feelings. For example, people rely upon phrases that subtly convey their prejudices, as well as solidifying intergroup distinctions, simplifying their understanding of the outgroup, and justifying discrimination. A communicator may, for example, claim that an outgroup member is "aggressive" rather than noting that "he hit someone yesterday." The former, abstract characterization provides a stable disposition for predicting future behavior and may help justify dealing with the outgroup through forceful means.

Other aspects of prejudiced communication occur at less interpersonal levels and instead are manifested at the level of culture or institution. For instance, people demand implicitly that outgroups adhere to the ingroup's language patterns, and negative consequences are imposed on the outgroup when it fails to do so. This preference for one's own cultural patterns also is part of prejudiced communication. Outgroup members with heavy accents, or who look away when spoken to or use variants on the language of the dominant group, are devalued, ridiculed, or experience discrimination when attempting to enter particular institutions. On a larger scale, dominant groups can use the mass media to protect their social power by portraying outgroups in a stereotypic fashion. The dominant group also may give trivial attention to outgroup concerns and issues, or may only discuss outgroup concerns when they can be linked to negative stereotypic qualities.

As implied by the opening examples, these topics all fall within the purview of prejudiced communication. However, they vary dramatically in how well social psychologists have addressed them. The purpose of this book is to compile a body of knowledge regarding prejudiced communication, drawing upon psychology, communication studies, political science, sociology, lifespan studies, cross-cultural psychology, and discourse analysis. This body of knowledge will be critiqued through the lens of social psychology, particularly linking the theoretical literature in social psychology to the phenomena discussed in these varying disciplines. By so doing, the book proposes to provide a richer understanding of the social psychology of prejudice and stereotyping. The book will consider how communication contributes to the existence of prejudice, how prejudice is maintained and transmitted through communication, and the extent to which the deleterious effects of prejudice can be undercut through communication.

Distinctions among Related Concepts

Different disciplines use identical terms in slightly different ways. Given that this book draws upon several disciplines, some definitions of the meanings used here—traditional definitions in social psychology—are warranted. First, a *stereotype* is a specific type of schema, which is a network of beliefs that specify characteristics describing a certain concept. A stereotype is a schema about members of a social group, whether that grouping is based on gender, ethnicity, sexual orientation, nationality, regionality, or the like. The stereotype may describe people who hold a particular job (e.g., librarians are quiet, intellectual people who like antique furniture), of a racial or ethnic group (e.g., white Anglo-Saxon Protestants—WASPs—are materialistic, stiff, and exclusionary) or of a gender group (e.g., women are intuitive, love children, and are lousy drivers). The attributes that compose the stereotype often are dispositional traits, but those traits subsume behavioral episodes that somebody, once or twice, presumably witnessed. However, perceivers may characterize a behavioral episode that they have witnessed in many ways. For example, epileptic seizures may be characterized as demon possession or a medical problem, spanking children may be characterized as child abuse or as discipline, and charging interest on a loan may be characterized as a greedy abuse of others' needs or as normal business practice.

Prejudice refers to the negative feelings associated with a particular group. These negative feelings may include anger, fear, disgust, or mere discomfort. In communication settings, prejudiced attitudes often are displayed through facial expressions and peripheral nonverbal behaviors, though they can be expressed verbally as well. Sympathy also can reflect prejudice. Unlike empathy, which involves feeling along with a person, sympathy implies a sense of superiority and disdain.

Finally, *discrimination* involves treating people unjustly because of their group membership. Discrimination can range from physical harm, evaluating someone negatively, not supporting affirmative action policies, or implicitly preventing a group from acquiring status or influence. Although many discriminatory behaviors "send a message," not all discriminatory acts are communicative ones. For example, a manager's decision to hire an ingroup member instead of an outgroup member has no obvious communicative aspects unless the manager discusses that decision with someone (e.g., justifying the decision to the Equal Employment Opportunity Commission [EEOC] officer) or the company's historical hiring practices become public and others construe this history as communication of prejudice.

The distinction among stereotyping, prejudice, and discrimination is theoretically important, and each of these topics can be studied outside communication settings. For example, researchers may examine personality dimensions associated prejudiced attitudes (e.g., authoritarianism; social dominance orientation) without considering communication. Similarly, the speed at which people recall stereotypic information and other "uses" of stereotypes may be examined with little or no reference to communication. Prejudiced communication is therefore a unique blend of stereotyping, prejudice, and discrimination. It explicitly or implicitly conveys stereotypic beliefs, prejudiced attitudes, or discriminatory intentions and may be inherently discriminatory itself; the mode of communication may be oral, written, or nonverbal, as well as apparent in visual media (e.g., film).

THE FUNCTIONS
OF PREJUDICED COMMUNICATION

Prejudiced communication is pervasive because it serves a variety of functions. Functional analysis in psychology proposes that needs and motivations underlie psychological phenomena. A critical aspect of this approach is the assumption that different motivations may manifest the same surface features (Snyder & Miene, 1994). For example, two people may have negative stereotypes about homeless people. For one individual, the stereotype may serve an ego-protective function, that is, the stereotype helps the individual feel more safe and secure. This individual might blame homeless people for their dire circumstances (e.g., they are alcoholics or mental incompetents), thereby convincing him- or herself that homelessness is not a personal risk. The same stereotype may serve a different function for another individual. Rather than being afraid of becoming homeless, this individual may want to devote cognitive energy to other tasks. Thinking about homeless persons in simple stereotypic terms and behaving toward them as that stereotype prescribes allow more time for other tasks. (If one considered homeless people as people like oneself, one might feel compelled to volunteer at the soup kitchen or write letters to one's congressional representatives, rather than examining one's stock portfolio.) Prejudiced communication also serves functions such as cognitive economy and ego-defensiveness. Five such functions are described here (see Table 1); these functions are not mutually exclusive, but instead often work in concert.

Cognitive Economy and Economy of Expression

People are bombarded with myriad social stimuli and are able to focus attention on only a fraction of these stimuli at any given time. The cog-

TABLE 1. Functions of Prejudiced Speech

Function	Examples	Elaboration
Economy of expression	Group labels such as "white trash" or "JAP"	Shorthand that evokes stereotype is efficient
Group enhancement	Hostile humor	Points out superiority of ingroup
Social functions	Delegitimization, rationalization	Keeps outgroup separate for reduced contact
Ingroup dominance	Control of media, controlling nonverbals	Perpetuate stereotypes and social structure to retain ingroup status
Impression management	Bifurcation, illusion of universality	Presents nonprejudiced image to the world

nitive miser metaphor portrays the social perceiver as an individual who looks for shortcuts to help filter through these myriad stimuli. The use of stereotypes is one such shortcut. Stereotypes render the world more predictable, by compacting some of this information into manageably sized units. The unique attributes of a particular person are lost during the compacting, but if the person is not deemed relevant, a stereotypic view is considered sufficient for present purposes (Fiske & Neuberg, 1990). By using a stereotype, social perceivers can turn attention elsewhere—toward stimuli currently more important to them (Macrae, Milne, & Bodenhausen, 1994). Returning to the earlier example, thinking about homeless people as alcoholic bums simplifies a heterogeneous group into a single prototype and enables the perceiver to turn attention toward his or her own personal concerns. Note that recognizing the utility of stereotypes does not excuse people from using them or imply that stereotypes must be adaptive in the long run (especially for the stereotyped target!). Instead, stereotypes exist because they provide something that the perceiver wants or, at least momentarily, needs (even if the stereotype is an inaccurate generalization).

Cognitive economy also is served by prejudiced communication, by providing communicators with economical expressions. Speakers follow implicit communication rules, which include saying only as much as needed to meet the communication goal. As discussed more thoroughly in Chapter 2, labels notoriously provide such economical expressions. Referring to someone as a nerd, jock, white trash, or Jewish American Princess ("JAP") evokes a vivid mental picture in the mind of the hearer, implies a host of dispositional traits and behaviors, and prescribes how to interact with the person (if interaction is necessary). A picture may convey a thousand words, but one word also can convey a 100,000-pixel image.

At least when conversing with fellow ingroup members, cognitive economy also is served by the presumption of shared stereotypes. By virtue of shared culture, people implicitly recognize that knowledge of certain stereotypes is shared. Two white coworkers with generally shared impressions of Latina women, for example, quickly can arrive at a consensus about the new Latina clerk by honing in on her stereotypic attributes or on attributes that are sufficiently ambiguous to be interpreted in a stereotypic fashion. The first worker may roll her eyes at the clerk's collection of salsa CDs, and the second worker may smile and then subtly gesture at a prominent golden necklace. The nonverbal communication between the two white coworkers is facilitated by the shared stereotype. They need few words to convey their disdain for the clerk and her culture, and may rely on the shared stereotype to inform later verbal conversations. Chapter 3 considers how these shared stereotypes may develop and how they are used by small groups.

In the case of mass communication, photographs and video images economically transmit sentiment, stereotypes, and overall perceptions of outgroup members. For example, as discussed in Chapter 7, television and film characters who conform to stereotypes are readily recognized by the audience and easily convey the filmmaker's message. Alternately, images in the news media (Chapter 6) can perpetuate stereotypes by presenting too few or too many of a particular type of image. Images of homeless individuals, for example, disproportionately represent African Americans (beyond actual statistics), perpetuating the association between poverty and ethnic minority status. Again, the use of such images need not be consciously intentioned. Instead, their use may reflect the goals of economical expression or simply reflect the fact that mass communicators, like most communicators, possess stereotypes and rely upon them when retelling a story or generating an image.

Ego Protection and Group Enhancement

A good deal of evidence suggests that people typically maintain positive illusions about their own qualities and about their prospects for a healthy and prosperous life (S. E. Taylor & Brown, 1988). By comparing the self to allegedly less fortunate others, people can feel superior and bolster their self-views. Some evidence suggests that people with high self-esteem are most likely to engage in downward social comparisons when coping with a threat (Gibbons & McCoy, 1991). In intergroup settings, downward social comparisons may be reflected in intergroup bias, which is a predilection to view the ingroup more positively than the outgroup. Given that group memberships often are important sources of self-esteem, intergroup bias sometimes increases under threat conditions (Thompson & Crocker, 1990). Interestingly, people with certain types of high self-esteem often are the most prejudiced (Crocker & Luhtanen, 1990), especially if they are from the ethnically dominant culture (Verkuyten, 1996).

Stereotypes arguably are part of a person's cultural worldview. A cultural worldview provides a set of standards by which individuals should live; if individuals abide by these standards, the worldview also provides a promise of real or symbolic immortality (Schimel et al., 1999). When the worldview is threatened by mortality salience, people lash out against outgroups who hold different worldviews. For example, mortality salience increases disparaging evaluation of religious outgroups (J. Greenberg et al., 1990) and ethnic outgroups (Schimel et al., 1999). Interestingly, outgroup members whose attributes are inconsistent with the cultural stereotype are disparaged most, presumably because they are most threatening to the person's worldview.

These ego-protective and group-enhancing functions easily are met via prejudiced communication. Ingroup members may discuss the outgroup among themselves, choosing expressions that bolster the ingroup and downgrade the outgroup (Chapter 2). Hostile humor pokes fun at the alleged foibles and shortcomings of outgroup members, and therefore also helps serve this function (Chapter 7). Tales of the Polish or blonde person's alleged idiocy, the Jewish American Princess's presumably crass materialism, and the homosexual man's supposedly effeminate proclivity for interior decorating may send members of their respective outgroups into gales of laughter, but also implicitly attest to the superiority of the ingroup's values and qualities. Conversing about the outgroup—through humor or otherwise—also validates an individual's viewpoints (Chapter 3). "Everybody" appears to perceive the outgroup as possessing negative qualities, so this assessment is presumed to be correct. Thus, not only is the ingroup deemed superior in its qualities, but its consensually validated judgments of others are taken to be beyond reproach.

Ingroup members also may intend that their prejudiced communications reach outgroup recipients. Outgroup members may be disparaged by subtly talking down to them, interrupting them (Chapter 4), or by displaying nonverbal postures that convey superiority such as folding the arms and not providing encouraging nods (Chapter 5). Outgroups may be "allowed" to overhear ingroup conversations about them in which they are described with derogatory group epithets or hostile humor. Persons in need of group enhancement or ego protection legally cannot cause physical harm to outgroup members or their property, terminate outgroup employees without just cause, or engage in many other forms of discrimination. But much prejudiced speech is protected under the First Amendment (Chapter 7), such as "allowing" an outgroup member to overhear a prejudiced joke, which makes prejudiced communication an ideal way to fulfill ego-defensive functions.

Not that only negative qualities of the outgroup are the focus of ingroup members. At times, the ingroup's self-protective needs may be served by pointing toward extremely positive outgroup qualities. When the positive qualities of a target are unambiguous and highly superior, people sometimes aggrandize the target (Alicke, LoSchiavo, Zerbst, & Zhang, 1997). Exalting the target allows individuals to create a believable story and appear magnanimous, while rendering the target as an inappropriate comparison to anyone, let alone the speaker. For example, a reasonably bright student would seem envious if he disparaged the intellect of the class valedictorian who won a series of awards and fellowships. By exaggerating the valedictorian's abilities and commitment (e.g., sincerely hypothesizing that she will find the cure for AIDS), the speaker suggests that the valedictorian is too gifted to serve as a fair comparison.

When that target is an outgroup member, additional group protective motives also may be apparent. Consider statements like Jimmy the Greek's claim that athletic prowess among blacks stemmed from slave owners' selective breeding processes. Although this statement acknowledges an alleged athletic superiority of African Americans (a strongly held stereotype among European Americans), the statement robs the particular African Americans who are stellar athletes of their accomplishments. From this viewpoint, their accomplishments stem from the "intelligence" of whites, rather than from the hard work and gifts of particular African American individuals. The self-esteem of nonathletic whites is preserved by alleging unusual circumstances that lead to black athletic superiority. Another example of this perverse logic is apparent in non-Jews' stereotype of Jews as clever. Jean-Paul Sartre notes that anti-Semitic individuals readily admit to the intelligence of Jewish people, because intelligence also means that Jews are dangerous. Dangerousness outweighs the potentially positive attribute of intellect, making the ingroup feel better about itself and, as seen in the next section, helps justify discriminatory behavior. Thus, even positive qualities can be given a negative slant, in order to help the ingroup defend its self-esteem.

The statements and conversation that ingroups share among

themselves not only allow the ingroup to portray itself in a (relatively more) favorable light. As detailed in Chapter 3, such conversations also help the ingroup define itself. When talking about outgroup members, people tend to focus on the qualities that differentiate "them" from "us." Like a T. S. Eliot poem, ingroups partially define themselves in terms of what they are not. For instance, during their rousing bout of male bashing, the women in the opening example point out a set of negative qualities that men presumably have and, by implication, that women do not possess. The ingroup is different, and overall it is deemed better than the outgroup.

Social Functions

Prejudiced language also serves several social functions: avoiding contact, detachment, and delegitimization. Avoiding contact with people from other groups is tolerated reasonably well by society (Graumann & Wintermantel, 1989) and often is not labeled as prejudice (Fiske & Ruscher, 1993). Instead, people can provide verbal accounts for their avoidance behavior that invoke nonprejudiced reasons that their ingroup audience, who also do not wish to appear prejudiced, readily may accept. A white couple that moves to a white suburb cites better schools there as necessitating the move, teenaged siblings avoid visiting their grandmother by claiming the need to do schoolwork, and a men's club alleges that admitting women would violate tradition. Admittedly, sometimes these reasons are genuine and nonprejudiced. However, it bears mentioning that these verbal accounts and denials of prejudice seem most prevalent exactly when the person already has decided to avoid the outgroup member (Ruscher, 1998). Interestingly, the reduced opportunity for contact also reduces avoidant individuals' perceptions of themselves as prejudiced. If one does not interact with outgroup members, one will not get into fights with them, fail to hire them, or say something that may be interpreted as discriminatory. The global act of avoiding contact, which is justified with other plausible explanations, ironically can convince the person that he or she is not prejudiced.

The separation into groups also creates detachment, which is maintained by prejudiced communication. People often experience fear or loathing of individuals whose circumstances are considerably worse than their own. To cope with these negative feelings, people detach themselves and cover their tracks with rhetoric. "Public housing" is the term used, more often than not, for a collection of buildings in poorly maintained neighborhoods inhabited by people from a specific ethnic or racial minority. "Nursing homes" and "acute care facilities" usually are places where elders spend their remaining days. People can avoid thinking about the poor and the aged by putting them in separate places and then explaining the reasons for institutionalizing the separation. Once people collectively stop thinking about such outgroups, they may fail to give serious consideration to alternative situations (e.g., assisted living facilities or home health care for elderly persons) that potentially are more beneficial and financially viable in the long run.

At the most extreme end of the social functions is delegitimization. Delegitimization involves the reconstruction of a group or individuals into something less than human or, at best, into people who are not part of society because they allegedly fail to act within the limits of accepted norms (Bar-Tal, 1989). For example, the delegitimized are labeled gooks, savages, imperialists, outcasts, and huns. The greater the physical and cultural differences are, the easier delegitimization appears to be (Bar-Tal, 1989); language helps emphasize these differences and transmit their apparent existence among individuals. Delegitimization also may be institutionalized, and used to justify mass killing or persecution. Adolf Hitler, for example, spoke of Jews in the following way:

> For hundreds of years Germany was good enough to receive these elements, although they possessed nothing except *infectious* political and physical diseases. (1939, cited in Baynes, 1942, p. 738, emphasis added)

To Hitler, the Jews were "elements" not people. Further, they were an infection, like so many rats who brought upon a plague. The most dramatic examples of delegitimization often are found during wartime, cutting across cultures and nations. Delegitimization is used to justify a range of extreme behaviors, such as the European and European American enslavement of Africans, the Nazi's extermination of the Jews, and the United States' forcing the Nisei (second-generation Japanese Americans) into camps during the Second World War. More contemporary examples, unfortunately, are not difficult to find. For example, criticized for napalming villages in Vietnam, U.S. Gen. William Westmoreland countered, "These Asians don't value life the way we do." By inferring that one's enemy possesses a nonhuman quality (not valuing life), killing seemingly is justified.

Protecting the Power of the Dominant Group

Another function of prejudiced communication is to protect the dominant group's privileged access to power and resources. For example, people from certain groups may be restricted from holding power. The expression the "white man's burden" implied that Native Americans, Africans, and other alleged "savages" lacked the moral and intellectual capabilities to control their own fates. Women and blacks traditionally have been referred to as "children," again explaining why they cannot wield power. Such powers include the right to vote and to own property, rights granted to most people only recently in the history of Western civilization. In the early 1990s, a major restaurant chain enjoined managers to "lighten up" the service staff, particularly waiters and waitresses, essentially restricting people of color to behind-the-scenes jobs or to no jobs with that company at all. Directly and intentionally, the ingroup protects its power.

Dominant groups also use more subtle means of communication to protect ingroup resources. For example, African Americans traditionally have had little influence over the news and media, and issues important to their culture receive less media attention than issues important to dominant groups (e.g., Daniel & Allen, 1988). The role of the media in serving this function will be considered more thoroughly in Chapter 6. In the realm of interpersonal communication, interviewees who are from the outgroup experience less encouraging interviews (Word, Zanna, & Cooper, 1974) or are evaluated poorly if they have a pronounced ethnic or regional accent (Cargile, 1997). As discussed in Chapter 5, such interpersonal communication behaviors and preferences can decrease the likelihood of employment and other types of success.

Despite the undeniable discrimination that people from particular groups experience, individuals often only recognize the discrimination that their *group* experiences. However, they tend to underestimate personal discrimination (D. M. Taylor, Wright, & Porter 1994). Prejudiced communication partly may be to blame, because the media usually highlights only profound examples of discrimination, so the individual may feel well off by comparison (D. M. Taylor et al., 1994). Another possibility is that, in this politically correct climate, people are more likely to be exposed to prejudiced communication that is directed at the group. Graffiti and propaganda often slander groups, not individuals; if these modes do target individuals, the odds are relatively low that the particular individual who is targeted is oneself. The impact that graffiti, propaganda, and overheard comments have on society is considered more completely in Chapter 7.

Impression Management

Finally, prejudiced communication may mask the appearance of prejudice and allow people to maintain valued egalitarian self-perceptions.

People often recognize that expressing prejudiced beliefs about many groups is unacceptable in contemporary society (Dunton & Fazio, 1997) and that sometimes there are social (and occasionally legal) sanctions against such expressions. Denying or masking prejudice through communication therefore seems a reasonable strategy. As already noted, people may deny prejudice or provide verbal accounts for alleged discrimination when observers are most likely to infer prejudice (Ruscher, 1998). In the stories that they tell, people portray themselves as innocent victims of the outgroup's inappropriate and bizarre behaviors (van Dijk, 1987). Examples of these stories appear in Chapter 2.

People also engage in bifurcation (Allport, 1954/1989) or concessions (van Dijk, 1984) when attempting to appear nonprejudiced. Bifurcation details a difference between some acceptable subgroup of the outgroup and its typically unacceptable members. Statements that begin with "Some of my best friends are . . . " often end by pointing out the negative qualities of the group. The speaker hopes to persuade the listener that prejudice only should be inferred if the entire group is disparaged. This verbal strategy resembles the cognitive strategy of subtyping or subgrouping, in which certain classes of the outgroup are cordoned off in order to preserve the overall stereotype. Another type of impression-managing communication is concession. A concession allows that a negative assertion about an outgroup occasionally describes the ingroup as well. For example, a Dutch communicator speaking about foreigners might say, "They ruin our park here. Of course, also some of the Dutch children do this" (van Dijk, 1984, p. 127). As with bifurcation, the speaker is trying to seem fair-minded and less prejudiced (but also to make a prejudiced point).

Finally, people mask their prejudice by providing "evidence" that their claims are true. They may cite statistics or case examples from the media, ignoring the possibility of inaccuracy in the evidence or that the evidence was collected in a biased fashion. The alleged consensus of others also provides evidence. Presumably unbiased others are called upon to vouch for the speaker's assertions (van Dijk, 1987). Alternatively, people may claim that "everybody thinks so." Allport called such claims the illusion of universality. Because consensus may be perceived as a proxy for accuracy (Funder, 1987), what "everybody" believes is presumed to be true and unbiased.

CHAPTER SUMMARY

Prejudiced communication encompasses a wide range of phenomena, from ethnic labeling and sexist humor to discouraging nonverbal behavior and propagandistic use of the mass media. Prejudiced communication allows communicators to convey their beliefs in a concise way, stirring negative feelings and eliciting prejudiced thoughts in the minds of their listeners. By pointing to alleged inferiorities of the outgroup, prejudiced communication also can help the ingroup maintain its self-esteem. The lines drawn between groups also allow ingroups to detach themselves from groups with whom they do not desire contact. In dramatic cases, rhetoric and labeling delegitimizes the outgroup and attempts to justify extermination, enslavement, and imprisonment. The ingroup also may use communication in more subtle ways, for the express purpose of protecting its own power, influence, and resources. Nonverbal behaviors elicit less than stellar performances from outgroup members, and seemingly vindicate the ingroup from appearing prejudiced for the negative decisions that it may make. Finally, prejudiced communication aids impression management efforts. The irony is that assertions denying or masking the appearance of prejudice often are, in and of themselves, prejudiced communications.

~

TWO

Language That Divides

Words, like Nature, half reveal and half conceal the Soul within.
—ALFRED LORD TENNYSON

LANGUAGE AS REPRESENTED THOUGHT

Two of the primary roles of language are to transmit information and to maintain social interactions (Kintsch, 1994). But when people desire to convey information or develop a shared understanding with someone, they are faced with an impressive array of possibilities regarding which particular words to use (Fromkin & Rodman, 1988). For example, in describing her new employer to a friend, a woman might claim that her employer either (1) is *smart* or *shrewd*, (2) is *aggressive* or *assertive*, or (3) *asks her to fetch coffee* or *treats her like a slave*. The italicized expressions within each of these pairs may reference the same objective behavior, but they certainly connote something different about the employer. The particular words may be selected by the woman to conjure up a specific image in the mind of her friend, but they also may reflect in part how the woman thinks about her new boss. Moreover, what the woman fails to mention might reflect what she prefers not to tell her friend, but may also indicate that certain aspects of her boss's personality or behavior have never grabbed her attention. She may not, for example, have paid much attention to her employer's apparent marital status, religious background, or skeptical nature, because these attributes may be unimportant to her; she may not use these qualities typically as dimensions or categories by which to form impressions.

Proponents of linguistic analysis argue that thoughts can be represented by verbal propositions, such as utterances and written communications (Chafe, 1979; McGuire, 1968). These verbal propositions can provide insight into how speakers view a target of the communication, as well as reflecting what they wish others to believe. Even though the translation from thought to language is imperfect, language can provide insight into how people mentally represent the social world (Krauss & Chiu, 1998).

Consider, for example, how people differentially view the self versus how they view other people. Compared to knowledge of other people, individuals possess more insight into the contextual reasons underlying their own actions. One also clearly experiences the self as an agent, that is, as acting from specific intentions in each given situation. Other people, in contrast, are simply part of one's situation. What others "do" is perceived less in terms of agency and more as a result of who they happen to be. Consequently, one tends to explain one's own actions in terms of the situation, while explaining other people's actions in term of their dispositional qualities. A first-year college student therefore might say, "I decided to attend Tulane because of its solid African-Diaspora Studies program. My new roommate is here because he's insecure about leaving the New Orleans area." This student explains his own college choice in terms of program attractiveness (situation) but his roommate's choice in terms of insecurity (disposition). This differential pattern of explanation is termed the actor-observer effect, and support for the effect is abundant (Fiske & Taylor, 1991).

If people think differently about the self versus how they think about others, then the particular words that they use might reflect this distinction. In one of the earliest systematic social psychological investigations of linguistics, William J. McGuire and Claire V. McGuire (1986) asked 1,000 participants to "tell us about your family" and "tell us about school." The researchers then examined what type of verbs participants used when they described the self versus when they described others. One of the most striking findings was that when participants described themselves they used proportionately more action verbs (e.g., "move," "helped") than when they described other people. A similar pattern emerged regardless of whether the response was oral (82% vs. 51%) or written (84% vs. 33%). Thus, the choice of verbs appears to reflect a perpetual recognition of one's own agency but a tendency to be less aware of others' agency. That is, language appears to mimic the actor-observer bias. The present chapter examines how similar logic regarding the thought–language relation is applied to representation of outgroup members.

REPRESENTATION OF OUTGROUP MEMBERS

How people think about outgroup members also may be betrayed by the particular words that they select for describing them. For example, descriptions of outgroup members parallel representations of "them" as being all alike and as possessing stereotypic qualities. Outgroups also may be portrayed less favorably than ingroups, or as barely worthy of attention. These differences correspond roughly to social psychological research regarding several phenomena: outgroup homogeneity effects, stereotyping, intergroup bias, and exclusion.

Outgroup Homogeneity and Noncomplexity

A considerable amount of research indicates that people construe outgroup members as "all alike" and in a relatively noncomplex fashion. People do not distinguish easily among outgroup members (Malpass & Kravitz, 1969) and perceive greater ingroup variability than outgroup variability. For example, men and women rate their gender outgroup as being more homogeneous than they rate their gender ingroup (Park & Rothbart, 1982). This differential perception of variability is termed the outgroup homogeneity effect, and it is relatively stronger than the corresponding ingroup heterogeneity effect (Mullen & Hu, 1989). The outgroup homogeneity effect also is relatively stronger and more consistently observed with naturally occurring groups such as different professions or colleges than with artificially created groups (Ostrom & Sedikides, 1992). Conceivably, construing true outgroup members as all alike provides a sense of welcome predictability: If natural outgroup members are seen as possessing similar characteristics, predicting behavior—and what that behavior might mean to the self and to the ingroup—is facilitated. Moreover, people may believe that real-world outgroups act as a group rather than as individuals, making differences among individual outgroup members seem unimportant (for a recent discussion, see M. B. Brewer & Harasty, 1996).

Less complex impressions of outgroup members than of ingroup members also is a common research finding. Complexity involves the use of fewer aspects to describe a concept, as well as more overlap among the dimensions of those aspects. For example, a employer might think about his secretary as (1) an employee who takes instructions well and is concerned about others and (2) a mother of two who does what her husband tells her to do and worries about her children. The qualities of these two roles overlap considerably, rendering the overall impression low in complexity. Conversely, the same employer

may view his romantic partner as (1) a lover who is giving and demanding, (2) a tennis player who is competitive and athletic, and (3) an
accountant who is detailed and committed to clients. This latter impression revolves around a greater number of roles, and the qualities
of those roles overlap very little. Compared to the perception of the
secretary, the impression of the romantic partner is more complex.

Consistent with the notion of less complex impressions of outgroups, older and younger people use fewer dimensions through
which to construe members of the other age group (Linville, 1982). In
similar fashion, people might think about their ingroup members with
respect to college major, favorite sports team, intelligence, and extra-
version (e.g., "My friend Jane is a really outgoing psychology major
who likes the Chicago Bulls"). Outgroup members, in contrast, are
viewed along fewer dimensions (e.g., "Jim, in Fraternity X, is a Dallas
Cowboys fan"). To the extent that ingroup members use the same few
dimensions for thinking about several members of the same outgroup,
those outgroup members are likely to seem relatively similar to one another. Noncomplex impressions therefore may contribute to perceptions of outgroup homogeneity.

INCLUSIVENESS

These perceptions of outgroup homogeneity and noncomplexity are
evident in statements that explicitly point to the similarities among
outgroup members. In his classic treatment of prejudice and stereotyping, *The Nature of Prejudice*, Allport (1954/1989, p. 196) observed,
"When a Jew of our acquaintance achieves a goal, we may say quite
automatically– 'the Jews are so clever.'" People orally express these
perceived—and stereotypic—similarities among outgroup members,
generalizing from the single instance to the group. In a systematic examination of this pattern using gender outgroups, Harasty (1997) recently provided empirical evidence for Allport's observation. In her
study, same-sex dyads discussed American men or American women
for 5 minutes, then discussed whichever group they had not yet discussed for an additional 5 minutes. Harasty expected that in these relatively unrestricted conversations, dyads would describe outgroups in
more inclusive terms than they would describe ingroup members.
Women, for example, would focus on men in general rather than on
particular men. The lowest level of inclusiveness characterizes the
behavior as pertaining to a specific individual, then proceeds toward
more abstract characterizations at the level of subgroups, social categories, and global levels. For example, if Ellen, a woman from a particular sorority, divulges personal information about a classmate, a nonin-

clusive statement might be "Ellen is gossipy." Proceeding to higher levels of inclusiveness, the statements might be "Women at that sorority are gossipy," then "Sorority women are gossipy," and, most globally, "Women are gossipy." As she expected, Harasty found that both men and women described gender outgroups with the most abstract global levels. She also found that these global comments tended to be negative, which suggests that outgroups not only are viewed as "all alike" but also may be seen with a negative slant—or at least as more negative than the ingroup.

Harasty (1997) also observed greater discussion of specific exemplars when the discussion concerned the outgroup than when the discussion centered on the ingroup. That is, people often discussed specific individuals who belonged to the gender outgroup. On the surface, this finding is at variance with theoretical models that would suggest knowledge of specific individuals could undercut perceptions of outgroup homogeneity. That is, if people have knowledge about specific outgroup members, why would they also speak about the outgroup in global terms? One possibility noted by Harasty is that knowledge of specific exemplars does not always erase the outgroup homogeneity effect (see also Park & Judd, 1989). She also noted that the type of outgroup exemplars mentioned may not be well differentiated and may only be known for a single attribute (i.e., the impressions of the particular individuals are not particularly complex). An alternative possibility is that outgroup exemplars are qualitatively different than ingroup exemplars, not necessarily in terms of differentiation but in terms of prototypicality; van Dijk (1984) notes, for example, that speakers invoke prototypical exemplars in order to illustrate the stereotypical qualities of the outgroup. Speculating with respect to Harasty's (1997) data, one possibility is that people describe the stereotypic behavior of a particular outgroup member in order to illustrate a global quality previously mentioned in the discussion. The exemplar is used as evidence that the general perception is veridical.

It also bears mentioning that, although some similarities among mental representations of and speech about many outgroups may exist, differences may exist for particular aspects of mental representation and speech. At least in the contemporary United States, individuals have a good deal of contact with members of each gender (i.e., cross-sex siblings play together; most schools and places of employment are gender integrated), so people typically possess more acquaintance exemplars for gender outgroups than they possess for racial, national, or socioeconomic outgroups (Fiske & Stevens, 1993). The media may provide additional exemplars from outgroups other than gender outgroups, but these exemplars may be stereotypic or, on average, less representative of the groups from which they purportedly hail (see Chapters 6 and 7). Conceivably, with outgroups for whom fewer exemplars genuinely are known, discussion of ingroup exemplars might exceed discussion of outgroup exemplars.

GROUP EPITHETS

The simplification of the outgroup also is manifested in the terms that people use to describe outgroup members. Group epithets, or "ethnophaulisms," are terms used to describe outgroup members, usually in a less than savory fashion. Ethnophaulisms (from the Greek *ethnos*, "nation" or "people," and *phaulizo*, "to disparage") specifically are ethnic slurs that reflect this simplification. Examples of group epithets include "micks" and "harps" as references to Irish persons, "bitches" and "skirts" as references to women, and "darkies" and "pickaninnies" as references to African American individuals.

Epithets boast varying etymologies, which provide insight into how outgroups are—or historically have been—perceived. For example, research demonstrates that perceivers are sensitive especially to characteristics that minimize within-group variability and maximize between-group variability (Wilder, 1981); that is, people hone in upon information that separates "us" from "them." Not surprisingly, then, a large number of epithets point out intergroup differences with respect to alleged physical characteristics (e.g., darkie, redshanks, skirt), cultural and eating practices (e.g., porker, spaghetti eater, frog), and names (e.g., Paddy, Heiny, Guido; for a review see Allen, 1990). The individual's unique qualities are ignored, and she or he can be construed instead through a simple stereotype. Group epithets therefore emphasize the person's group membership rather than the person's individuality. They are the epitome of economical expression because, in time, ingroup members know what they connote, how the speaker feels about the group, and how the speaker intends that the group be treated.

Group epithets are observed in majority or dominant groups, as well as in groups that are numerical minorities or who possess relatively less sociopolitical power (Allen, 1990). Allen notes, for example, that African Americans and Spanish-speaking Americans historically have used insulting expressions for European Americans (e.g., marshmallow, white meat, gringo). Group epithets also are not a uniquely American phenomenon. For instance, native Japanese individuals were less than welcoming of the first Christian missionaries to Japan, which was reflected in the Japanese word for Christians: *Kirisutan*. *Kirisutan* (from *kiri*, to cut, and *suto*, person) essentially translates as someone who should be cut into pieces and so holds a negative connotation to Japanese individuals. The use of epithets therefore appears to range across cultures and statuses.

Some epithets seem to reduce outgroups to the social roles that the ingroup believes outgroup members hold, again implying *what* rather than *who* an outgroup member is. Outgroup members are tools to be used by the ingroup, rather than as individuals who possess unique qualities, needs, and gifts. For instance, many terms for women are highly sexualized (Allen, 1990); there are 220 English words for sexually promiscuous females, compared to 20 for sexually promiscuous males (J. Stanley, 1973, cited in Spender, 1980). The implication is that women are viewed often as sexual objects or in sexualized roles. A woman may be called a "piece of ass" and "tail," along with more taboo expressions. African American women are called "dark meat" and "brown sugar." Women of Asian descent sometimes are called "cherry blossoms," pairing the meekness of the Asian female stereotype with a pun on virginity. Sexualized terms for men, although they exist, are relatively fewer than sexualized terms for women. Beyond gender outgroups, ethnic outgroups also may be referenced in terms of the purposes that they serve for the ingroup. Terms like "cotton picker" or "coolie," for example, focus on the use of African American individuals and Chinese immigrants, respectively, as sources of cheap (and historically exploited) labor.

Many epithets, at face value, may not seem provocative or insulting to individuals who do not belong to the group at which they are directed. The receiver's perception that the speaker is using the term as an insult—or its underlying implications—is what makes a term especially provocative. The expression "boy" may seem quite neutral out of context, but it takes on a particularly negative connotation when used by a European American to address an African American male (Fromkin & Rodman, 1988). Like many terms for African Americans, "boy" implies that the individual is a child and needs to be governed. He cannot make his own decisions correctly, is a slave to his passions and superstitions, and is subordinate to the speaker. In addition, whites once commonly referred to black males, irrespective of age, as "boys," so the term also alludes to blacks once being slaves and second-class citizens. In other cases, epithets are bastardized versions of concepts or words that are important to the group, essentially robbing the group of important sources of pride and identity (or at least sullying those sources). For example, the expression "wop" used in reference to Italian Americans may derive from the word "guapo," meaning a handsome young man. Italians in the United States apparently used the expression "guapo" as a greeting, much as people contemporarily might greet a friend with "Hey, man. How you doing?" The expression was shortened by non-Italians, not in a well-meaning fashion, to "wop." "Wop" eventually then developed a dual meaning "*with-out-papers*," implying that Italians attempted to enter the United States by illegal means (Allen, 1990).

Expressions referring to outgroup members eventually may be adapted into common parlance, even when outgroup members are not the specific topic of conversation (Allen, 1990). Reneging on a bet is "welshing," financially cheating or unfairly bargaining is "jewing someone down," and the foolhardiness accompanying inebriation is called "dutch courage." Any reckless person may be termed an "Indian," a cruel person may be called a "Turk," and an unintelligent person may be called a "Polack." Although not directed specifically at the outgroup, the use of these expressions in communication helps a culture maintain a link between negative attributes and a particular group.

Until recently, most of the scholarly work on group epithets has been largely descriptive. Most importantly, very little work addresses how the use of such terms reflect variations in underlying representations, both with respect to the particular flavor of the epithet and the underlying complexity. For example, people with particular kinds of beliefs about outgroups conceivably would use group epithets akin to those beliefs. For example, in their discussion of ambivalent sexism, Peter Glick and Susan T. Fiske (1996) argue that some male sexism toward women reflects an idealization of and a desire to care for women; they term this form of sexism "benevolent." Other sexism is "hostile," reflecting a view of relations with women as conflictual and a distaste for women's attempts to obtain or wield power. One might expect that individuals high in benevolent sexism would use epithets that imply femininity, idealization, or women's need to receive care and protection (e.g., skirt, angel, dolls). Conversely, individuals high in hostile sexism probably would use hostile epithets (e.g., bitch, femi-nazi) that reflect the presumed conflict between the sexes. Such findings therefore would demonstrate not only that people use group epithets in their descriptions of outgroup members but that they use the epithets that best correspond to their particular underlying cognitive representation of the group.

Another individual difference in proclivity toward using group epithets, at least in describing individual outgroup members, might be impression complexity or impression stereotypicness. People can and do form nonstereotypic impressions of particular outgroup members, typically when they are dependent upon those individuals for desired outcomes or when they must justify their impressions to an important third party (for a review see Fiske & Neuberg, 1990). From the perceiver's point of view, stereotyping such an outgroup member risks not understanding his or her unique qualities, qualities that potentially will help obtain the desired outcomes or that may have been considered by the third-party judge. Under such conditions, although the group to which the target belongs remain part of the impression, it ceases to serve as the organizing theme for the impression. Presumably, once the target no longer is construed as a typical member of her or his group, group epithets are deemed less appropriate. And, given that many group epithets carry a negative connotation, they probably are used less for outgroup members who are not only individuated but also well liked.

Mullen and his colleagues (see Mullen, 1991; Mullen & Johnson, 1993) have taken a rare empirical approach to understanding the relation between group epithets and underlying representation. Mullen has argued that as the proportionate size of the ingroup increases, the outgroup is perceived as increasingly homogeneous. If a group is more homogeneous, fewer types of ethnic epithets will be used. For example, if only a few individuals in one's social world hail from a particular ethnic group, the ingroup might characterize them along physical traits only, rather than adding terms concerning the kinds of food that they eat or proposing surname commonalties. That is, group size should covary with cognitive complexity, the extent to which a concept is viewed in a multidimensional, integrated fashion (see Figure 1). In a pair of studies, Mullen and Johnson (1993) found support for this latter proposition. In the first study, they considered the ethnophaulisms identified by Allen (1983) with respect to the group size (as indexed by the U.S. Census reports of 1880, 1930, and 1970). Their analysis demonstrated clearly that group size predicted the complexity of the labels used to describe outgroup members. Groups whose representation in the United States was proportionately small (e.g., Australians, Saudi Arabians, Ukrainians) were described by fewer types of ethnophaulisms than groups whose representation was proportionately larger (e.g., Irish, Italians).

The arrangement of the ovals in Figure 1 reflect the distinction between a noncomplex (and smaller) group and a complex (and larger) group. Group epithets for the smaller group of Australians cluster around names and behaviors, but there are relatively few epithets of either type. In contrast, group epithets for the larger group (Irish) are abundant; these epithets cluster around a greater number of types (i.e. names, foods, and behaviors), and there are numerous examples within in each type.

In their second study, Mullen and Johnson (1993) selected five eth-

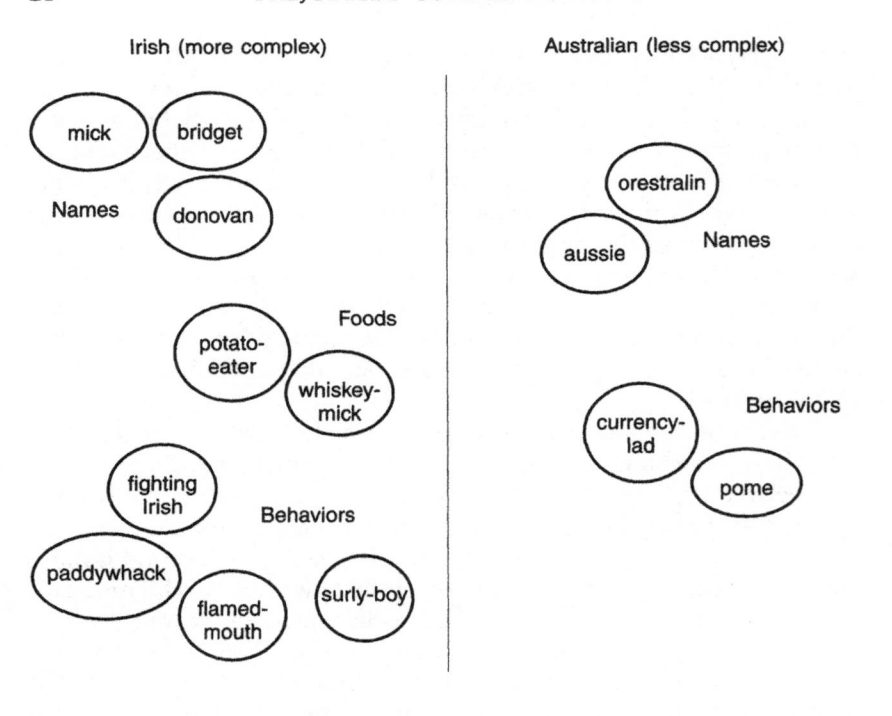

FIGURE 1. Ethnophaulisms clustered by type. More types are used for large groups such as the Irish, indicating greater complexity.

nic groups that had cultural similarities but who were geographically dispersed (Australians, British Canadians, English, Scots, and Welsh). Participants at a university in the United States then received a sheet of stickers that contained the ethnophaulisms for one of the five groups. The researchers asked participants to place the terms that were central to their idea of the group near the center of the page (and the least central further away) and to put the similar terms close together. As expected, cognitive complexity and group size were strongly related. Larger groups such as the English and the British Canadians, for example, tended to have a more complex array of ethnophaulisms than did smaller groups such as the Welsh.

The reduced complexity in representation of smaller groups implies that they are mentally represented as prototypes, that is, as typical instances of a category rather than as exemplars or as unique individuals. Work on ethnophaulisms therefore provides some evidence that people from smaller groups are perceived as mere members of their social group. Moreover, if members of smaller outgroups are represented as prototypes, they conceivably may be more likely to be called by group epithets in natural discourse. At present, this hypothesis has not been tested in a direct experimental fashion. Less directly but no less interesting, Mullen, Rozell, and Johnson (1996) demonstrated this pattern in Shakespeare's plays. For example, the greater the number of Christian characters present on stage during *The Merchant of Venice*, the more likely that the Jewish character Shylock is described with an ethnophaulism (e.g., infidel). The appearance of this pattern in another time and through a different research medium indirectly supports the size–complexity relation. At the very least, the appearance of group epithets in Shakespeare (and other literature) indicates that communicators think about outgroup members at a group level, essentially implying that outgroup members should be dealt with as a member of that group—with coercion or manipulative force, rather than with reason or cooperation (Rothbart & Hallmark, 1988).

If members of smaller groups are represented as prototypes, is the converse—that members of larger groups are individuated—necessarily the case? Conceivably, members of larger outgroups still may be stereotyped, but the perceiver simply may have a more clear appreciation of within-group variability. Perceivers may create subgroups of outgroup members who are seen as especially similar to one another, even though they still are seen as reflecting particular aspects of the stereotype (Mauer, Park, & Rothbart, 1995). For example, European Americans cognitively may cluster African Americans into several subgroups, such as black athletes, inner-city blacks, and militant political and religious leaders. These subgroups, based on the increasing number of black exemplars that European Americans may have in contemporary society, reflect increased recognition of within-group variability. But these subgroups do not necessarily mean that stereotyping of members from larger groups does not occur.

SUMMARY

People apparently describe outgroups in ways that emphasize outgroup homogeneity and noncomplexity. Outgroups are described more often at the most abstract group levels rather than at the individual level. A woman says "men are like that," when her friend's husband forgets a birthday; a non-Jew says "Jews are money grubbing" when the proprietor of a Jewish deli raises prices; and a European American insinuates that "blacks are pushy" when a black man applies for a job in a traditionally white company. The entire group is implicated in the single behavior of one of its members (Henderson-King & Nisbett, 1996), and the speaker's message is clear. If no reprisals are feared from the audience, the outgroup may be called by a group epi-thet: kikes, micks, or tails. From a functional perspective, such labels epitomize economical expression. The person is reduced to a word, al-beit one that is affectively charged and calls forth numerous associa-tions. The simplistic terms and group level characterizations attest that they are all alike, they have negative qualities, and they most certainly are not like us.

In a broad sense, the use of group epithets does correspond to mental representations of outgroups: both mental representations and outgroup epithets are abstract, emphasize homogeneity and non-complexity, and often have undesirable connotations. Little empirical work has addressed these parallels, with the notable exception of Mullen and Johnson's (1993) work on group size and perceived com-plexity. Empirical work regarding the link between individual cogni-tive representations and use of group of epithets appears to be nonex-istent. This link may prove useful in elucidating the relation between group epithets and acts of intergroup violence or discrimination, to be considered in Chapter 7.

Stereotypic Descriptions

In addition to being described in relatively noncomplex terms and in ways that emphasize within-group similarities, outgroups are de-scribed in ways that highlight their stereotypic qualities. For exam-ple, heterosexual individuals often expect homosexual men to be artsy or effeminate but not to be interpersonally aggressive. In keep-ing with their stereotypes, individuals who are prejudiced against heterosexual men select words that emphasize (or at least betray) un-derlying stereotypes, and ways that "explain away" potential contra-dictions.

LINGUISTIC INTERGROUP BIAS

A major way that stereotypic beliefs are expressed in language is through the linguistic intergroup bias, a pattern of describing ingroup versus outgroup behaviors in ways that maintain group stereotypes (Maass, Salvi, Arcuri, & Semin, 1989; for a review see Maass, 1999). In general, behaviors that are congruent with stereotypes are described with abstract terms whereas stereotype-incongruent behaviors are de-scribed with more concrete terms. For example, European Americans might describe an African American who takes a break at the water cooler as "lazy" rather than as "stopped working" or "got a drink of water." The same individual's attainment of an A on a test, in contrast, might be characterized as "getting a good grade on this test" rather than as "intelligent."

Certainly, "stopped working" and "intelligent" are more favorable descriptions than "lazy" and "got a good grade." And, intuitively, one might imagine using the former descriptions when describing fellow ingroup members than when describing outgroup members. But what makes one description more favorable than another, and what differentiates these descriptions as more or less abstract? The linguistic intergroup bias actually is an application of the linguistic category model (Semin & Fiedler, 1988), which classifies verbs along varying levels of abstractness. An examination of this model provides insight into how the linguistic intergroup bias operates. After this model is examined in detail, a more thorough discussion of the linguistic intergroup bias can follow.

The linguistic category model proposes that behaviors may be characterized by one of four linguistic categories that fall along a continuum of abstractness (see Table 2). At the most concrete level, descriptive action verbs refer to specific objects and specific observable behaviors. This description also is devoid of evaluative connotation (e.g., touch, hit). Proceeding to the next level of abstractness, interpretive action verbs also refer to specific objects and behaviors but are colored by an evaluative interpretation (e.g., caress, pummel). At a third level, state verbs refer to a particular object but are more abstract in that they imply enduring states (e.g., love, hate). Finally, adjectives are

TABLE 2. The Linguistic Category Model

Abstraction level	Description	Examples
Descriptive action verb	Reference to specific behavior, without interpretation	"Joe hit Jim." "Mary touches Bill."
Interpretative action verb	Reference to specific behavior, with interpretation	"Joe pummels Jim." "Mary caresses Bill."
State verb	Reference to specific object, but inference of actor's internal enduring state	"Joe hates Jim." "Mary loves Bill."
Adjective	Reference to actor's internal disposition without reference to specific behavior or objects	"Joe is aggressive." "Mary is affectionate."

the most abstract characterization, because they are detached entirely from specific behaviors or objects (e.g., romantic, aggressive).

Descriptive action verbs and interpretive action verbs "stick to the facts" more closely than do state verbs and adjectives. Consider what this distinction means, then, for the linguistic intergroup bias. Stereotypes about a group tend to be relatively abstract, so behaviors matching those stereotypes likewise are described in a more abstract fashion. Stereotype-congruent behaviors are construed as reflecting the typical behavioral tendencies of the person. Thus, to members of their respective outgroups, African Americans are lazy, physically challenged individuals are determined, alcoholics are disagreeable, and lesbians are argumentative. The more abstract types of speech (state verbs and adjectives) therefore are common when the speaker refers to stereotype-congruent behavior; they are verbally economical and to the point, with the capacity to encompass a broad range of behaviors in a word or two. But when the behaviors challenge stereotypes, a concrete characterization minimizes the need to revise the stereotype and casts the behavior in ephemeral terms. Thus, the more concrete types of speech characterize discussion of stereotype-incongruent behaviors. For example, consider these comments as to various outgroups: an African American "looked at a newspaper," rather than "is well informed"; a physically challenged person "failed to say hello," rather than "is unfriendly"; and an alcoholic "went to work at 7:00 a.m. every day," rather than "is disciplined." Unless the stereotype-incongruent behaviors are quite extreme (in which case it is nearly impossible to characterize them in a concrete fashion), characterizing incongruent behaviors in a more concrete fashion helps maintain stereotypic beliefs (Karpinski & von Hippel, 1996). Thus, the traditional linguistic intergroup bias finding shows more abstract characterizations of behavior that are congruent with stereotypic beliefs about ingroup and outgroup behavior.

For many naturally occurring outgroups, evaluative connotation and stereotypicness often are confounded. That is, people tend to expect negative behaviors from outgroup members but positive behavior from ingroup members. Not surprisingly, then, the original formulation of the linguistic intergroup bias (Maass et al., 1989) did not unconfound evaluative connotation and the stereotype. In a later study, Maass, Milesi, Zabbini, and Stahlberg (1995) showed that stereotypic expectancies were sufficient to produce the bias. In their sample, Italian perceivers presumed southern Italians to possess both negative (e.g., intrusive) and positive (e.g., warm) qualities and presumed northern Italians also to possess both negative (e.g., intolerant) and positive (e.g., industrious) qualities. These authors found that, irrespective of the behavior's evaluative connotation or the perceiver's group membership, more abstract terms were used to describe stereotype-congruent behaviors whereas less abstract terms were used to describe stereotype-incongruent behaviors.

ADDITIONAL EVIDENCE FOR THE LINGUISTIC INTERGROUP BIAS

Among the research on stereotyping and communication conducted by social psychologists, the linguistic intergroup bias arguably has been studied the most. Although the majority of the research derives from the aforementioned work of Maass and her colleagues in Italy, independent laboratories have conceptually replicated their findings in the United States (Ruscher & Duval, 1998; Schnake & Ruscher, 1998; von Hippel, Sekaquaptewa, & Vargas, 1997; Webster, Kruglanski, & Pattison, 1997), Spain (Valencia, Gil de Montes, Arruti, & Carbonell, 1998), and China (Ng & Chan, 1996). The examined stereotypes range from those of rival horse-racing groups (Maass et al., 1989), northern versus southern Italians (Maass et al., 1995), environmentalists versus hunters (Maass, Ceccarelli, & Rudin, 1996), and African Americans versus European Americans (Schnake & Ruscher, 1998; von Hippel et al., 1997), as well as paraplegics and alcoholics (Ruscher & Duval, 1998). The bias also is found using age cohorts (Ng & Chan, 1996), political affiliations (Karpinski & von Hippel, 1996; Maass, Corvino, & Arcuri, 1994) and friends versus enemies (Karpinski & von Hippel, 1996; Maass et al., 1995). The fact that the linguistic intergroup bias replicates across researchers, nationalities, and types of stereotypes and expectancies is important because these replications render the possibility of chance findings and artifacts rather unlikely. Moreover, to the extent that language provides insight into cognitive representation, this generality may even suggest that people universally store at least some information about groups in abstract form.

To date, the linguistic intergroup bias has been tested in a variety of ways. The most common way of examining the bias is to present research participants with a series of cartoons or phony newspaper clippings, each of which depicts members of the ingroup (or outgroup) engaged in a particular behavior (e.g., Maass et al., 1989, 1995). Below each cartoon or clipping appears four possible descriptions, one at each level of linguistic abstraction (the order of the four descriptions varies across trials, of course). Then, participants choose the description that they believe best fits each picture. In a variant on this procedure, von Hippel et al. (1997) asked participants to rate the extent to which each of the descriptions fit the newspaper clipping. This latter procedure potentially allows greater measurement sensitivity by providing multiple data points on each behavior and by providing interval-ratio data.

Given these methods of choosing or rating a description, one well may wonder whether the linguistic intergroup bias really is a communication bias—a way that people actually describe others—or whether the researchers simply are putting words in participants' mouths. After all, participants simply might select the description that they think the researcher wants them to select, or they might evidence another kind of experimental demand characteristic. Fortunately, several studies indicate that the linguistic intergroup bias does emerge in less restricted formats. Maass et al. (1989) and Webster et al. (1997), for example, asked participants to write a description in their own words. Most recently, Ruscher and Duval (1998) and Schnake and Ruscher (1998) asked participants to communicate orally their impressions of a target. All of these more naturalistic procedures also detected the linguistic intergroup bias. Thus, regardless of how it is measured, the linguistic intergroup bias consistently is observed.

MODERATORS OF THE LINGUISTIC INTERGROUP BIAS

The extent to which communicators exhibit the linguistic intergroup bias is influenced by dispositional and situational constraints. One might predict, for example, that bigoted individuals would show the linguistic intergroup bias more than would less prejudiced individuals. Although both highly prejudiced and less prejudiced individuals are presumed to hold stereotypic beliefs at least unconsciously (e.g., Devine, 1989), less prejudiced individuals conceivably attach a lower probability between outgroup membership and possessing a given trait or, at the least, lower prejudiced individuals consciously inhibit stereotypic thoughts when they are aware of having them. Consequently, less prejudiced individuals might be less likely to manifest the linguistic intergroup bias than their more prejudiced counterparts.

One widely used index of individual differences in the level of prejudice is the modern racism scale (discussed below; see McConahay, 1986). Modern racism—and modern prejudice in general—deals with the fact that people in contemporary society often recognize that overt prejudice is socially inappropriate and conflicts with consciously espoused egalitarian ideals (e.g., everyone should have equal opportunity for jobs). Concurrently, however, many people retain residual negative affect toward particular social groups. Whites high in modern racism do not admit to "old-fashioned" racist beliefs such as genetically based intellectual inferiority of blacks, but instead believe that racism is a thing of the past, that blacks are pushing too hard for additional rights, and that the anger of black people is unwarranted. Armed with these beliefs, modern racists discriminate against

African Americans if and only if they can point to a race-irrelevant reason such as mediocre grades or failing to persevere at a task. If a white target has mediocre grades or does not persevere, however, modern racists overlook these negative attributes and do not discriminate against him or her; instead modern racists treat the mediocre white target better than a mediocre black target. Thus, modern racists primarily hold African American targets accountable for slipups and inadequacies but seem to forgive their fellow European Americans. Racism slips out when the situation is ambiguous or when an alleged justification is available.

Individuals who are high in modern racism subscribe more strongly to their stereotypes than do less racist individuals (Kawakami, Dion, & Dovidio, 1998). Accordingly, they particularly should evidence the linguistic intergroup bias. To examine this hypothesis, Schnake and Ruscher (1998) distinguished European Americans as high or low in modern racism by using the modern racism scale (McConahay, 1986). This scale is a personality dimension that taps the extent to which whites espouse the aforementioned tenets of modern racism. After rendering this distinction, participants orally described the behavior of several African American men depicted in sketches to a fellow European American student. As expected, the terms that participants high in modern racism used to describe stereotype-congruent behaviors were more abstract than the terms used by participants low in modern racism. For high modern racists, African Americans' behaviors were seen as confirming their stereotypes, and they conveyed that impression to their audience.

Thus, individuals low in dispositional prejudice exhibit the linguistic intergroup bias more strongly than do more prejudiced individuals. Does this finding suggest that the linguistic intergroup bias is under conscious control? Not necessarily. Franco and Maass (1996) explicitly argued and presented evidence that the linguistic intergroup bias does not seem to be under as much conscious control as other forms of intergroup differentiation (e.g., reward allocation). They showed that aggressive basketball fans differed from nonaggressive fans with respect to reward allocation but not with respect to their use of the linguistic intergroup bias.

Rather than conclude that the linguistic intergroup bias per se is under conscious control, a more likely interpretation of Schnake and Ruscher's (1998) findings is that individuals who are low in modern racism are motivated not to stereotype African Americans. (Basketball fans, in contrast, may not feel pressured to avoid stereotyping outgroups fans and teams.) Devine (1989) argues that low-prejudiced individuals actually suppress the stereotypes that they may have learned, and instead initially bring to mind the nonprejudiced beliefs that are central to their self-concepts. These beliefs include viewing the person as an individual rather than as a mere member of a particular social group. Put another way, low-prejudiced individuals may be concerned with being accurate about the particular person in question. They actively try to avoid stereotyping others, and this effort causes them to think about stereotypic behaviors as not reflective of an overall tendency (and, in turn, they do not characterize the behavior in as abstract a fashion). Thus, it may be that a conscious suppression of a stereotype inhibits stereotypic thoughts, which in turn attenuates the linguistic intergroup bias. That is, people may not consciously control their use of the linguistic intergroup directly, but they may be able to exercise conscious control over one of its distal causes.

Congruent with this interpretation, an explicit motivation to be accurate can undercut the linguistic intergroup bias. Ruscher and Duval (1998) induced accuracy motivation in pairs of acquaintances who were communicating their impressions of an alcoholic or a paraplegic target to another friend. The communicators either received identical or different information about the target. If they possessed identical information, the communicators tended to feel that their job was to provide a shared impression to their audience. If they possessed different information, the communicators felt that their job was to each provide a unique perspective on the target person. This latter orientation encouraged them to think more about the target, and to try to be accurate and complete. Doing so discouraged their jumping to conclusions about the target's stereotype-incongruent behaviors, and ultimately encouraged those behaviors being characterized in an abstract fashion. For example, when the alcoholic studied from 7:00 until 9:00 every night, the communicators pointed out that he was "organized," a quality incongruent with the alcoholic stereotypic and also at the highest level of linguistic abstraction. The accuracy-oriented communicators also spent a great deal of time describing the incongruent behaviors, again suggesting their desire not to jump to hasty conclusions but instead to think about how the stereotype-incongruent behaviors actually might reflect internal dispositions and states.

Interestingly, as a result of describing the alcoholic target in this fashion, both the communicators themselves and their receivers came to view him in a less stereotypic fashion. Thus, accuracy motivation may encourage people to think about—and talk about—others more like the way they talk about ingroup members: as individuals, not mere group members. Because using dispositional adjectives to describe stereotype-incongruent behavior is counter to perceivers' usual way of talking about outgroup members, doing so typically requires time and cognitive effort. In fact, perceivers take this effortful route when it is counterproductive to think about the target at a group level and when instead their outcomes depend on knowing the person as an individual (Fiske & Von Hendy, 1992; Ruscher & Fiske, 1990).

Additional evidence, from another laboratory, indirectly points to the importance of accuracy motivation in attenuating the linguistic intergroup bias. Webster et al. (1997) reasoned that "Need for Closure" would magnify the linguistic intergroup bias. (Need for Closure is an individual difference dimension that reflects a desire for a definite answer and causes the participants to be biased against information that would change answers on which they already had decided.) Given that abstract stereotypic attributes are the product of general social consensus, one imagines that people high in Need for Closure would be inclined to rely on these stereotypes to provide abstract characterizations for expected outgroup behavior. That is, people who want a definitive answer find stereotypes perfect for meeting that need. As expected, high Need for Closure participants exhibited the linguistic intergroup bias more strongly than did low Need for Closure participants. In a conceptual replication, Webster et al. situationally induced need for closure by running a noisy dot-matrix printer during the experimental session; participants in the low Need for Closure condition were not exposed to this environmental noise. Presumably, being distracted prompts people to want a quick decision and interferes with thinking ability; again stereotypes are quick and easy ways to think about others. As expected, the noise pressured participants to come to a decision quickly about the target, and they therefore relied on their stereotypic expectations. Consequently, participants exposed to noise exhibited the linguistic intergroup bias more than did participants not exposed to noise.

SUMMARY

The work on the linguistic intergroup bias indicates that language reflects and maintains the stereotypes that people hold about groups: a woman is gossipy, rather than tells a story about someone else; an African American is lazy, rather than takes a break from work; an Asian student is curve-busting smart, rather than obtains a good grade. The way in which ingroups describe outgroups betrays their stereotypic beliefs about the outgroup and the outgroup target in question. The observation of the linguistic intergroup bias across various languages, with numerous types of stereotypes and expectancies and using various methodologies, attests to it robustness.

A number of factors moderate the magnitude of the linguistic intergroup bias. Dispositional prejudice and a need to make quick judgments exacerbate the linguistic intergroup bias, while implicit and explicit motivations to be accurate attenuate it. Despite these moderators, the linguistic intergroup bias itself still is construed as something that operates largely outside conscious awareness. Instead, the magnitude of the bias conceivably is pushed around by distal factors that may or may not be under conscious control. At least until people become acutely aware of this differential communication pattern and perhaps bring it under conscious control, the linguistic intergroup bias should provide a useful tool for examining stereotyping and prejudice.

Intergroup Bias

Although current research on the linguistic intergroup bias focuses on its role in stereotype maintenance, the bias originally specified differential expectancies with respect to evaluation. That is, the linguistic intergroup bias predicted that negative outgroup behaviors and positive ingroup behaviors would be seen abstractly whereas positive outgroup behaviors and negative ingroup behaviors would be seen in a more concrete fashion (Maass et al., 1989). All things being equal, people are more likely to expect negative qualities from outgroups than from ingroups (Howard & Rothbart, 1980), so stereotypic expectancies and valence often are confounded in natural settings. For example, although European Americans expect African Americans to be musically or athletically inclined, the majority of the attributes associated with the African American stereotype are negative. Thus, negative behaviors of the ingroup are explained away while positive behaviors are claimed as descriptive of the group. Conversely, positive behaviors of the outgroup are explained away while negative behaviors are accepted.

This self-serving pattern presumably stems from the desire to hold positive beliefs about one's ingroup and therefore serves the group-enhancing function discussed in Chapter 1. According to social identity theory (Tajfel & Turner, 1979), the groups to which people belong are important sources of identity and self-esteem. Given this central importance, the ingroup often is favored above the outgroup when resources are allocated (Jetten, Spears, & Manstead, 1996), when personality traits are judged (e.g., D. M. Taylor & Jaggi, 1974), and when the quality of each group's work product is judged (J. D. Brown, Schmidt, & Collins, 1988; see M. B. Brewer & Brown, 1998, for a review of intergroup bias). Interestingly, the ingroup need not receive any tangible benefit for intergroup discrimination to occur (J. D. Brown et al., 1988). Moreover, intergroup bias is not only evident in "real-world" groups that are divided on the basis of ethnicity, university, social club, or nationality. Ad hoc groups created in the laboratory by entirely random procedures also show ingroup bias. Groups might be formed by random assignment to green versus red jerseys, an alleged preference for a particular modern artist, or an alleged predilection for focusing on the figure versus the ground of a picture. Thus, mere categorization into groups alone—not any preexisting stereotypes or conflict—is sufficient to produce intergroup bias.

The original formulation of the linguistic intergroup bias is one example of the intergroup bias in language. As discussed above, its later refinements show that stereotypes are important, even if those stereotypes occasionally are positive (e.g., African Americans as athletic; Jews as clever). Maass and her colleagues recognize, however, that the preference to view the ingroup in a positive fashion still may play a role in linguistic abstraction. They note that when the ingroup is threatened, the linguistic intergroup bias is accentuated (Maass et al., 1996). That is, even if differential stereotypes are sufficient to produce the linguistic intergroup bias, the desire to see the ingroup in a favorable light remains a relevant motive. People may admit that outgroups possess positive qualities, but they require more evidence before they will accept those qualities with confidence. Conversely, people more readily believe that the outgroup possesses negative qualities, and they require considerable evidence to disconfirm those negative qualities (Maass, Montalcini, & Biciotti, 1998; cf. Leyens & Yzerbyt, 1992). When it comes to the outgroup, people resist seeing what they prefer not to see . . . and see what they prefer to see. Language clearly reflects this bias.

US VERSUS THEM

The separation into "us" and "them" is a clear source of intergroup bias. Even the vocalizations of nonhuman primates distinguish between members of the ingroup and outsiders (Cheney & Seyfarth, 1982), suggesting that ingroup–outgroup distinctions may be fundamental to social existence. In ancient times, strong ties to the ingroup may have helped specific kingroups (and their genes) survive. From a sociobiological perspective, then, the pervasive tendency to overvalue the ingroup may be part of our genetic heritage. That tendency now may be less adaptive than it once was and, in many cases, counterproductive. In many respects, our biological evolution has not kept pace with our social evolution.

This distinction between ingroups and outgroups, and the differential evaluation of these groups, again is evidenced in human language, particularly in the use of pronouns associated with those groups. The first person plurals (we, us) reflect a sense of ingroup cohesion, belongingness, and positive evaluation of the ingroup. Couples in satisfied marriages (Sillars, Shellen, McIntosh, & Pomegranate, 1997), Italian adolescent newscasters of a news program for other adolescents (Mininni & Annese, 1997), mothers who are verbally responsive to their children (Laks, Beckwith, & Cohen, 1990), and close-knit families (Dreyer, Dreyer, & Davis, 1987) all use the first person plural in conversation with ingroup members.

Over time, the first person plural—and the implied ingroup— becomes mentally associated with positive evaluation; the third person plural tends to become associated with the outgroup and consequently with negative evaluation. A set of provocative studies (Perdue, Dovidio, Gurtman, & Tyler, 1990) demonstrate this association quite well. In one study, a computer presented participants with a nonsense syllable (e.g., xeh, wuh, giw) that was paired randomly with either a first person plural pronoun (us, we, ours), a third person plural pronoun (them, they, theirs), or another pronoun (he, she, hers, his, me, you, mine); these last-named pronouns served as the control group. Although participants believed that the study tested their verbal skills, the real purpose was to assess their evaluation of each syllable. Participants rated syllables paired with the first person plural as more pleasant than the control pronouns or third person plurals. Thus, first person plurals—pronouns typically associated with the ingroup—imply more favorable feelings than third persons plurals, which are better associated with the outgroup. It bears mentioning that, although the difference between first person plurals and control pronouns was statistically significant, the difference between third person plurals and control pronouns did not reflect a significant difference. That is, pronouns such as "they" did not produce a less favorable reaction than pronouns such as "she" or "his." This disparity may reflect ingroup love being stronger than outgroup hate. Alternatively, this disparity may reflect the fact that third person plurals do not always reflect an outgroup; as discussed further below, recent conventions use "they" as a gender-neutral pronoun in lieu of "s/he" or "he or she." "We," in contrast, more often typifies an ingroup.

At times, differential use of the first person plural can designate efforts to increase or decrease association with a group. Because groups are an important source of self-esteem, people's level of identification with a group often waxes and wanes with the degree to which the group helps meet self-esteem needs. For example, after a sporting event, fans of the winning team often are observed to claim "we won," whereas fans of the losing team claim "they lost." In one of the earliest social psychology studies on pronoun use (Cialdini et al., 1976), nearly 200 randomly selected college students were interviewed regarding the outcome of a football game; the students' home team either had won or lost that particular game. In their responses, participants relied on the first person plural for victories but tended to rely on the third person plural for losses. This linguistic pattern, at least temporarily, renders the losing team as the outgroup and the winning team as the ingroup, and functions to protect group-level self-esteem. Is this pattern really reflective of ingroup identification, or is it merely an interesting phenomenon? Cialdini and colleagues also reported that, after victories, college students at six major U.S. universities were more likely to wear apparel that contained their own school's name or logo than when no victory occurred. Given that this behavior strongly reflects identification, the similar pattern in use of the first person plural presumably signifies identification as well.

CONVERSATIONAL CONVENTIONS AND INTERGROUP BIAS

Howard and Rothbart (1980) argued that people typically expect more negative behaviors from outgroups than ingroups, and Maass and colleagues' (1995) findings are congruent with their assessment. Put another way, ingroups do not give outgroups the benefit of the doubt. As discussed below, the failure to give outgroup members the benefit of the doubt also emerges in a rather selective use of conversational conventions.

Conversational conventions are based on the implicit communication rules that speakers and listeners typically follow. These implicit rules encourage speakers to provide relevant information and only as much information as is needed to understand the message; listeners presume that speakers follow these rules (Grice, 1975; Higgins, 1981; Schwarz, 1994). The upshot of this expectation is that listeners attach more weight to communicated information that appears late in the message. Consider, for example, someone who is describing her decision to buy one of two cars (Krosnick, Li, & Lehman, 1990). If an advantage of one model precedes a disadvantage, listeners will presume that she did not purchase that model (e.g., "The X model was not expensive, but it didn't have power windows"). If the disadvantage precedes the advantage, listeners will presume that she bought that particular model (e.g., "The X model didn't have power windows, but it was not expensive"). Listeners presumably reason that the speaker would not mention the additional information unless it was highly relevant, so they place more weight on that late information. Importantly, this finding does not rely on the use of disjunctions such as "but" or "however." Even when such disjunctions are omitted, the latter information receives greater weight.

This order effect potentially is important when people are speaking about outgroup members, because people tend to prefer multiple explanations over single explanations when explaining outgroup behavior (Hewstone, Gale, & Purkhardt, 1990; Jackson, Sullivan, & Hodge, 1993). On the surface, presenting multiple explanations might help the communicator seem less judgmental when speaking about an outgroup member. For example, a European American teacher might comment on an African American student's poor grade by noting, "The test was hard, but she didn't study." The initial admission of a difficult test seems to imply that the teacher recognizes external factors, and at the surface it sounds as though he has given some thought to the source of the student's poor performance. The emphasis of his statement, however, is on the latter part of the sentence, which blames the student for the failure.

Even if people prefer multiple explanations for outgroup behaviors, the attributions that they make typically reflect intergroup bias. Research shows that the ingroup is credited for its successes while failures are explained away. The outgroup, conversely, is blamed for its failures while successes are explained away. Pettigrew (1979) termed this pattern "the ultimate attribution error," an attributional pattern of intergroup bias that replicates across countries and behavioral domains (e.g., Ben-Ari, Schwarzwald, & Horiner-Levi, 1994; Hewstone, Jaspars, & Lalljee, 1982; D. M. Taylor & Jaggi, 1974). Although conversational conventions suggest that greater emphasis should be placed on later appearing explanations, the ultimate attribution error suggests that preferred explanations for outgroup behavior might override that convention. Take, for example, a statement such as "Bill called his sister a rude name. He has a bit of a temper. She'd been teasing him." If Bill is cast as an ingroup member, he probably will be forgiven for the offending behavior (i.e., receivers follow conversational conventions and will weight the latter information more heavily in their impressions). If, however, Bill is cast as an outgroup member, an audience probably will ignore conversational convention and focus on the preferred detrimental attribution.

Recent evidence indicates that listeners do rely more heavily on the intergroup bias than on conversational conventions when hearing about the behaviors of outgroup members (Beal, Ruscher, & Schnake, in press). European American participants were exposed to statements similar to "Bill called his sister a rude name. He has a bit of a temper. She'd been teasing him." The statements varied with respect to the evaluative connotation of the behavior (positive or negative), the order in which the explanations appeared (internal, external), and whether the name of the person implied a particular ethnicity or a name that pretested as likely to refer to a white student (e.g., José or Keisha vs. Matt or Hillary). Congruent with intergroup bias, the addition of mitigating explanations for negative behaviors did not help actors with names that implied ethnicity other than white. Similarly, the addition of crediting explanations for positive behaviors essentially was ignored for these actors. Actors with white names, however, received the benefit of the doubt. A follow-up study using only African American actors replicated these findings, but only among European Americans high in modern racism (Ruscher, Beal, & Schnake, 1999). Thus, it appears that European Americans hear what they prefer to hear about ethnic outgroups.

SUMMARY

Intergroup bias is a predilection to view the ingroup more positively than the outgroup. This pattern emerges in the original formulation of the linguistic intergroup bias; for example, people characterize ingroup positive and outgroup negative behaviors abstractly, reflecting their positive versus negative expectations of the ingroup and outgroup, respectively. The increased use of first person plurals in cohesive groups, and the positivity implied by those pronouns (e.g., "we") further reflects a favorable bias toward the ingroup. This favorability bias is not extended to the outgroup and, indeed, they do not receive the benefit of the doubt. People ignore conversational convention and instead rely on intergroup bias when judging explanations for outgroup behaviors. All in all, the love that people communicate for their ingroups is counterbalanced by the disdain—or at least apathy—that they communicate for the outgroup. Language therefore can be used strategically in the service of group enhancement.

Exclusion

What people *fail* to say also provides some insight into how they view other groups. Groups that are not even acknowledged are, implicitly, invisible or unimportant. Even in today's politically correct climate, people in male-dominated companies still may receive an invitation addressed to "employees and their wives," a slight against the companies' female employees. Although somewhat less insulting to most women, "employees and their spouses" ignores individuals—heterosexual and homosexual—who are in committed but unformalized relationships. (Indeed, the invitation probably does not consider the possibility of a gay or lesbian marriage.) Even if the majority of the people in the organization have traditional heterosexual marriages, some individuals implicitly are excluded. The excluded individuals are left to wonder whether the person issuing the invitation will be offended by the appearance of a dating partner, same sex spouse, or other guest, as well as their appearing alone without any guest or partner. True, the speaker may not have had a conscious intention to be exclusive, anymore than speakers consciously manifest the linguistic intergroup bias. Even so, such an invitation implies that the speaker was not thinking about potentially excluded individuals, that these individuals are invisible, or simply not worth the effort of creating a more inclusively worded invitation.

Gender-biased language is thus far the best-researched area on language and exclusion, and is recognized as a form of prejudiced communication (Graumann & Wintermantel, 1989). But even here the work is limited, perhaps because studying the absence of something is awkward or not sufficiently salient to attract research attention. At the grossest level, gender-biased language implies that people are male unless "proven" to be female. Female gender may be designated by either tagging on a feminine descriptor (e.g., lady professor, women doctor, female engineer) or by belonging to a stereotypically female group (e.g., kindergarten teacher, social worker). Critics of efforts to use more inclusive language argue that expressions such as "mankind" or "brotherhood" include women, but they seem to ignore the imbalance in those expressions. For example, if "brotherhood" implicitly includes women, why does "sisterhood" not include men? Until recent years, women were excluded from various societies using the expression "brotherhood," which casts doubt on the term's inclusiveness. And, given that women in most Western countries earned the right to vote—and many other rights—less than a hundred years ago, statements that use the masculine terms historically often did not refer to both women and men. Efforts toward inclusiveness convey the message that the speaker recognizes the importance of the typically excluded group or, at least, recognizes that exclusion is socially unacceptable in the present climate.

Not surprisingly, then, the desire and propensity to minimize gender-biased language varies across interest groups and occupations (Harrigan & Lucic, 1988); psychologists, for example, have explicit guidelines for minimizing sexist or gender-biased language (American Psychological Association, 1994). Individual differences in prejudice also affect the use of biased language. For example, Cralley and Ruscher (2000) demonstrated that sexist men are more likely to use terms such as "girl" or "lady" rather than "she" or "woman" to describe adult female targets. The former terms imply the passive qualities inherent in the gender role stereotype for women (Eagly & Crowley, 1986) and presumably bring to mind different representations than the more neutral terms (Krauss & Chiu, 1998). Similarly, people who subscribe to traditional sex roles distinguish among the expressions "chairman," "chair," and "chairperson." These terms are seen as reflecting increasingly greater feminine qualities and decreasingly less masculine qualities. Less traditional men and women draw no such distinction among such terms with respect to femininity or masculinity (McConnell & Fazio, 1996). At least for traditional individuals, then, chairman apparently calls to mind a man, whereas chairperson calls to mind a woman. Such findings further call into question whether using masculine expressions as generic terms (e.g., man, brotherhood) actually serve the purpose of gender neutrality. Being corrected for using gender-biased language does help minimize its use, although attitudes toward language reform may not change as a function of correction (Prentice, 1994). It remains to be seen whether changes in the long run will come as a result of increased use of gender-neutral terms.

Of course, nouns are relatively easy to adapt into gender-neutral expressions and seem to serve their goal of being gender neutral. Mailman becomes postal worker, poetess becomes poet, and stewardess becomes flight attendant. The selection of generic singular pronouns, unfortunately, is more difficult than adapting nouns. Masculine singular pronouns (him, he, his) currently are supposed to serve as generic singular terms, but their adequacy to the task is questionable. These masculine terms apparently bring to mind persons of male gender, rather than both male and female individuals. For example, if "he" is used when describing a possible occupation, rather than "he or she," individuals are less likely to believe that a woman can perform the job well (Hyde, 1984). Similarly, the use of masculine pronouns does not call to mind females as easily as neutral pronouns do. In one study, for example, participants read the statement, "In a large coeducational institution the average student will feel isolated in his (his or her) introductory courses." Participants then wrote a story in response to this theme. If presented with "his," men included females in their stories 16% of the time whereas women included females 48% of the time. If presented with "his or her," men included females 23% of the time whereas women included females 78% of the time (C. M. Cole, Hill, & Dayley, 1983). At least some researchers therefore believe that the continued use of "he" is problematic, if the goal is to provide a gender-neutral singular pronoun.

Grammarians increasingly accept the third person plural (e.g., "they") as the generic singular for expressions that could imply groups of individuals (e.g., "Everybody brought their book"). "Everybody" implies more than one person is present. Even so, the third person plural (they, their) is the most popular candidate for any singular generic pronoun when actor gender is unknown. For example, rather than say, "The student brought his/her book to class," someone might say, "The student brought their book to class." In spoken English, students often use "they" and "their" as the singular generic but will use "he or she" and "his or her" when writing (Martyna, 1978). This pattern suggests a growing desire for reducing gender-biased language among young people in the United States, but also a preference for nonawkward phrases.

Does the use of "they" do any good? Recent evidence suggests that the third person plural is a mixed bag. For stereotypically male occupations, "they" is read as quickly as "he." Conversely, for stereotypically female occupations, "they" is read as quickly as "she" (Foertsch & Gernsbacher, 1997). Consequently, "they" can substitute for a gender-specific pronoun when the actor's gender implicitly is understood. Unfortunately, "they" does not really solve the problem of a gender-inclusive pronoun. To hear "A truck driver should never drive when sleepy, even if they may be struggling to make a delivery on time" still probably conjures up a male truck driver in the mind of the listener. That is, "they" only is an adequate substitute for "he" in a masculine-stereotypic position. Indeed, when a pronoun does not match the gender stereotype of an occupation, people are surprised, as evidenced by increased brainwave activity (Osterhout, Bersick, & McLaughlin, 1997). The search for gender-inclusive expression therefore continues.

SUMMARY

Observation suggests that language implicitly can exclude particular groups on the basis of their gender, sexual orientation, physical challenges, and ethnic groups. Recent work on gender-biased language specifically addresses the implicit exclusion of women. Although grammatically correct, the use of masculine expressions as generic terms (e.g., mankind, he, chairmen) primarily may bring to mind males rather than males and females. Expressions that exclude members of particular group help serve some of the social functions of prejudiced language. For example, an invitation to faculty and their wives or a statement that the office is "undermanned" implicitly suggest where women do and do not belong. College students preference toward using the third person plural, at least in oral expression, suggests that acceptance of gender-biased language is changing.

Individual differences in sexism, occupation, and adherence to traditional sex roles is associated with a predilection for gender-biased language. This finding suggests that women are represented primarily in stereotypic roles among certain individuals or that images of women are not accessible when particular issues are under consideration. The implications of this work is not simply that some individuals will be offended by sexist language. Gender-biased language could influence judgments of employability (and therefore who is interviewed; Hyde, 1984). In addition, gender-biased language could influence psychology practitioners' interpretations of psychological instruments such as the Draw-a-Person Test. Women are more likely than men to draw opposite-gender figures, which may reflect language bias more than gender identification (Merritt & Kok, 1997). Future work on biased language needs to consider additional often excluded groups, as well as consider the ramifications of that language for real-world concerns.

CHAPTER SUMMARY

The particular words that people select betray their beliefs about outgroup members. Group epithets reflect the relatively noncomplex and homogeneous perceptions that ingroups hold of outgroups; often, these epithets are less than flattering, so they also reflect the general negative beliefs about outgroups. Group epithets also point to intergroup differences—of what separates "us" from "them." The stereotypic beliefs that people hold about outgroups also emerge in language, most notably through the linguistic intergroup bias. By abstractly characterizing behaviors, the stereotypic expectations people hold can be preserved.

Language also reflects categorization into ingroups and outgroups, and the implicit evaluation associated with each group. "We" is applied to cohesive ingroups and groups with which one identifies; "they" is applied to outgroups and groups from whom one desires distance. The negative evaluation of the outgroup also is reflected in the selective use of conversational conventions and the deleterious slant of many group epithets. Finally, language suggests that some groups are invisible or unimportant. True, there is not a one-to-one correspondence between thought and language. However, research does show striking parallels among the beliefs about, treatment of, and communication about outgroup members.

THREE

Developing and Using
Shared Stereotypes

Two cultivated middle-aged women were discussing the high
cost of cut flowers. One spoke of a lavish floral display at a
Jewish wedding, and added, "I don't know how they afford it.
They must doctor their income tax returns." The other replied,
"Yes, they must."
                                    —ALLPORT (1954/1989, p. 49)

Although particular individuals possess stereotypes, stereotypes are
not developed or expressed in a social vacuum. Stereotypes are shared,
developing through communication with other people. In addition,
through communication, people use shared stereotypes to validate
their beliefs about outgroups and to sustain ingroup harmony. For example, in the above snippet from Allport's *The Nature of Prejudice*, if the
second woman's stereotype of Jewish individuals initially did not include beliefs related to avarice or shrewdness, the first woman's comment might foster the development of such beliefs. Alternatively, if
both women already shared a stereotype for Jews, the conversation
might allow them mutually to validate those shared beliefs. Indeed, as
Allport suggests, conversing about shared stereotypic beliefs might
help sustain a friendly acquaintance by centering the conversation
around a topic about which both women easily can agree.

Shared stereotypes also can help conversing individuals develop
shared impressions of individual outgroup members. These women
might, for example, refer back to this conversation later when they en-

counter another Jewish person. They could rely on this instance as a basis for comparison or, alternatively, use the shared impression to provide "evidence" of a generally perceived consensus about the characteristics of Jews. In addition, they might rely on the shared stereotype to define norms for dealing with newly encountered Jewish persons. If, for example, a group of non-Jews came to believe that Jews are dishonest when dealing with money, they might be disinclined to invite their new Jewish coworker to join their expedition to a new restaurant or tavern. The shared stereotype might lead them to reason that she would not pay her appropriate portion of the bill or, at least, skimp on her portion of the gratuity. Once such a norm develops, it might be maintained by group storytelling or myths. The present chapter examines these various points. After defining shared stereotypes and discussing their measurement, the chapter examines the development of shared stereotypes through interpersonal communication, primarily in dyads. Having examined the development of shared stereotypes and stereotypic impressions, the chapter next considers how those shared viewpoints may spread among the larger social group of which the dyad or intimately sized group is a part. Finally, the chapter examines how shared stereotypes and shared stereotypic impressions help the ingroup develop strategies for dealing with outgroup members.

WHAT ARE SHARED STEREOTYPES?

As discussed in Chapter 1, stereotypes are a specific type of cognitive schema that describe people from a particular social group. Stereotypes need not develop through first-hand encounters with the target group. Instead, stereotypes may be spread or develop through interpersonal or mass communication. For example, heterosexuals who are unaware that any of their acquaintances are homosexual, whites who have never met blacks, and Christians who have never met Jews may be well aware of the stereotypes of these respective groups. Such individuals "learn" about their respective outgroups by talking with peers, listening to their parents, watching television, and reading the news.

Theorists vary with respect to whether they believe that a stereotype must involve consensually held beliefs (for discussions, see Gardner, 1994; Haslam, Turner, Oakes, McGarty, & Reynolds, 1998). At one end of the debate, consensuality is not a necessary aspect of a stereotype because, outside the realm of science fiction, beliefs and thoughts reside in the minds of isolated individuals. Theoretically, then, each individual has her or his own schema for group X, with potentially no overlap among these individual schemas. From this perspective, other aspects of the stereotype are more critical. For example, the more important feature of a stereotype might be the extent to which it is applied indiscriminately to members of a particular group. At the other end of the debate, stereotypes by definition are consensual. All or most of the attributes of one person's schema for group X are represented in the schemas that most other people have for group X. Consistent with the lay notion of a stereotype, a group of people must share similar beliefs for a schema to be a stereotype.

Assuming that at least some stereotypes are shared, what makes them consensual? Gardner (1994) indicates that consensual stereotypes reflect the set of beliefs shared within a particular group. Southern whites in the nineteenth century historically believed in the intellectual inferiority of blacks, members of sorority Alpha Alpha may believe that members of fraternity Beta Beta are drunken idiots, and many heterosexual men believe that gay men are effeminate. Intuitively, although the notion of shared stereotypes makes a fuzzy kind of sense, defining the term "shared stereotype" can carry both conceptual and methodological problems. Does consensus require that all individuals in the group hold the stereotype, or does a majority rule apply? For example, must *all* heterosexual men believe that gay men are effeminate, can a *subset* of heterosexual men hold the belief (e.g., just those who are highly prejudiced or the 20-odd members of a homophobic bowling team), or does consensus imply the belief among *most* heterosexual men? Alternatively, does consensus require that the individuals in the particular group apply the stereotype indiscriminately to all members of the other group, or does consensus mean only that most outgroup members are perceived as conforming to the stereotype? Are all members of fraternity Beta Beta presumed to be drunken idiots, or just most of them? Does consensus preclude a recognition of degrees of drunken idiocy, or does it require all members to be extreme on this dimension?

Methods of assessing consensual stereotypes vary in their ability to address these concerns. For instance, in the classic work on consensual stereotypes (Katz & Braly, 1933; see G. M. Gilbert, 1951, and Karlins, Coffman, & Walters, 1969, for follow-up studies) participants selected which among 84 adjectives best described each of 10 ethnic groups. The 12 attributes selected with the greatest frequency purportedly reflected consensual stereotypes. For example, in 1933, Chinese people were considered to be very religious and conservative. The problem with the results using this method, though, was that the actual number of participants who endorsed particular attributes objectively was rather low. As Gardner (1994) points out, only 7 of the possible 120 attributes were endorsed by at least 50% of the participants. These included Italians as artistic (53%), "Negroes" as superstitious and lazy (84% and 75%, respectively), Jews as shrewd (79%), Germans as scientifically minded and industrious (78% and 65%, respectively), and the English as sportsmanlike (53%). Other than these few attributes, the typical agreement among 10–30% of a population seems only modest evidence of shared beliefs at best.

The original Katz and Braly (1933) method also does not indicate the extent to which people acknowledge within-group variation. That is, if 65% of respondents indicate that Germans are industrious, does that mean that they believe all Germans to be so? Could some of the Germans be nonindustrious? To deal with this issue, Brigham (1971) asked participants to indicate what percentage of a group possessed a given trait; percentages that exceeded 80% (or fell below 20%) were designated as "unjustified generalizations." Even so, these judgments did not assess consensual beliefs, but rather the perspectives of specific individuals. Do a large percentage of people agree that 80% or more Germans are industrious, or is this a belief only held by two or three people?

More recent methods attempt to consider both the magnitude of consensus among respondents and the extremity of the belief. For example, Gardner's (1994; Gardner, Kirby, & Finlay, 1973) method presents participants with 25–30 bipolar traits and requires them to rate the degree to which these attributes describe a target group. Attributes whose ratings differ significantly from the hypothetical scale midpoint (in a one-sample t test) are designated as consensual stereotypes. For example, using this type of method to select stereotypic attributes of alcoholics, Ruscher and Hammer (1994) selected 4 traits from an original pool of 136 traits. Participants rated each trait along a 9-point Likert-type scale. Selected traits (crisis-prone, paranoid, disagreeable, forgetful) each differed significantly from the hypothetical scale midpoint of 4.5 ($M = 7.03$). This method takes into account several conceptually important facets of a consensual stereotype. First, it accounts for the extent to which the population of raters agree with one another, that is, the degree to which consensus is achieved. If raters disagreed radically with one another, a trait would not emerge as statistically different from the hypothetical scale midpoint (i.e., because the denominator in the t test is a variance estimate; for a different interpretation, see Conway & Schaller, 1998). In this respect, then, this procedure taps consensuality. Second, the method accounts for the degree to which the stereotype is endorsed. Are alcoholics presumed to be very forgetful or just mildly forgetful? This method, or at least some variation upon it, contemporarily seems common in selecting stereotypic descriptions to be used in social psychological research. Note that this method does not address a fundamental concern raised by Brigham (1971): the percentage of group members assumed to possess the trait.

An alternate estimate of consensus uses the intraclass correlation coefficient (Griffin & Gonzalez, 1995) or some variation upon it. The intraclass correlation indicates the extent to which dyad members' scores on a variable are not independent of one another. For example, two close friends both might rate their new psychology professor in a similar fashion on course evaluations, because of their shared slant on things: they both compare him to their mutual psychology professor last year, they have come to look for similar things in a professor, and they have discussed him before completing the ratings. Their ratings have been influenced by each other in a way that they would not been influenced by a randomly selected stranger.

Thus, shared impressions—and shared stereotypes—might stem from extensive past conversations about a group, participation in the same basic culture, or any number of other factors. The intraclass correlation is restricted to two-person groups, although statistical procedures that allow extensions to larger groups exist (Kenny & La Voie, 1984). These methods can only be used if the dyad members are indistinguishable; that is, the only way to distinguish members of the dyads is through some arbitrary characteristic (e.g., friend #1 and friend #2). If the members are distinguishable (e.g., husband–wife, teacher–learner), the researcher can use one type of members' scores as the predictor variable and the other type of members' scores as the criterion variable. For example, the husbands' scores might be predicted from the wives' scores, allowing an ordinary zero-order correlation to be computed as an index of consensus. In contrast, with indistinguishable dyads, the assignment of one member's score to the predictor and the other member's score to the criterion is arbitrary. For example, in a study in which two people discuss and then rate a target person but who have no expressly defined roles (e.g., Hammer & Ruscher, 1997), the members are indistinguishable and the intraclass correlation is appropriate.

Finally, a very different way of demonstrating that stereotypes are consensual is to ascertain the ease with which people make connections between stereotypic attributes and their presumed categories. For instance, a person described as quick tempered and as aroused by sadomasochistic fantasies is easily labeled as a child abuser (Nisbett, Zukier, & Lemley, 1981). The logic here is that, if people generally agree as to what constitutes a child abuser, providing the requisite attributes should allow categorization as such. Indoctrination into one's culture also might mediate the development of a consensus. Consequently, the consensus among generated labels should be better as children become older. Supporting this idea, Gardner et al. (1973) found that fourth-year high school students evidenced more consensus than first-year high school students in their perceptions of various social groups. Admittedly, people are quicker to form impressions of targets described with both a label and label-congruent attributes than of targets described by attributes alone (Fiske & Neuberg, 1990). However, they still spontaneously can categorize people on the basis of attributes alone—and arrive with synonymous categories. All these various methodologies—selecting attributes for categories, rating the degree to which attributes fit a category, and selecting categories for attributes—provide evidence that stereotypes are beliefs shared among individuals with a similar history.

Summary

Several theorists have argued that consensuality is not a fundamental quality of stereotypes, and the debate has sparked a number of different ways to assess shared stereotypes. But people at least operate as though stereotypes are shared and assume that others understand the content of particular stereotypes. Two heterosexuals nod knowingly at one another when a male hairdresser strolls by, two film critics complain that a film has stereotyped female characters and expect that filmgoers will know what they mean, and people make sweeping statements like "you know how they are" about outgroup members. People may not hold jargon-laden discussions of what constitutes a stereotype or how consensuality is assessed, but they are aware implicitly that stereotypic information is consensual. People recognize, for example, that stereotypic qualities are likely to elicit agreement from communication partners and that they will be understood with ease (Ruscher & Duval, 1998). Almost without thinking, people assume that stereotypes are mutually understood.

MECHANISMS FOR DEVELOPING
SHARED STEREOTYPES

If shared stereotypes do exist, how are they developed? Certainly, people might develop shared stereotypes when they undergo similar experiences with an outgroup. If José and Alphonso are excluded from a group predominantly comprising individuals of Northern European descent, they conceivably both may conclude that "WASPs" are exclusionistic. If the two are acquainted with one another and are properly miffed at the exclusion, the event probably does not go unmentioned.

If they mutually discover the similar experience, they may discuss it with each other. Alternatively, each man may tell older friends and family members, who then may be reminded of similar experiences that they have had or about which they have heard. As the story spreads, the stereotype develops and becomes shared among the group (see Schaller & Conway, 1999). This shared reality reinforces the belief that the event is not a random occurrence and is not just in the individual person's mind (Hardin & Higgins, 1996). Even if a world filled with self-serving outgroup members is not a benign one, the shared reality of what "they" are like renders that world more predictable. This sense of predictability conceivably helps the group develop strategies for coping.

In order to develop shared stereotypes through conversation, conversing individuals must negotiate what, exactly, they believe. How will they refer to the outgroup, and do they both agree on the outgroup's general characteristics? Does a newly encountered individual belong in the outgroup, and how like the outgroup is he? Should he be treated as such? What does the ingroup know about the outgroup really, and what have they heard from other people? At least three types of literature are relevant to the negotiation of shared stereotypes: grounding, the reliance on stereotypic information, and storytelling.

Grounding

"Do you know what I mean?"
"He did what, you say?"
"Uh-huh."
"I know what you mean."

Statements and questions like the preceding ones are typical of conversing individuals' efforts to "ground" their conversation. Individuals attempt to establish that what has been said actually has been understood. Statements such as "Uh-huh" and "I know what you mean," as well as nonverbal cues such as nods are taken as evidence that the message has been understood. Questions such as "He did what?" or perplexed facial expressions imply failed understanding. Basic as it sounds, without such efforts to ascertain what has and has not been understood, a conversation is not really a conversation. Instead, it is more like parallel play in children: two or more individuals talking, perhaps even in turn, but with little connection between their statements. Grounding is the sine qua non of shared understanding.

These apparently simple aspects of conversation seem to be important for developing shared stereotypic impressions. When the subject of the conversation is an outgroup member, conversing individuals tend to develop consensus around stereotypic information. Such information is, after all, the information upon which people are most likely to agree (Ruscher & Duval, 1998). Asking questions about stereotypic attributes in order to solicit shared understanding, as well as providing back-channel information, helps a dyad achieve consensus:

ADAM: O'Malley is getting so forgetful.

AGNES: How do you mean?

ADAM: He forgot to return that thingamajig he borrowed.

AGNES: (*nodding*) Yeah. Well, he forgets a lot of things after a night out at the pub.

Agnes's question prompts Adam to elaborate on his assertion, and ultimately prompts her both to agree with him and then to link the behavior to alcohol abuse. The conversation leads them to a shared, albeit stereotypic, view of the Irish-descended O'Malley. Dyads who evidence these conversational patterns are more likely to achieve shared stereotypic impressions than dyads in whom these behaviors are rare (Ruscher, Hammer, & Hammer, 1996). The nonrhetorical questioning about potentially stereotyped qualities, as well as statements of agreement regarding them, essentially are the glue that holds a shared impression together. Although the conversation that endeavors to develop a shared impression may take some work in the short run, in the long run the conversation serves the economy function: the conversation participants know what each person believes and knows, what their shared impression is, and how they arrived at that impression. In later conversations about the person or group, the groundwork for understanding already is laid.

Economy is most evident in the establishment of referential identities in various ways (Clark & Brennan, 1991). First, conversing individuals might use alternate descriptions for the person or thing being described. One speaker might remark, "Ann always makes all those femi-nazi comments in Sociology." The other speaker might respond, "She and her femi-nazi followers make class so annoying." As the conversation progresses, Ann is referenced as "the head femi-nazi" rather than by her name, meaningful to the conversing individuals but an unclear reference to naive listeners. Second, conversing individuals might use gestures or other nonverbal cues to reference the topic of conversation. They might point or cock their heads meaningfully to denote the person in question. Alternatively, they might mimic a behavior or create an appearance that is stereotypically associated with the individual or group (e.g., creating the appearance of slanted eyes; effeminately displaying a limp-wristed hand). Finally, conversing individuals often establish which individual or thing is being discussed before elaborating about it. For instance, the first speaker says, "You know, she used to be a reporter on Channel 4, the black woman with the foreign-sounding name?" The second speaker replies, "Uh-huh. Hoda Kotb." Then the first speaker can say, "Well, she's taken a job with a cable network." These various ways of grounding help the conversing individuals ascertain whether each is following what the other has said.

Alternate references apparently become more brief over time, and may underlie, at least in part, the development of group epithets and the derogatory names used for individual outgroup members. Work by Krauss and Fussell (1991) on the naming of nonsocial objects provides a clue as to how alternate references develop and shorten. Their research paradigm requires individuals to describe or name nonsense figures in such a way that a partner can understand them. The initial references are detailed (e.g, Mardi Gras mask–shaped thing with elf boots), then shortened to minimal detail (e.g., the Mardi Gras mask), and finally shortened to a single referent (e.g., the mask). Similarly, for the conversationalists of the previous paragraph, "in-your-face militant feminist propaganda" has become "nazi feminism," and finally "femi-nazism." At the individual level, Ann is first described as "that annoying woman in Sociology who makes femi-nazi comments and has lots of followers," but eventually the label is shortened to "the head femi-nazi." Once the people involved in the conversation have developed one of these short labels, this label will organize their understanding of the person. Moreover, this label will be available to people who join or overhear the conversation, and therefore may provide a filter through which they think about the person or group. Like the group epithets discussed in Chapter 2, these idiosyncratic referents provide an oral shorthand that conveys a host of ideas and shared understandings with a minimum of words.

Efforts to create common-ground understanding depend considerably upon the inferences that conversing individuals make regarding their existing degree of shared knowledge. If the conversing individuals share a common experience or one individual tells the others something, this information is assumed to be known throughout the conversation. For example, if three clerks (of northern European descent) all were present when their supervisor introduced their new (Latina) coworker, their subsequent discussion of the secretary assumes that they all heard the same information at the introduction. This assumption, of course, may be incorrect: one person might have failed to infer that the new secretary is Latina; another might have failed to notice her wedding ring; and another might have misinterpreted something said about her previous employment situation. But the conversation will operate as though knowledge of these attributes is shared unless a question is raised.

Conversing individuals also may make suppositions about each other's knowledge, based upon various qualities of the others in the group (e.g., social group membership; the degree of their friendship). These suppositions may help ground the conversation more quickly, or they may suggest in what areas additional grounding is needed. One of the aforementioned individuals easily might presume, for example, that her fellow coworkers share her prejudice against Hispanic individuals. This presumption might lead her to make a prejudiced wisecrack. As discussed further in Chapter 7, such an attempt at humor may be an attempt to create a favorable impression. The speaker wishes to show off her terrific sense of humor, show her allegiance to the ingroup, or foster a sense of camaraderie. Although prejudiced comments are rare in laboratory settings, or in other settings in which people are concerned about being labeled as prejudiced, with friends and ingroup members such comments probably are fairly common. Then, again, the presumption of common ground need not be accurate: the speaker's coworkers may not understand the joke or may find it grossly inappropriate. People are pretty good at understanding their friends' idiosyncratic references (Krauss & Fussell, 1991), so more often than not one might expect a wisecrack shared among group members to be understood. If there is risk of failed understanding, the speaker mindful of impression management concerns might preface the joke with the stereotypic information necessary to understand it (e.g., "You know how Hispanics are supposed to be X? Well, the new secretary . . . "). As for the acceptance of the wisecrack as funny versus inappropriate, people assume consensual attitudes of peers (Marks & Miller, 1987), but perhaps are more accurate regarding the attitudes of close acquaintances. For present purposes, it is reasonable to assume that people make assumptions about the knowledge base, stereotypes, and attitudes held by the others with whom they converse. And, over time, many learn when to keep their mouths shut.

The presumptions that people bring to their conversations and their efforts to ground their messages are instrumental in the development of shared understanding. When people communicate about outgroup members for whom stereotypes already are held, a considerable amount of common ground already may exist. Still, people may need to negotiate the degree to which an existing stereotype fits a particular individual and the degree to which fellow communicators buy into the stereotype. They also may need to develop a common understanding of how they should deal with outgroup members (see below). When stereotypes initially are developing, work on grounding may provide insight into how group epithets are created (see also Chapter 2), as well as which attributes survive to form the stereotype (i.e., those attributes which are communicated and readily understood).

The Role of Stereotypic Information

To say that stereotypic information plays a special role in the development of shared stereotypic impressions is like saying that cream plays a special role in creating crème brûlée for dessert. But, depending on the dietary needs of one's dinner guests, one can substitute half-and-half or whole milk for some of the heavy cream; one might also use smaller custard cups to reduce the amount of artery-clogging cream ingested. Crème brûlée also is shared with particular guests, such as guests on whom one wishes to make a splendid impression or with whom a special bond is desired. Analogously, the degree to which stereotypic information is used to create shared stereotypic impressions varies across situations, and these impressions are created in particular situations and with particular people. Specifically, shared stereotypic impressions develop when consensus is implicitly or explicitly required, when maintaining a cohesive relationship is desired, and sometimes even when accuracy goals are activated. Finally, just as a broiler unable to generate sufficient heat interferes with the crowning stage of crème brûlée, constraints such as cognitive distraction or personality factors can interfere with the development of shared stereotypic impressions.

Culinary metaphors aside, some existing overlap in stereotypes is likely among conversing individuals from the same culture. However, as noted earlier, the extent to which they apply the same stereotype to a particular individual is critical for the development of shared stereotypic impressions. For example, consider the category of elderly persons. Younger people's stereotype of older adults may include attributes such as forgetfulness, conservatism, and slowness to learn new things. But people rarely think at such high levels of the hierarchy. Instead, they think at the level of various subtypes: grandmother, crotchety neighbor, or bus-touring retiree. Initially, the same elderly individual might remind one conversing individual of her prim and proper third-grade teacher but remind another individual of a grandmother-type character on last night's television program. Each person categorizes the target as "elderly," and each may retain some unique slant on her. In the course of their conversation, though, they need to negotiate a shared understanding of the particular target. They rehash their impressions and experience, developing a shared understanding of the target or, at the very least, an understanding of each other's idiosyncratic viewpoints. In both cases, stereotype-congruent information is the glue that congeals that shared understanding.

CONSENSUS MOTIVATION

People's subjective assessments about the opinions of others can influence their own opinions. Put another way, we tend to drift toward the perceived consensus of others. For example, if white individuals learn that their ingroup holds more (or less) stereotypic beliefs about African Americans than they originally believed, those white individuals will adjust their own stereotypic beliefs accordingly. If "everybody" seems to think African Americans are moderately high in hostility, for example, individuals will exaggerate their own estimates of hostility (Stangor, Sechrist, & Jost, in press). Moreover, beliefs that have been consensually validated are resistant to change (Stangor et al., in press). People not only wish to hold correct viewpoints; impression management concerns lead people to avoid espousing overly deviant beliefs.

When consensual validation is not immediately forthcoming, people intentionally may seek it. During conversation, conversing individuals may work toward the development of shared understandings in order to ground their conversations, to validate their own viewpoints, and to garner social support (Festinger, 1954). Although groups tend to lean toward consensus even in the absence of explicit instructions to do so, situational and dispositional factors can magnify or attenuate this desire. Implicitly or explicitly, the motivation to reach consensus especially directs attention to stereotype-congruent information. Without the motivation to reach a consensus, conversing individuals simply voice their idiosyncratic views or even argue with one another about the target's qualities; in this case, no particular type of information is highly favored. As shown in Figure 2, the desire to reach consensus theoretically could lead to consensual impressions that are counterstereotypic in nature if conversing individuals actively work to avoid stereotypic impressions because they are low in prejudice toward the group or have been warned to avoid prejudiced judgments. Although some data bearing indirectly on this notion are discussed below, the hypothesis yet requires direct examination. To date, studies demonstrate that consensus-oriented dyads typically focus on the stereotype-congruent information that is easy to agree upon (Ruscher & Duval, 1998) and that is implicitly shared (see Stasser, Taylor, &

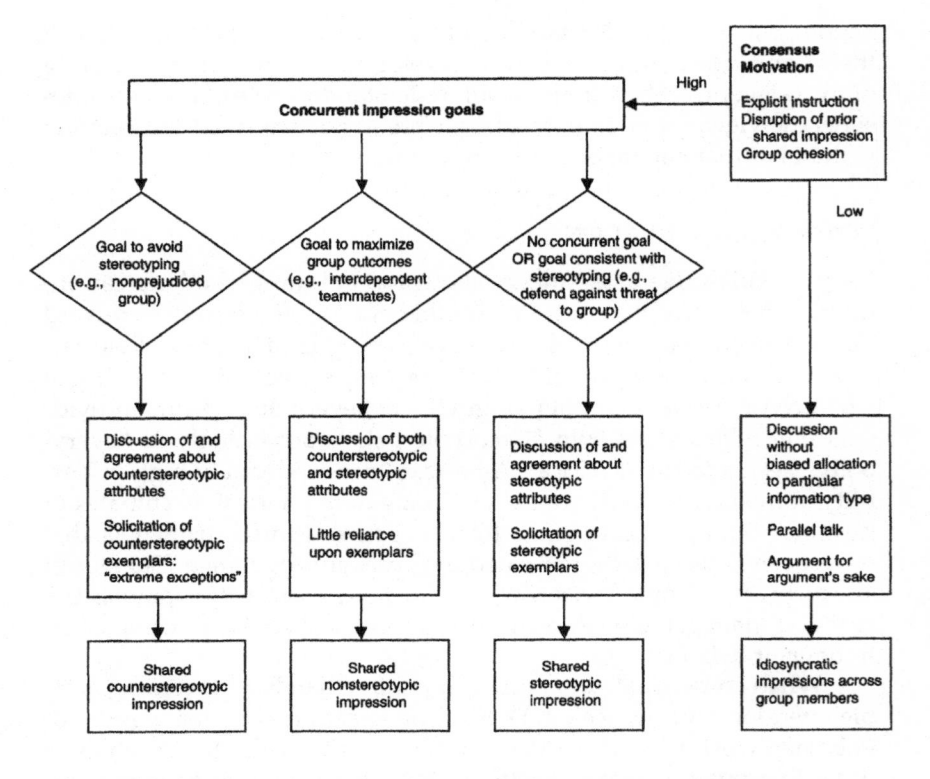

FIGURE 2. A model of the development of shared impressions.

Hanna, 1989). In the normative case, then, shared impressions tend toward the stereotypic.

Whether they are working to reach strict unanimity or simple majority, conversing individuals sometimes adopt an explicit consensus rule for making judgments about others. "Greek" societies discuss which college students will be admitted to the house, faculty search committees lobby for particular candidates to be invited for interviews, and juries debate the innocence of alleged criminals. Powerful third parties or group leaders explicitly may require consensus of the conversing individuals, subsequently directing attention toward stereotype-congruent information. Ultimately, conversational focus on stereotypic information encourages the development of shared stereotypic impressions. Examining this topic, Ruscher et al. (1996) presented same-sex undergraduate dyads with audiotaped descriptions of an alcoholic. These descriptions included characteristics that were stereotype congruent (e.g., disagreeable) and stereotype incongruent (e.g., optimistic). After hearing each description, dyads discussed their impressions of the target; half of the dyads explicitly were encouraged to work toward a consensual impression, whereas the other half were not so encouraged.

So how did the consensus-oriented dyads go about reaching consensus? Although they *could* have focused their conversation around anything that they knew about the target, the consensus-oriented dyads focused on the stereotype-congruent characteristics. The absolute difference between the impression formed by each dyad member (an index of consensus) was predicted by focus on congruent information, suggesting that congruent information helped impressions become more shared. Unfortunately, focusing on congruent information did not predict whether impressions became more stereotypic. That is, impressions under consensus motivation were shared as a function of focus on congruent information, but not necessarily shared stereotypic impressions. To investigate this possibility further, the companion study also measured impressions before the discussion occurred. By taking these initial impressions into account, the study could better examine the true relation between focus on stereotypic information and impression stereotypicness. Once these initial impressions were partialed out, focus on stereotypic information predicted both impression disparity and impression stereotypicness. That is, the more time that dyads spent discussing stereotypic attributes, the more dyads developed stereotypic impressions that were similar.

The motivation to reach consensus also can be more implicit, as when an apparent consensus is jeopardized. For example, the disruption of a previously shared impression may encourage people to reestablish their shared understanding of the person. One major disruption to an existing impression is the revelation of a previously unknown stigma: students learn that a classmate has dyslexia; a couple discovers that their neighbor beats his wife; and coworkers realize that a colleague is an alcoholic. Even if each member of the group is aware of the stigma, none can be certain that everyone has reached the same revised impression. One person might have missed some critical information, whereas another person might have better insight into the particular stigma. If the alcoholism of a coworker is revealed, for instance, one person might note that his compulsive gambling the previous evening seems typical of an alcoholic. Another person might interject that, since learning about the alcoholism, he has been noticing the Monday morning grouchiness. The group members will pool their inferences and experiences, trying to find a new shared impression of their coworker. The disruption, then, acts as an implicit motivation to reach consensus, and to think about how recalled and newly encountered information fits the stigma. Under such circumstances, conversing individuals allocate the majority of their discussion time to stereotype-congruent information, discuss how this information "fits" the stigma, and point to other individuals with the same or similar stigmas (Ruscher & Hammer, 1994).

Cohesive dyads also appear more inclined to work toward stereotypic consensus than less-cohesive dyads. In a recent study (Ruscher, Cralley, & O'Farrell, 1999), the cohesiveness of previously unacquainted female dyads was manipulated using a modification of a procedure developed by Arthur Aron and his colleagues (Aron, Melinat, Aron, Vallone, & Bator, 1997). In this modified procedure, dyads labeled as cohesive mutually disclosed intimate information; noncohesive dyads simply wrote down the intimate information while in the same room but did not exchange it with their partner. Dyads then listened to an audiotaped description of an elderly woman, then independently rated her on scales concerning negative stereotypes of elderly people and judged how typical she was of her age group. Intraclass correlations (discussed earlier) indicated that dyad members evidenced considerable overlap in their impressions of the elderly woman. More interesting, however, the cohesive dyads also perceived the target more stereotypically and as more typical of her age group than did the noncohesive dyads. That is, their shared impressions were more stereotypic, as a function of how much time they spent discussing stereotypic information. Creating cohesiveness therefore appears to operate very much like explicit or implicit consensus motivation.

The cohesion-stereotyping relation raises interesting questions about what functions are being served in these dyadic conversations. One possibility is that expressing stereotypic beliefs about an outgroup serves ego-protecting—or at least group-enhancing—functions. Cohesiveness that is based on social attraction, such as pride in the group's accomplishments, tends to stifle individuality and dissent (Hogg & Hains, 1998) and encourage efforts to protect the group's self-image (Turner, Pratkanis, Probasco, & Leve, 1992). Members of the ingroup may feel better about themselves or feel a more clear sense of camaraderie and "we-ness" when they express stereotypic beliefs about outgroups. Alternatively, to the extent that socially based cohesion limits freedom to express dissenting opinions, expressing stereotypic beliefs may reflect certain aspects of impression management. In the cohesive group, it may be important to be perceived as a person who tries to get along as a team player and as someone who accepts the opinions of other group members as valid. The functions are not mutually exclusive, of course. An individual may desire to bolster the group, his or her own self-esteem, and to appear an easygoing team player.

An intriguing variation on the cohesion → stereotyping association is the possibility that stereotyping also may enhance cohesion. Dyad members who echo each other's shared perceptions are viewed as more knowledgeable and competent than dyad members who assert unique information (Wittenbaum, Hubbell, & Zuckerman, 1999). Conceivably, such effects would extend to communication about stereotypes. A new communicator partner who echoes one's stereotypic views may be liked and respected. The initial spark of cohesiveness, then, could be driven by expressing stereotypic and prejudiced beliefs. Community, to paraphrase Jean-Paul Sartre, may be fostered by prejudice against an outgroup.

MUST CONSENSUS MOTIVATION LEAD TO STEREOTYPING?

Technically speaking, conversing individuals could develop shared nonstereotypic or counterstereotypic impressions. Figure 2 proposes some conditions under which such impressions could emerge. But the ease with which stereotypic information is understood and agreed upon, as well as the general tendency of groups to discuss implicitly or explicitly shared information, simply make it more likely that consensus will develop around stereotypic attributes in the absence of competing goals. To date, research primarily supports a link between consensus motivation and shared stereotypic impressions, but—as suggested by work with individual perceivers—several potential factors may undercut this tendency.

With individual perceivers, increasing accuracy motivation is known to attenuate stereotypic impressions. When perceiver and target are cooperating as teammates, for example, accuracy motivations are activated and the perceiver is encouraged to incorporate stereotype-incongruent information into impressions. Stereotype-congruent information is not ignored, nor is the stereotype label. Instead, the accuracy-oriented perceiver comes to see the target as an individual, who admittedly is a member of group X but who also has stereotype-incongruent features. The resulting individuated impression need not be counterstereotypic per se, just less stereotypic than an impression based on stereotype-congruent information alone. Telling individuals to be accurate (Neuberg & Fiske, 1987) or indicating that their judgments will be compared to those of an expert (Tetlock, 1983) mimic the effects of cooperation, encouraging efforts toward accuracy.

Curiously, the effects of these latter two methods do not extend directly to shared impression formation. Asking groups to strive toward accuracy or telling them that their judgments will be compared to those of an expert seems to encourage them to use consensus as a proxy for accuracy (for a discussion, see Funder, 1987). Consensus, as noted earlier, is most readily developed around stereotypic information. Groups conceivably see consensual viewpoints as valid ones, and may presume that their consensus approximates the experts' judgments and is their best estimate of accuracy. Ruscher and colleagues' (1996) study, discussed earlier, produced results that are consistent with this notion. In addition to manipulating consensus motivation, Ruscher et al. also manipulated accuracy motivation; in the first study, the experimenter enjoined some dyads to try to be accurate, whereas in the second study the experimenter indicated that impressions would be compared to those of an expert. Both accuracy manipulations encouraged the conversing dyads to discuss stereotype-incongruent as well as stereotype-congruent information, which suggested that dyads were trying, at least, to be thorough. However, their resulting shared impressions remained stereotypic. The incongruent information apparently was not integrated into shared impressions.

To date, the effects of cooperation on shared impression formation have not been examined. Conceivably, such situations might prove better at encouraging more individuated impressions. In the existing studies on shared impressions, the relationship between perceivers and targets is nondependent. The targets in these studies are of no real importance to the perceivers: they are not coworkers, fellow members of a sports team, or roommates in a college dorm. The target cannot influence perceivers' outcomes in any way. Perceivers typically rely on their stereotypes in nondependent situations, and the motivation to reach a consensus simply may magnify this tendency. Moreover, the perceiver–target relationship should be symmetrical. In the existing studies, dyads discuss and evaluate a target rather than vice versa. All things being equal, the impressions of the party with more power tend toward the stereotypic. If the target were a peer coworker of the conversing individuals or had more power than them (e.g., a new boss), shared impressions might be less inclined toward the stereotypic and derive from efforts to find a shared individuated impression. Consensus, in such cases, might be less likely to serve as a proxy for accuracy.

Finally, shared impressions need not be only stereotypic or individuated; they might also be counterstereotypic. Such impressions may develop not out of accuracy goals per se but from goals to actively avoid developing stereotypic impressions. For example, if the group comprised individuals who wish to avoid being prejudiced against the target's outgroup, they actively might avoid allowing stereotypic impressions to develop. They might draw to mind extreme counterstereotypic exemplars from the target's group to solidify their view that the stereotype is inaccurate. Stereotypic information, if discussed, probably would be challenged or summarily dismissed. Either dispositional or situational factors presumably could engender the desire to develop counterstereotypic impressions.

Storytelling

Much of the work on communicated impressions requests communicators to share their impressions of targets or to hear other people present their impressions. True, people do share what they heard other people say, and they do convey impressions based on written information that they have received. But in many situations people observe real behavior. In these situations, communicators may convey their impressions through storytelling rather than primarily through abstract descriptions or gut-level impressions. Communicators provide narrative accounts of their own lives and of the lives of other people, including accompanying inferences and emotional reactions (Wyer & Gruenfeld, 1995). A communicator may give an abstraction (e.g., "Hank is a real loser"), but unless the meaning of this statement is readily apparent to the audience, the communicator will then most likely detail one or two episodes that illustrate Hank's loser qualities. The retelling of these episodes may be slanted to meet the particular goals of the speaker and, as a consequence of the biased retelling, eventually may distort the communicator's memory for the original events (see Higgins & Rholes, 1978).

Like other types of communicated impressions, the goals of storytelling may vary from impression management to group indoctrination. People tell stories that illustrate the negative stereotypic qualities of particular outgroup members, and these stories purportedly help justify prejudice toward the group. In one of van Dijk's (1988) examples, a Dutch couple relay a story about a Turkish neighbor who illegally slaughtered a sheep in the bathtub during Ramadan. The couple describe how pieces of the sheep became clogged in the drain and began to rot, and then how the police "finally" came to investigate. The couple interject their own inferences and reactions into the story, questioning what kind of people would slaughter an animal in their own home and questioning who ultimately will cover the damages. The story provides an illustration of the outgroup as unintelligent, unclean, and irresponsible. Although this particular story was told in response to an interviewer's query, it just as easily could have been told to warn newcomers to the neighborhood about the troubles allegedly caused by Turks, to seek validation of the experience from the listener, or to support policies not beneficial to immigrants. But clearly this is a story about outgroup members, not a simple list of their qualities or inferred qualities.

Along with any number of potential concurrent goals, an implicit goal of storytelling is telling a *good* story. At a minimum, a good story needs to be coherent. If the story is explanatory in nature, it also needs to account for additional known or inferred pieces of information (see Pennington & Hastie, 1992). For example, imagine that Nancy, a supervisor, fires a subordinate. Nancy is white and John, the subordinate, is black. She infers that her colleagues are curious regarding the termination of employment and, in addition, fears being labeled as prejudiced by them. She needs to tell a story to account for this negative and perhaps unexpected event and to protect her public image. Consequently, during a coffee break, Nancy tells the following story to a coworker at a similar level of the organizational hierarchy:

> "I had to fire John yesterday morning. You've seen his performance appraisals? No? Well, they've been going steadily downhill for the last 18 months. I know that he's had some problems at home but, fact of the matter is, the work isn't getting done. Earlier in the week, I found six errors in the B-6 report the morning it went to Richardson's office. That was a close one! Eve's been trying to clean up after him, but that's not her job . . . and anyway, she's in line to be promoted so no one is going to be there to tow the line for him. I feel really bad, though. He's a nice guy."

The story here is quite simple: John's past and present performance allegedly is inferior, and personal feelings are irrelevant to the decision. His success in maintaining even a minimum standard of performance is attributed to both the supervisor and his peer covering up his mistakes. The magnitude of the poor performance is emphasized with the reference to seemingly objective performance appraisals and the near-miss episode with the ominous Richardson. If this story provides a more comprehensive and coherent explanation of the event than competing stories, it should be accepted by the group. In effect, the story will become the generally shared account of how John's employment was terminated. The story also helps Nancy's impression management goals by shifting any apparent blame to John. The group then may rely upon this story when they are called upon to provide judgments about Nancy, about Eve, about former employees, or about black employees.

Finally, the purpose of some good storytelling is largely to entertain. Listeners enjoy stories of the bizarre and unexpected, of people getting their just deserts, and even of random acts of kindness. Like evidencing a delightful sense of humor, the ability to tell a good story is a socially desirable characteristic and helps portray a favorable impression. Because the primary goal is not necessarily accuracy, the communicator may take some liberties with the story to render it both more colorful and more coherent. For example, a coworker who disliked John (talking to a like-minded coworker) might omit the difficulties at home, embellish upon the ominous near miss with Richardson, and hypothesize about some ways that Eve covered for him. For prejudiced communicators, these "liberties" probably emphasize the stereotypic and therefore help perpetuate generally prejudiced impressions.

Summary

Grounding, the reliance on stereotypic information, and storytelling are not mutually exclusive devices used by people who develop shared impressions. Instead, their separation here reflects different research traditions more than fundamentally different processes. Storytelling, for example, requires the speaker to develop a common ground with the audience, filling in the setting and background plot for naive listeners, making certain that the thrust of the story is not missed. Similarly, when outgroup members are the topic of discussion, storytelling probably relies quite heavily on stereotypic information. And, as noted earlier, grounding conversations about outgroup members may occur primarily around stereotypic information. Undoubtedly, there are other micro-level aspects of conversation that serve the development of shared stereotypes and shared stereotypic impressions. For example, the linguistic choices that people make (Chapter 2), their nonverbal behaviors (Chapter 5), and use of group-disparaging humor (Chapter 7) also may help people develop shared understanding of outgroup members. The above sampling provides a flavor of how conversing individuals do what they do, but it is by no means an exhaustive list.

STEREOTYPE TRANSMISSION

Shared impressions may not remain isolated between a dyad or among members of some other small group. Instead, they may be transmitted among larger social groups to which the smaller group belongs. Members of a small work group, for example, may communicate primarily with each other, but each member may have one or two additional work contacts with whom she or he regularly communicates. Alternatively, people might converse most often with individuals in the closest physical proximity, so the person nearest a public place (e.g., stairwells, rest rooms, the main department office) may have numerous communication partners. Persons with social centrality (e.g., the shared secretary or the person on all major committees) also may have more different partners than peers. These central individuals simply have more opportunities to transmit their own stereotypic beliefs (and the beliefs that they have developed with others) to new people. If these beliefs are viewed as informative and are communicated with ease, they will be transmitted into the larger social setting (see Schaller & Latané, 1996). As a result of communication, and depending on the type of social space that prevails, the viewpoint that originally reflected the majority viewpoint (e.g., a stereotype) may become even more widely accepted than it originally was (Latané & L'Herrou, 1996).

Besides wanting to ground their communication and develop shared understanding, why do people transmit their stereotypes? And, assuming that the recipients are not simply passive receivers of information, what possesses them to take the message to heart? A few potential goals already have been mentioned, namely, the desire to build cohesion, to tell a good story, and to justify apparently prejudiced actions. Because interest in stereotype transmission is relatively recent, only a few potential goals have received empirical attention. Among these goals are group indoctrination, the motivation (or lack thereof) to provide one's own idiosyncratic slant on the target, and impression management.

Group Socialization and Identification

When an individual joins a social group, the group indoctrinates the individual by sharing norms and expectations. Formal and informal indoctrination sessions, as well as mentors, pass along this knowledge to the new group member (for a review see Moreland & Levine, 1982). Included in this information are the shared attitudes toward outgroups and about issues relevant to outgroups. These specific aspects of the indoctrination process serve the social function of prejudiced communication, namely, helping the new group member learn ingroup values as well as norms for dealing with the outgroup. A newly hired organizational psychologist, for example, might be "taught" by more senior members of the department that the historians are prima donnas, the biologists are resource grabbers, and the counseling psychologists are deadweight. She acquires this knowledge in a variety of ways—through overheard conversations, as the recipient of storytelling and warnings, by inferences drawn from the nonverbal behavior of her colleagues, and via other means. Initially, she may try to suspend judgment in the interest of fairness. Over time, however, her acceptance as a full-fledged and influential member of the group depends in part upon her adopting these beliefs. To the extent that the group wants her to fit in and be successful, it believes that the imparted "knowledge" will help her devise strategies for interacting with these other groups. Moreover, although they may or may not be conscious of it, the sense of ingroup identity also may be strengthened by explicitly differentiating the ingroup from other groups. Put another way, transmitting the stereotypic beliefs functions to distinguish the ingroup from the outgroup. Finally, these beliefs express the values of the ingroup, focusing on group-enhancing characteristics. With respect to the example above, the new person learns that her ingroup prides itself on being modest, fair about resource allocation, and particularly on its productivity. The new person may not come to share *all* of these beliefs, but at the very least she needs to operate with full cognizance of the ingroups' values and beliefs about its various outgroups.

Recent studies, primarily conducted by Guimond and his colleagues, address the social transmission of such attitudes with longitudinal designs. One such study (Guimond & Palmer, 1996) examined the attitudes of social science majors versus commerce majors during their first year versus their third year in college. In their curriculum, social science students are exposed to the structural and situational pressures that influence groups and individuals. Commerce students, in contrast, learn about the factors that encourage economic growth and financial success. On the average, then, social science students may be expected to become more "liberal" whereas commerce students may become expected to be more "conservative" with respect to social and political issues. Interestingly, students from the two groups in this study did not differ in their first year with respect to their attitudes toward socialists, unions, and capitalists. Consequently, any observed changes in attitudes over time are unlikely to stem from initial selection of major. By their third year, marked changes in attitude had occurred: Compared to social science students, commerce students' attitudes toward unions and socialists had become less favorable whereas their attitudes toward capitalists had become more favorable.

How did transmission of these attitudes occur? Reported sources of influence ranged from course content to professors to peers. With respect to peers, students reported that peers from their same discipline had affected their attitudes. Undoubtedly, at least some of the peers' influence occurred via interpersonal communication. Course content also was targeted as an influence source, and presumably included readings, class discussions, lectures, and films. The more that social science students believed that they were influenced by course content, the less they blamed impoverished or unemployed individuals for their bleak situations. Admittedly, participants may not be able to identify with perfect accuracy the influences on their own attitudes (Nisbett & Wilson, 1977). However, it is not unreasonable to think that these various sources exerted some influence. Interpersonal communication alone, of course, may not be the only (or even the most important) factor driving social transmission. Individuals simply might model the behavior of peer and reference groups (e.g., be socially reinforced for excluding members of the disparaged group). Alternatively, socialization by professors and more advanced students might lead them to encounter members of the disparaged groups in different settings. For example, students undergoing "liberal" training might join volunteer groups in which they have first-hand encounters with impoverished individuals; such encounters may develop both a better appreciation for the difficulties of living within a restricted income as well as viewing people in these situations as individuals.

Although some form of social transmission of normative beliefs occurs among members of a group, not all recipients of those beliefs take them to heart. Instead, those individuals who most strongly identify with the group are most inclined to adopt the beliefs of their group. This point is addressed in a longitudinal study of English-speaking students at a Canadian military college (Guimond, 2000). Initially, these Anglophones held more positive attitudes toward both Anglophones and Francophones than did their counterparts at a non-military university, but otherwise they evidenced similar intergroup attitudes (e.g., regarding immigrants). Guimond surveyed the military students' attitudes toward Francophones, immigrants, Anglophones, and civilians during their first and final years of college; he also examined their social identification as military officers during their third year. Certainly, changes in attitudes would be expected over time as a result of social transmission (see Guimond & Palmer, 1996). But Guimond reasoned that the degree of social identification might underlie those changes. Supporting this idea, Guimond found that increased social identification as a military officer predicted more negative attitudes toward Francophones, civilians, and immigrants, above and beyond initial attitudes; social identification did not underlie changes in attitudes toward the ingroup (Anglophones). As people become more tied to the ingroup, they adopt the ingroup's shared belief system. One further might expect that these highly identified individuals, in turn, express the stereotypic beliefs that indoctrinate new group members; doing so would serve social functions of group differentiation, as well as possibly enhancing group-based self-esteem.

Impression Management

Guimond's work, just discussed, suggests that a need to belong prompts individuals to accept the beliefs of their adopted groups. Conceivably, such a need to belong or a desire to be seen in a favorable light could prompt both the acceptance of stereotypic beliefs and their transmission. People do, for example, tailor their communicated impressions to suit the evaluative preferences of their audiences (Higgins & Rholes, 1978). Perhaps one of the reasons that communicators tailor their messages is an implicit recognition that similar values and attitudes are associated with increased liking (Byrne, 1971). Creating a favorable impression indeed can encourage stereotype transmission. As discussed in Chapter 1, for instance, communicators may try to project a nonprejudiced self-image. Alternatively, communicators may hope that their humorously embellished and bizarre story about an outgroup will make them seem humorous, witty, and insightful.

Along that vein, Schaller and Conway (1999) explicitly examined impression management goals and communicated stereotypes in a series of experiments. In one of these experiments, dyads were lead to believe that people who talked about negative (or positive) qualities of other people typically became successful in later life. Thus, in order to portray themselves in a favorable light, they should communicate primarily about the attributes allegedly diagnostic of future success. Dyad members received information about two groups. The majority of the members in the first group were both more aggressive and more creative than members of the other group. Dyad members communicated their impressions to each other via note cards, then rated the groups on aggression-relevant and creativity-relevant adjectives as an index of stereotyping. As expected, the evaluative slant of participants' communications reflected impression management goals; participants who believed that communicating negative information was associated with later success focused on the negative information, and vice versa for participants who believed in the association between positive information and success. The former individuals also came to see the group with a majority of aggressive individuals as more aggressive than did their counterparts. These impressions of aggressivity did not stem entirely from participants' initial impressions, but derived at least in part from interpersonal communication. Thus, impression management goals can influence the communication of at least negative stereotypes.

That interpersonal communication only partially mediated the effect of impression management goals on stereotyping lead Schaller and Conway to conduct another experiment to ascertain whether interpersonal communication per se was truly critical (e.g., rather than being driven by one's own impressions). In this experiment, dyads were assigned to one of four conditions. One condition mimicked a condition in the previous study, in which both dyad members could write notes and both were encouraged to convey a negative impression. Another condition allowed mutual communication but manipulated no impression management goal (which provided a control condition). A third condition manipulated impression management goals but only allowed participants to receive written notes from previous participants; this condition could help rule out the possibility that participants only were responding as they thought the experimenter wanted them to do. The final condition manipulated impression management goals and only allowed participants to write messages but not receive them; this condition could help rule out one-way communication as the main source of stereotyping rather than interpersonal communication. As expected, participants with an impression management goal who were permitted mutual communication stereotyped more than any other participants. This result provides strong support that interpersonal communication in the service of an impression management goal encourages people to transmit stereotypic beliefs.

Being Coherent versus Accurate

An implicit communication rule presumably encourages communicators to be accurate and truthful when constructing their messages (Grice, 1975; Higgins, 1981). Be that as it may, trying to be accurate may conflict with other communication goals. Telling the *whole* truth can muddy an otherwise tidy story. Incongruent and counterstereotypic information is not only harder to understand, it jeopardizes the coherence of a stereotypic description. To maintain coherence for the listener, incongruencies, if mentioned at all, must be resolved (Cummings & Ruscher, 1994). Coherence seems to be the overriding goal, so telling the whole truth may only occur under certain circumstances.

Addressing this issue, Ruscher and Duval (1998) examined how previously acquainted dyads transmitted impressions of an alcoholic or a paraplegic to a third party. Like Schaller and Conway (1999), Ruscher and Duval presented half of their communicators with an implicit communication goal. In this case, the communication goal was to convey an accurate impression that conveyed each dyad member's perspective, that is, to tell the whole truth. To encourage this goal in half of the dyads, target information was divided between the dyad members. These dyad members should (and did) feel pressured to convey their own idiosyncratic impressions, increasing the likelihood that they would describe the stereotype-incongruent attributes that were implicitly and explicitly unshared. In effect, these individuals felt pressured to be both accurate and coherent. The remaining dyads shared all the information and therefore presumably would focus their communication around the stereotype-congruent information about which they easily could agree; this information also potentially provided the most coherent description for their audience. Their communicated impressions of the alcoholic (or paraplegic) therefore would be relatively stereotypic and would engender stereotypic impressions in the message recipient.

As expected, the dyad members with unique information allocated more time to describing stereotype-incongruent information. They also characterized these attributes in a very abstract fashion, which served to undercut the stereotype. For example, they described the alcoholic as "motivated"—an attribute incongruent with the alcoholic stereotype—rather than simply noting that he worked during his lunch hour (see Chapter 2 for more discussion of the linguistic intergroup bias). Most interesting, however, was the impact of these communicated impressions on receivers. Ruscher and Duval (1998) yoked one naive participant to each communication, then assessed his or her stereotypic impressions of the target. That is, the transmission of each communicating dyad was received by one individual. As anticipated, the less that the descriptions focused on stereotype-incongruent information (and characterized these attributes in an abstract, stereotype-refuting fashion), the more receivers' impressions became stereotypic. Without stereotype-refuting information, the transmitted impressions engendered stereotypic impressions in the receivers.

More recently, Wigboldus, Semin, and Spears (2000) asked participants to write four true stories about a close friend of the same or other gender, in which their friend displayed behaviors that varied in desirability and typicality for their gender. Each participant then read the set of stories written by another participant, thereby serving as communicators and receivers. Communicated stories were more linguistically abstract when describing gender-congruent behaviors (e.g., a woman friend who performed a typically female behavior). The dispositional inferences that communicators' stories produced in receivers were mediated by the level of linguistic abstraction conveyed. That is, if a woman was described stereotypically (e.g., "maternal" rather than as "watched her niece on Saturday"), receivers' inferences about the woman were more dispositional. This effect was replicated conceptually in an additional study using Dutch versus Flemish targets, further supporting the importance of linguistic abstraction in the communication of stereotypes. Like Schaller and Conway's (1999) and Ruscher and Duval's (1998) research, the work of Wigboldus et al. (2000) lends insight into how stereotypes are communicated among individuals: Communicators focus on stereotypic information, characterize that information in ways that emphasize the stereotype, and ignore potential incongruities. As discussed next, what the receiver obtains is a compact slanted view on the outgroup and outgroup member. Small wonder that stereotypes are alive and kicking.

The Problem of Secondhand Information

Communicated impressions and stereotypes are, essentially, secondhand information. As the story replicates from individual to individual, only the most stereotypic information may be passed along. In general, recipients of secondhand target information form more extreme impressions of targets than do recipients of firsthand information. In the initial studies on this topic, Gilovich (1987) allowed half of his participants (first-generation participants) to form an impression of videotaped targets who described actions of which they were not proud (e.g., betraying a confidence). The descriptions included details of these negative behaviors as well as mitigating circumstances. The first-generation participants then recounted their impression of the target onto an audio-recording; each audio-recorded impression was played for one of the remaining participants (second-generation participants). As expected, the second-generation participants' impressions were more negative than those of their first-generation counterparts.

One potential explanation for this "teller–listener extremity effect" is that the first-generation tellers tend to omit the mitigating information that might temper the negativity of the impression (just as people communicating about outgroups tend to omit counterstereotypic information). Without mitigating information available to them, the listeners exposed primarily to negative actions infer underlying dispositional causes for the behavior. That is, they tend to make the fundamental attribution error. Although Gilovich's (1987) study does not examine the communication of stereotypic perceptions per se, a parallel is easy to see. A good deal of stereotype-congruent information is dispositional in nature. As perceived by their respective outgroups, women are gossipy, blacks are lazy, and elderly neighbors are stubbornly old-fashioned. These inferences initially may be based on specific stereotype-congruent behaviors, respectively: a woman telling a story about a neighbor, an African American worker who arrives to work late one day, or an 75-year-old woman who refuses to surf the

Internet. But these specific behaviors get lost in the stereotype, and the circumstances during which they were enacted are forgotten. When people retell stories about outgroup members, then, they may focus more on stereotypic dispositional information than the situational factors that might temper application of the stereotype. Consistent with this notion, Hammer (1996) showed that European Americans who were thinking aloud about an African American individual's stereotypic behaviors drew dispositional inferences about those behaviors. Subsequent acknowledgment of situational constraints occurred only when the participants were low in prejudice toward blacks and not experiencing a simultaneous cognitive load. Thus, one might expect that prejudiced communicators generally focus on stereotype-congruent dispositional information and omit situational constraints. Consequently, listeners should be more likely to develop extreme stereotypic impressions.

Additional indirect evidence supports the notion that secondhand impressions tend to be more stereotypic than the impressions implied by the original message. Duval, Ruscher, Welsh, and Catanese (2000) required college-aged participants to listen to a college-aged or elderly speaker describe three elderly people in a stereotypic fashion. Although these descriptions were not generated by participants, the description mimics the "first-generation impressions" in Gilovich's original study. Descriptions comprised three stereotypic attributes (one evaluatively positive, one negative, and one neutral) and one stereotype-irrelevant but evaluatively neutral attribute. With the inclusion of the stereotype-irrelevant attribute, which "diluted" the stereotypicness of the message, the average stereotypicality of these descriptions was 2.98 on a 5-point scale. The stereotypicality of *listeners'* think-aloud impressions of these targets later were judged for stereotypicality. When the original speaker was a fellow college-aged student, the stereotypicality of the listeners' think-aloud impressions was 3.14—quite similar. If the original speaker was an elderly person, however, the stereotypicality jumped to 3.93. The listeners' impressions therefore seemed to become more stereotypic than the original message implied, especially if the speaker was a member of the described group. Duval et al. (2000) suggest that the elderly person was viewed as a sort of "expert" on other elderly people and therefore was more influential on listeners' impressions than a peer would be. Although the study did not provide a statistical comparison of tellers and listeners, the descriptive findings are consistent with the notion that stereotypic impressions may become more extreme when they are communicated and that who transmits the impressions is of import.

Summary

Interpersonal communication is an important vehicle for the transmission of stereotypes. When new group members are indoctrinated into a group culture, the norms to which they are exposed include normative beliefs about outgroups. Among other things, the goal of such indoctrination is to smooth the new group member's transition into a full-fledged member and to validate the identity of the ingroup. Stereotypic impressions of groups also are transmitted to serve impression management goals as well as the standard communication goal of striking a balance between accuracy and coherence when conveying information. Finally, communicated stereotypes and stereotypic impressions represent secondhand (or even third- or fourthhand) information. Communicators typically may omit stereotype-diluting situational information, counterstereotypic information, or other discrepancies in order to convey a more coherent message for their audience. On average, then, one might expect that, just as shared impressions typically develop around stereotypic information, the impressions that are transmitted to other individuals or the larger group will tend to be stereotypic.

SHARED STEREOTYPES
AND GROUP DECISION MAKING

As groups with shared stereotypic impressions, people presumably rely upon these shared perceptions to make group decisions about how to deal with outgroup members. When or how a turf war should begin; whether "they" will be admitted to certain social clubs; and how to cope with the organization's aggressive new affirmative action policy—at least in part, decision makers will fall back upon shared stereotypes. This final section considers a few arenas in which stereotypes may be used in group decision making: group entry and juridic decision making.

Group Entry and Promotion

Groups vary considerably with respect to the permeability of their boundaries. Some groups can be joined simply by remitting a nominal application fee, typing one's name on an Internet webpage, or showing up at an open meeting. The criteria for admission to extremely permeable groups are minimal. At the extremely nonpermeable end of the continuum, the criteria for admission are much more stringent. The person seeking admission must meet certain prescribed characteristics (e.g., gender, ethnicity, religious background) or achievements (e.g., an advanced degree, national reputation) to be considered for admission. Shared stereotypes both may affect the creation of the criteria that exclude or include certain types of individuals, as well as how those criteria are applied.

For instance, some public school systems include particular schools that boast attractive qualities such as high standardized test scores or a small teacher–student ratio, but admission to these schools is not based solely on residency in the district. Such schools often are called "access" or "magnate" schools or, alternatively, "schools of choice." Students within the district have the first opportunity for admission, with students outside the district being admitted if there is room and if they meet certain criteria. Assume for a moment that the individuals who originally propose the locations for the access schools largely hail from a particular ethnic or socioeconomic background. The designated access schools may then tend to be located in districts in which individuals from that particular ethnic or socioeconomic background tend to live. Although the decision may be based both on efforts to retain valued resources for one's own group (i.e., the resource protect function), shared stereotypes may affect this decision as well. For example, a high-status group of decision makers may believe that individuals from lower socioeconomic status or different ethnic groups generally are less hardworking or less intelligent. Their stereotypes may lead them to conclude that such individuals will be unable to maintain the high standards of the school, dooming it to fail.

Once a norm for admitting individuals into a particular group is created, the norm may take on a life of its own. With access schools, for example, the younger siblings of current students typically receive high priority for admission, even if they reside outside the district. In Orleans Parish, which includes the city of New Orleans, this admissions policy was not examined thoroughly until 1998, when some residents questioned whether that policy was biased against African American students. (The inquiry found no evidence for bias from this particular policy.) But norms that seem "reasonable" may be passed across generations without question. Nielsen and Miller (1997), for instance, examined the transmission of norms for hiring recommendations made by three-person groups. During the first session, the person who presumably was the second most senior person (actually a confederate) indicated that the previous groups had followed either a seniority rule or majority rule in making the hiring recommendations. After the set of decisions was made, the most senior person of the group (also a confederate) was replaced by a real participant. Once the

confederates were gone, the most senior person in the group was replaced by a new participant, either until the rule changed or for no
more than 10 generations. The study found that groups adhered to the
seniority rule norm for an average of 2.15 generations, usually changing the norm during the third generation when the confederates both
had left the group. In contrast, the majority rule lasted an average of
9.95 generations.

Nielsen and Miller (1997) point to the possibility that these female
college students probably were very familiar with majority rule and
may have disliked the nonegalitarian system of decision making implied by the seniority rule. Their focus therefore is on the failure of the
seniority rule to persist as long as the majority rule. For present purposes, however, the persistence of the majority rule is perhaps more interesting. Shared stereotypes presumably reflect the majority's view of
a particular group and therefore could be the source of a group norm.
A majority of individuals in an all-male organization, for example,
may hold negative stereotypes of women and consequently be opposed to their membership in the organization. If the shared stereotype
fails to change and the majority rule persists, the all-male organization
may continue to oppose female membership in the organization. Even
if the organization eventually is forced to admit some women, it may
develop or invoke esoteric criteria that minimize the number of
women admitted. The majority rule regarding admission certainly
may seem fair to the admitting group but may not be fair to certain individuals seeking admission.

It bears mentioning that even small differences in preferential admission or hiring may have important long-term consequences. Many
organizations have a pyramidal structure, with fewer potential opportunities at the top of the organization than at the bottom. Moreover,
early success at lower levels is critical for possible movement into upper levels. Martell, Lane, and Emrich (1996) demonstrated this phenomena with a Monte Carlo computer simulation. The simulation began with an equal number of men and women in each of eight
hierarchical levels, with 500 positions at the bottom and 10 positions at
the top. Each person was randomly assigned a performance evaluation
score, and the distributions of the men and the women at this initial
stage were identical. Then the simulation removed 15% of the participants (mimicking workplace attrition). The positions "vacated" by
these participants were filled by the person with the highest evaluation
at the position just below in the hierarchy (mimicking workplace promotion).

Given the similarity of male and female employees, the distribution of men and women within each level of the hierarchy remained
the same. But then Martell et al. (1996) added "bias points" to the

performance score of each man. In one of the simulations, they added points that accounted for only 1% of the variance, making the differences between the men and women very trivial—trivial, that is, until the cycle of attrition and promotion continued until an entirely new set of employees had been "hired." Even with the tiny advantage of men over women, women in the organization eventually comprised 53% of the bottom level positions but only 35% of the top positions. Even small biases—derived from shared stereotypes, hiring norms, or other factors—ultimately can have dramatic effects. If the majority of the ingroup implicitly agrees that members of a particular group are better suited for promotion, a small bias—too small to arouse the attention of the equal opportunity officer—may have a substantial impact.

Although Martell et al. (1996) targeted their discussion to employment settings, the logic of their argument and the computer simulation extends to educational settings as well. Fewer individuals complete baccalaureate degrees than complete high school, and fewer still complete advanced degrees such as the doctor of philosophy. And most individuals who are academically unsuccessful early on fail to find their way into institutions of higher learning. Even small biases against a particular group at early education levels ultimately should reduce that group's representation in upper education levels. These biases might include admissions policies, but also the encouragement (or lack thereof) extended to individuals from particular groups. For example, in today's climate, educators perhaps are wary about directly informing females that they are unsuited for neuroscience or higher mathematics. But the validation of the stereotypes that they receive from their peers might lead some educators not to push females as hard as they push males, or not to reinforce female performance in "male" arenas as much as they reinforce allegedly gender-appropriate arenas. Women medical students, for example, may be "encouraged" toward pediatrics or gynecology but not encouraged toward neurosurgery. As Martell and colleagues' simulation suggests, these biases do not need to be large to have dramatic effects at higher levels. The advent of mentoring programs in male-dominated occupations (e.g., the Women in Neurosurgery Society) in part endeavor to counteract the discouragement deriving from shared stereotypes.

Not all admissions or promotions decisions are made by groups, of course. But the groups probably play a large part in the development of policies and norms that, once in effect, may persist for some time. Moreover, even when such decisions are made by individuals, the general sense that one's peers share one's stereotypes—and the opportunity to discuss outgroup members in a stereotypic fashion—presumably is quite validating.

Jury Decision Making

Stereotypes also may exert their influence on group decision making within the judicial system. For cases that go to trial, a 6- or 12-person jury typically is selected to provide a verdict to the court. Especially in situations in which the evidence is ambiguous or weak, extralegal factors such as shared stereotypes may come into play. For example, if the evidence in a trial is ambiguous, juries' postdeliberation decisions give more benefit of the doubt to attractive versus unattractive defendants (MacCoun, 1990). Similarly, when each of two eyewitnesses provide little detail (i.e., weak and ambiguous evidence), white jurors' decisions are more negative against Hispanic than non-Hispanic defendants; when one witness provides considerable detail, that detailed information rather than stereotypes influences jurors' decisions (M. Jones, 1997). People therefore appear to resort to their shared stereotypes when individuating information is unavailable or unclear. But they also resort to their stereotypes when using the stereotype seems valid: Mock jurors are more harsh when the crime is stereotypically associated with the defendant's ethnic group, that is, when the criminal "fits" the crime (Bodenhausen & Wyer, 1985).

A considerable amount of research on juridic decision making focuses on mock jurors, who make their decisions in isolation, rather than mock juries, who deliver their decisions after deliberating with fellow jurors. At times, the decisions rendered by juries differ from those rendered by individual jurors (Kerwin & Shaffer, 1994). The deliberation process changes the decision given. One explanation derives from the work on group polarization, which is the tendency of a group's initial leanings to become more extreme following deliberation. Because groups tend to center their discussions around shared information (Stasser et al., 1989), the majority viewpoint will be most likely to be expressed. The repeated exposure to such arguments presumably validates the majority viewpoint, and people shift their opinions further toward the extreme (Vinokur & Burnstein, 1974). People also might value the more extreme viewpoints that are expressed ("Now there's a *real* liberal!") and accordingly shift their opinions (Zuber, Crott, & Werner, 1992).

Imagine, then, a jury in which a large majority share certain stereotypes. All things being equal, the opinions that are consistent with those stereotypes should receive the most airtime. This is not to suggest that jurors necessarily will make group-derogatory or even stereotypic statements, but rather that they will focus their conversations on evidence and observations that are consistent with their stereotypes. For example, a jury comprising a non-Hispanic majority repeatedly might focus its conversation around stereotype-consistent characteristics of a Hispanic defendant: the neighbor's testimony that he was always picking fights, the main eyewitness's testimony that the defendant became furious over a minor insult, or the girlfriend's barely disguised black eye. Stereotypes would have influenced the initial encoding of this stereotype-congruent information by individual jurors; then presumably the stereotypic evidence would receive the lion's share of deliberation time. If so, their resulting shared impression should be of the Hispanic defendant as a volatile menace to society. At least in situations in which the jurors are unconcerned about the allegation of group bias, shared stereotyping might encourage a verdict that is consistent with the stereotypic assessment.

Jurors may be sensitive in particular to the expressed or imagined opinions of specific other jurors, especially jurors who apparently belong to the same group as the defendant. The presence of such jurors may encourage voiced opinions that are intended not to anger or offend their fellow jurors. For example, a male juror might expect that the women jurors generally are unsympathetic to a male defendant in an acquaintance rape case; in a jury comprising mostly women, the male juror might be more careful about what he says and be less inclined to vote for acquittal (see Fischer, 1997). Similarly, white jurors who are high in modern racism might be cautious about voicing negative opinions regarding a black defendant for fear that other people might perceive them as racists.

Research by Dovidio, Smith, Donnella, and Gaertner (1997) bears on this latter possibility. Dovidio et al. informed white participants that they were part of a six-person jury. On videotape, each jury member advocated the death penalty. For half of the participants, one fellow juror was black and the other jurors were white; for the remaining participants, all jurors were white. Among old-fashioned racists, the racial composition of the jury mattered little: Recommendations for the death penalty were more pronounced if the defendant was black rather than white. Among the less old-fashioned but aversive racists, racial composition mattered considerably when the defendant was black. Specifically, if the black juror advocated the death penalty, these individuals more strongly recommended the death penalty than if the jury was entirely white. Presumably, the black juror's advocacy of the death penalty undercut the potential attribution of racism. That is, if the black juror would advocate the death penalty for another black person, a white juror doing likewise could be presumed to be responding on the basis of the defendant's guilt rather than his race.

In Dovidio and colleagues' (1997) study, aversive racists who were faced with an all-white jury recommending the death penalty for a black defendant did not have a face-saving justification for sharing their recommendation. If these juries actually had met, however, perhaps the verdict would have proceeded in a different fashion. Holding one's own in face-to-face social influence attempts is difficult, especially if unanimity is required. Face-to-face deliberation may allow the other jurors to argue for the viability of alternative face-saving explanations for a harsh sentence (e.g., irrefutable evidence). Alternatively, the other jurors may be able to portray themselves as attitudinally similar to the opinion minority (i.e., express egalitarian ideals and deny racial prejudice) but as having reached the negative decision through hours of soul searching. They may point out that, on a previous trial that month, they had voted for a lighter sentence for another black defendant but that the death penalty was warranted in the present case. Although face-to-face deliberation perhaps would not convince the person to recommend the death penalty, it might make the person more inclined to support other harsh sentences (e.g., life imprisonment). The conversation therefore might encourage the opinion minority to activate aspects of the stereotype held in common with other jurors and to apply that stereotype in making decisions.

Finally, it bears mentioning that juries also develop and use shared stereotypes of parties other than the defendant. Witnesses who are unattractive, are legal minors, are from a particular ethnic group, or have "crooked" faces all might be stereotyped by the jury and their testimony be weighted accordingly. Similarly, juries may apply their shared stereotypes to the prosecuting and defense attorneys, and become more or less sympathetic to the case presented by female, Jewish, black, or high-powered white lawyers. Juries who come to dislike and discredit a lawyer may, by extension, become biased against that lawyer's client. Given that juries discuss not only evidence but also witness credibility, defendant character, and defendant motives, shared stereotypes no doubt play a role in the juridic arena.

Summary

When group decision making involves the judgment of other people, shared stereotypes are likely to influence decisions. Groups often provide recommendations about which person should be hired or promoted, which person is guilty or not guilty, which person lives and which person dies. If the decision targets belong to a traditionally stereotyped group, individual stereotypes can affect how and which decisions are made. Communication with others can allow a validation of one's stereotypes as veridical. Indirectly, then, shared stereotypes are likely to affect these kinds of group decisions.

CHAPTER SUMMARY

Stereotypes can be construed as culturally shared beliefs, representing what a group believes about another group. Although later chapters consider how mass media and other larger cultural forces may foster and maintain these consensual beliefs, the present chapter has focused on the role of interpersonal communication in developing and transmitting shared beliefs. Factors such as the desire to get along with other group members, to be understood with ease, or to create a good impression all can encourage people to develop or transmit shared stereotypes.

With the exception of classic origins in attitude and value transmission (e.g., Newcomb, 1961) and the group mind (for a discussion see Wegner, 1987), work on the development and transmission of shared beliefs is relatively recent in social psychology. More research is necessary on the factors that encourage and discourage the development of shared stereotypes, as well as their role in group decision making. Relevant work on jury decision making and on hiring decisions suggests that such endeavors may well be fruitful.

FOUR

Talking Down
to Outgroup Members

Isn't it nice that she knows her name and address?
—STORE CLERK TO THE MOTHER OF A WOMAN WITH
CEREBRAL PALSY (cited in E. E. Jones et al., 1984, p. 159)

People's expectations regarding the intellectual capacity of outgroup members often are low, especially when outgroup members appear to belong to a lower-status group. Regardless of actual abilities (or actual status for that matter), individuals who apparently belong to a lower-status group are presumed to possess less competence than individuals who apparently belong to higher-status groups. According to expectation states theory (e.g., Berger, Wagner, & Zelditch, 1985), social categories such as race, age, and gender serve as diffuse status cues. For example, in the United States, without explicit information about status, women are presumed to hold less status than men, African Americans are presumed to hold less status than European Americans, and the extremely aged are presumed to hold less status than middle-aged adults. These implicit status cues often lead communicators to conclude that targets lack competence and, consequently, communications directed toward such targets differs from communications directed toward (allegedly competent) peers.

The presumption of incompetence is particularly apparent in two classes of verbal behavior: patronizing speech and performance feedback. Speakers often patronize allegedly lower-status individuals by using secondary baby talk or inappropriately controlling talk. That is, people talk down to others by being overly simplistic, or by attempting to control the conversation and the other person's behavior through communicative acts. Researchers also have investigated the delivery of performance feedback, although a limited amount of this research directly addresses differential feedback as a function of demographic characteristics. In both cases, the communicator either holds or adopts higher status than the person from the traditionally disadvantaged group; the limitations of examining only this particular asymmetrical relationship are considered toward the end of this chapter.

PATRONIZING TALK

As discussed previously, people try to follow implicit communication rules. One of these rules enjoins speakers to take audience characteristics into account when they are crafting their message. If, for example, speakers do not know an audience's opinion about the message issue, the speakers resist being one sided and instead try to present a more balanced perspective (e.g., Tetlock, Sitka, & Boettger, 1989). Similarly, speakers adjust their communications to match the knowledge that they presume their audience possesses. For instance, if a man's accent implies that he hails from another geographic area, residents provide more detailed directions than if the accent implies that he is from a local area (D. Kingsbury, 1968, cited in Krauss & Fussell, 1991). Such accommodation efforts therefore are understandable and generally well intended (for a review of speech accommodation theory, see Giles, Coupland, & Coupland, 1991).

The problem, of course, is that speakers sometimes overaccommodate or hypercorrect their speech, basing their communication strategy on apparent status and on stereotypic assumptions. Being unnecessarily repetitive or detailed violates communication rules regarding conciseness and therefore can be perceived by the communication target as inappropriate or insulting. Moreover, speakers sometimes adjust qualities of their speech that are not particularly helpful for comprehension. Sighted persons, for instance, occasionally speak more loudly to persons with visual impairments (see Ferguson, 1979). Or, as in the opening example, able-bodied speakers may presume that an individual with cerebral palsy is mentally incompetent, often by overgeneralizing from the atypical speech patterns that may accompany the disease (see Lass, Ruscello, Harkins, & Blankenship, 1993).

In their work concerning patronizing speech directed toward elderly people, Hummert and Ryan (1996) distinguish among four different types of patronizing talk. They suggest that patronizing speech varies along two dimensions: controllingness and care. "Baby talk" is high in controllingness and also high in care; "directive talk" is low in care but also controlling; "overly personal talk" is high in care but low in control, whereas "superficial talk" is low on both dimensions.

The majority of the literature on speech directed toward out-groups is focused around baby talk and directive talk. Baby talk (which resembles speech addressed toward young children) typically is addressed toward adults whom the speakers surmise require their care or who may have difficulty comprehending native adult speech: elderly individuals, foreigners, and mentally retarded individuals. To the speaker, the lower status of the listener is not in question, and the listener is expected to make no efforts toward equalizing the conversational playing field. Directive talk, in contrast, lacks the care dimension. The targets of directive talk also are presumed incompetent, but the speaker apparently realizes at some level that the listeners want to be equals or already consider themselves as equals. Not surprisingly, then, directive talk appears to be addressed toward individuals who technically may have equal status but who the speaker prefers to shift to (or at least maintain at) lower status: women and ethnic outgroups.

Secondary Baby Talk

The original work on baby talk considered the special register with which parents speak to young children; presumably, the purpose of baby talk in this context is to facilitate acquisition of the native language. A speech register comprises distinct structural features (e.g., pitch, syntax, lexicon) and is used for particular purposes with particular audiences. For example, when speaking in their respective roles, television newscasters and storytellers use distinct registers that contrast with "normal" conversation between adults. Similarly, the baby talk register is lexically and paralinguistically distinct from language addressed toward adults. For example, cute or simplified words (e.g., choo-choo, tummy) might substitute for more proper terms in the available lexicon (e.g., locomotive, stomach). Along paralinguistic dimensions, baby talk includes higher pitch, shorter sentences, and exaggerated prosody (i.e., intonation and stress placed on particular words).

Secondary baby talk involves the use of the baby talk register, or at least an extremely similar register, when a person is speaking to targets other than very young children. Secondary baby talk is addressed to pets, houseplants, romantic partners, mentally retarded adults, foreigners, and elderly individuals (for a discussion see Caporael, 1981). Even older children who have "baby faces" are more likely to be the targets of baby talk than are more mature-faced children (Zebrowitz,

Brownlow, & Olson, 1992). Given this array of targets, the purposes of secondary baby talk clearly extend beyond efforts to aid language acquisition. Instead, secondary baby talk may be intended as sarcasm or affection, or may reflect overgeneralized efforts to aid listener comprehension. As discussed later, intent and effect do not always go hand in hand.

NON-NATIVE SPEAKERS

Imagine for a moment living in a foreign country where English (if that is your native language) is not the primary language spoken and in whose language you are not fluent. The professor is lecturing in this other language, and you must use this language to write course papers and to comment in class. No one where you work after class speaks English, so the extent to which you are understood and can understand is limited. Being in such a situation, one would be quick to recognize that any detriments in performance stem not from lack of intelligence but instead from the situation. Unfortunately, native speakers often fail to be as understanding when they encounter non-native speakers; they underestimate the power of the situation on others' behavior. In Great Britain, for example, immigrants often have as much as or even more formal education than natives. The challenges of living in a new culture and speaking a new language are grossly underestimated by natives, and the immigrants may be perceived as incompetent and stupid (Roberts, Davies, & Jupp, 1992).

"Foreigner talk" differs from speech addressed to fellow native speakers in several ways. Researchers report that foreigner talk includes several features that presumably might aid comprehension, such as a slower speech rate (e.g., more pauses) and efforts to maintain attention (e.g., use of shorter sentences). But speakers also adapt their speech in ways that serve no obvious purpose. For example, they speak louder, exaggerate stress, and vary pitch more with foreigners than with native adults (e.g., Woolfson, 1991). To some extent, speakers do differentiate among foreigners based on their linguistic sophistication. For example, dropping words like "it" or tense markers ("Is good for you?") is observed more commonly with less linguistically sophisticated foreigners than with more sophisticated ones (as noted in DePaulo & Coleman, 1986). Another example of this differentiation involves a study of Dutch municipal employees interviewing foreign immigrants (Snow, van Eeden, & Muysken, 1981). The extent to which the Dutch speakers used foreigner talk was related strongly to the extent to which the immigrants produced Dutch speech errors. Indeed, foreigner talk characteristics closely resembled the kind of speech errors that the speakers made, suggesting that foreigner talk can be an attempt to improve communication.

Although foreigner talk is sometimes well intended, a conclusion that it is primarily beneficial or benignly intended is premature. With more linguistically sophisticated foreigners, for example, native speakers are relatively repetitive. These native speakers are not, however, aware that they are being unnecessarily repetitive (DePaulo & Coleman, 1986). At initial stages of a relationship, perhaps between individuals acting as representatives of their countries or among newly acquainted colleagues, repetitiveness might be interpreted as condescending and start the relationship off on bad footing. Put another way, the linguistically sophisticated non-native speaker conceivably infers that overaccommodation reflects efforts by the native speaking group to assert status and to maintain social dominance. But perhaps the larger problem in foreigner talk may lie with speech directed toward less linguistically sophisticated foreigners. Despite solid education in their own language, such immigrants initially may take low-status jobs in which they have little contact with native speakers. Limited contact not only will reinforce their idiosyncratic speech pattern (Jupp, Roberts, & Cook-Gumperz, 1982). Limited contact also may reinforce social stereotypes. The continued pairing of individuals with less language sophistication with low-level jobs may lead perceivers to conclude erroneously that people from particular immigrant groups lack natural intelligence. Indeed, some theorists have gone as far as to suggest that foreigner speech is a mechanism for maintaining foreigners' inferior social position (for a discussion, see Valdman, 1981). That is, by failing to assist non-natives in learning the dominant speech patterns, foreigner speech serves the functions of social separation and of maintaining the power of the dominant group.

INDIVIDUALS WITH MENTAL RETARDATION

As with talk addressed to non-native speakers, talk addressed to individuals with mental retardation partially could reflect efforts to ease comprehension. Apparent in DePaulo's (e.g., DePaulo & Coleman, 1986) and Caporael's (e.g., Caporael, 1981) work, talk addressed to retarded adults involves clarification (e.g., repetition) and simplification (e.g., preference for common vocabulary). Rather than slowing the speech tempo (e.g., pausing), speech directed at retarded adults is relatively quick, perhaps because nonretarded individuals believe that pausing would allow retarded individuals' attention to wander.

At least among teachers or among people taking on a teacher role, speech directed toward retarded individuals tends to have a nurturing flavor. For example, teachers' nonverbal behavior toward children who have been labeled as retarded (but actually are not) is more warm and open than their nonverbal behavior toward children not so labeled (Kurtz, Harrison, Neisworth, & Jones, 1977). Less linguistically and cognitively sophisticated retarded adults also are treated with increas-. ingly more warmth than are more sophisticated retarded adults; these more sophisticated retarded adults are treated with as much warmth as children and non-native speakers of the language (DePaulo & Coleman, 1987). Thus, although adults treat retarded individuals differently than they treat other individuals, there is little evidence of animosity. Again, this pattern may hold because the speaker experiences no threat to relative status.

Nonretarded children, on the other hand, may not like peers who have been labeled as retarded as much as they like nonlabeled peers (Milich, McAninch, & Harris, 1992). Cooperation sometimes eases the use of stereotypes and encourages more intergroup friendships (e.g., Johnson, Johnson, & Maruyama, 1984) but at other times fails to produce the hoped-for positive effects (Gresham, 1984). If there are differences in how children versus adults treat retarded individuals, from what sources might those differences arise? One possibility is that nonretarded individuals genuinely "grow out of" the discomfort that they experience with retarded individuals. Another possibility is that the sense of "political correctness" is more developed in adulthood than in childhood and that nonretarded adults' behavior toward their retarded peers may not be entirely genuine. But, given some difficulty in monitoring one's own nonverbal behavior, this possibility does not seem very plausible in light of adults' nonverbal and paralinguistic warmth toward retarded individuals.

A more likely possibility is that childrens' cross-group relationships are at least intended to be equal status, whereas the relationships between nonretarded adults and retarded adults are rarely so intended. Although equal status contact can undercut stereotype use, it does not necessarily ensure liking (for reviews see Fiske & Neuberg, 1990). Indeed, the cooperative relationship is often thrust upon the children by well-intentioned third parties; at some level, the nonretarded children may resent the requirement of treating the retarded child as an equal. Nonretarded adults, in contrast, may more clearly see themselves in the higher-status role and as a caregiver. Perhaps in situations that accord retarded adults more equal footing—say, with a third party's sanction—nonretarded adults would be somewhat less nurturing toward retarded individuals.

ELDERLY ADULTS

The most extensively studied work on secondary baby talk involves the work on "elderspeak," the speech register directed toward elderly adults by younger caregivers. Although several subgroups are identifiable within stereotypes of elderly individuals (e.g., elder statesman, grandmother; M. B. Brewer, Dull, & Lui, 1981), the qualities associated with these stereotypes become more negative as age increases (Hummert, Garstka, Shaner, & Strahm, 1995). These stereotypes can be activated by various characteristics, such as facial appearance (Hummert, 1994) and speech cues (Mulac & Giles, 1996; Ruscher & Hurley, 2000). Once activated, these stereotypes guide younger speakers toward using stereotype-based communication strategies with elderly individuals, including elderspeak and other types of patronizing language.

As with other forms of secondary baby talk (i.e., foreigner talk), the communicator's purpose—at least at some level—is enhanced understanding. And, indeed, some qualities are helpful for the listener. For example, younger speakers reduce the complexity of their utterances, are more repetitive, and slow their speech rate (Kemper, 1994), all of which aid understanding. Elderspeak also includes a wider range of pitches (Caporeal, 1981), but unfortunately speakers may change their pitch to place emphasis on inappropriate parts of the message. Speakers also tend to reduce the number of associations among the various concepts that they relay to older listeners, which makes the message less cohesive and harder to understand (Kemper, 1994).

Unlike foreigner talk and talk addressed to retarded individuals, however, speakers apparently do not differentiate among degrees of listener competence among elderly listeners. Elderspeak is used whether or not the listener is institutionalized or community dwelling, irrespective of mental competence, and irrespective of the listener's level of physical functioning (Caporeal, 1981; Kemper, 1994). Some aspects of elderspeak do change when the listener appears to suffer from dementia, but these are not always qualities that would help a demented listener. For example, repetition (helpful) increases with demented listeners, but prosody (also helpful) does not vary (Kemper, Finter-Urczyk, Ferrell, Harden, & Billington, 1998). Thus, the stereotypes of elderly persons as weak and dependent appear to be quite strong in the communication strategies that they elicit. Kemper (1994) argues that the use of secondary baby talk not only reflects the use of stereotypes but also can foster a sense of dependency in elderly adults. If the elderly person's resulting behavior helps reinforce negative stereotypes, opportunities for normal communication and interaction may be reduced. These reductions in normal communication can exacerbate further decline. Indeed, speakers who believe that they are instructing an elderly (vs. younger) person are less friendly and often teach less material, which in turn results in less understanding from the learner (M. J. Harris, Moniz, Sowards, & Krane, 1994). Thus, perceiver expectancies can actually change the behavior of the target via self-fulfilling prophecy (see Chapter 5). Even if not consciously intended, such speech may function to keep elderly persons isolated in contemporary Western society.

Aside from its mixed efficacy in terms of comprehension, how is elderspeak perceived? The answer, of course, depends entirely upon who is making the judgment. Caregivers, especially those with relatively low expectations for elderly people, believe that elderly people will like hearing baby talk addressed to them (Caporeal, Lukaszewski, & Culbertson, 1983). Similarly, college-aged students do not perceive the tone of elderspeak as condescending, but rather as soothing (Caporael, 1981). In contrast, elderly recipients of elderspeak may find it patronizing, although higher functioning elderly adults find it most offensive (Caporeal et al., 1983). Given this finding, one presumes that most linguistically or cognitively sophisticated recipients of secondary baby talk, including non-native speakers, baby-faced children, and mentally retarded individuals, would find such communications offensive. Research into this specific topic has been lacking.

It bears mentioning that younger speakers addressing elderly adults do not have the corner on the patronizing market. Elders sometimes patronize young people, and young people experience this patronizing behavior in a negative fashion (Giles & Williams, 1994). As discussed in Chapter 2, older and younger individuals possess clear stereotypes of each other and regard members of the other group in relatively simplistic terms (Linville, 1982). Thus, whether the speakers are old or young, negative stereotypes regarding lowered competence apparently influence differential speech patterns.

SUMMARY

The use of secondary baby talk apparently is most common when speakers believe that the target requires their care in some form. That speakers often overcompensate for the presumed incompetence of their listeners is evident in secondary baby talk addressed to foreigners and elderly adults. At least among elderly recipients who are high in cognitive and linguistic functioning, secondary baby talk is experienced negatively, even though observers do not find it so. Presumably, other recipients of secondary baby talk also would judge it to be patronizing.

Controlling Talk

Like secondary baby talk, controlling talk presumes incompetence on the part of the listener and endeavors to assert control over the listener's speech as well as other behaviors. However, controlling talk typically fails to impart the caring flavor of secondary baby talk. It therefore is similar to what Hummert and Ryan (1996) call "directive talk," but also includes other efforts to control the conversation such as ignoring the target's attempts to contribute to the conversation. Controlling talk with members of different gender, national, or ethnic groups appears to resemble the talk addressed to lower-status individuals (who do not seem to require care). Given its similarity to high-status talk, it is conceivable that controlling talk reflects an implicit recognition that the allegedly lower-status person may desire higher status—at least in other settings if not in the present one. Controlling talk therefore explicitly functions to keep low-status individuals "in their place."

PRESUMPTUOUSNESS

One type of controlling speech is presumptuousness. Presumptuousness involves the higher-status person issuing commands or suggesting a course of action, interpreting and evaluating the other person, and restating or clarifying major points in the conversation (Cansler & Stiles, 1981). The higher-status person controls the conversation and "presumes" the qualifications to provide direction. In one study on presumptuousness, Cansler and Stiles (1981) paired senior college students with a first-year college student for one conversation, and also with a professor for another conversation. With the first-year college student the senior possessed relatively greater status, whereas with the professor the senior possessed relatively less status. As expected, the seniors were more presumptuous with first-year students than with professors. For instance, seniors evaluated and suggested courses of action for first-year students more than with professors. Interestingly, the professors and seniors behaved in remarkably similar fashion when they held higher status, and the first-year students and seniors behaved quite similarly when they held lower status.

Whether a presumptuous style constitutes prejudiced communication is a matter of degree and appropriateness to the setting. If one asks another person for advice—at least temporarily relegating higher status to her or him—one probably expects or even desires suggestions and interpretations. But sometimes communicators behave more presumptuously than their actual status warrants. For instance, Schnake

(1998) asked European American college students to act as peer counselors to a fellow student. This alleged fellow student happened to be an African American who purportedly had performed a mixture of negative and positive stereotypical behaviors on which the peer counselor was to advise him. Certainly, the peer counselor setting is likely to evoke suggestions and interpretations, but some participants took an overzealous approach to their role, namely, individuals high in modern racism (see also Chapter 2).

Specifically, the high modern racists were especially presumptuous to the African American target when discussing his negative behaviors but not so presumptuous when discussing his positive behaviors. Low modern racists were not at all presumptuous when talking to the African American target. High modern racists, for example, chastised their counselee for being aggressive and lazy, and advised him to avoid negative behavior in the future. According to the modern prejudice perspective, high modern racists believe that blacks are pushing too hard to obtain equal rights and that racism is no longer a problem in the United States. Implicitly, then, high modern racists attribute many successes of African Americans to factors like affirmative action policies rather than hard work and deservedness. In contrast, any failures of an African American are doubly bad because the target presumably has received so many unfair advantages that such failures seem inexcusable; a guiding hand therefore seems necessary. Thus, presumptuousness sometimes may reflect prejudiced communication, above and beyond simple differences in status.

CONTROLLING COMMUNICATION FLOW

Another kind of controlling talk is interruption (Roberts et al., 1992). Like presumptuousness, interruption is evident when speakers either implicitly hold high status or are trying to acquire it. For example, individuals who use interruption in order to obtain the floor are perceived as possessing high status in their conversing group (Ng, Bell, & Brooke, 1993). Given that in the absence of explicit status information men are perceived as possessing higher status than women (Berger et al., 1985), it is not surprising that men interrupt more than women do, as long as the topic is one on which neither gender is a clear expert (C. E. Brown, Dovidio, & Ellyson, 1990). Interrupting successfully implies that listeners either believe that the speaker will make a meritorious contribution or that the speaker somehow possesses the capacity to punish them for not yielding the floor.

Speakers also can retain control of the conversation by insulting or ignoring others' attempts at contribution. In nonconflictual conversations, people typically respect the norms of neutral coherence and local coherence. Neutral coherence implicitly requires a relatively polite response, or at least a noninsulting response, to the previous speaker. Local coherence implicitly requires a response to the previous speaker that links his or her comment to one's own comment. For example, Mary may begin by saying to her classmates, "I'm going to rent a movie tonight." Jane then may interject, "I think that *The Big Easy* is a good film to rent." If Mary's next statement is "Movies that stereotype New Orleans aren't worth renting," she has violated neutral coherence by essentially insulting Jane's contribution to the conversation. If her next statement is "Or maybe I'll go shopping instead," she has violated local coherence by essentially ignoring Mary's suggestion and behaving as though Mary did not speak at all.

Öhlschlegel and Piontkowski (1997) examined such violations of coherence during intergroup discussions. They created 20 four-person groups, each group comprising two West Germans and two East Germans. To manipulate group salience, participants either were asked to speak as representatives of their own region or received no such instructions. Violations of coherence overall were greater with outgroups; violations of neutral coherence in particular were exaggerated when group membership was salient. Thus, not allowing interruptions from outgroup members and successfully making interruptions when outgroup members were speaking can put the outgroup members "in their place." Although this behavior perhaps does not convey global incompetence, it certainly suggests that contributions to conversation made by members of the outgroup do not merit attention. In other words, such behavior attempts to assert and maintain status.

EXCESSIVE DETAIL IN DIRECTIONS

Both the notions of controlling talk and of presumptuousness include giving commands or directions. The use of imperative verbs, that is, verbs that take the form of a command (e.g., "Close the window"), can reflect this kind of controlling talk. Alternate ways of making the request are less forceful, such as "Close the window, please"; "Would you close the window?"; or "It's getting rather cold in here, isn't it?" (Ng & Bradac, 1993). In addition to being a forceful variation of speech, the increased use of imperative verbs when a person is teaching someone to perform a task implicitly can suggest that the receiver has little knowledge of the task and may have difficulty performing it. For example, someone poorly acquainted with a cooking task must think about each specific step (e.g., brown the butter, add flour, stir constantly at low heat, add chopped onions when the mixture looks like

peanut butter), whereas people well acquainted with such a task com-
bine a sequence of actions into a single rapidly flowing procedure (see
Vallacher & Wegner, 1987). Thus, instructing someone to "make a roux,
then add onions" assumes that the receiver knows what constitutes a
roux and can recognize its appropriate texture and color). In contrast,
an increased sequence of imperatives suggests that the receiver needs
each specific step outlined.

As always, when this sort of detail is warranted and desired by
the receiver, it probably does not reflect prejudiced communication.
However, as with other forms of patronizing talk, people sometimes
overaccommodate based on status cues that may, in turn, help preserve status differences between groups. For example, the Heimlich
maneuver is considered a gender-neutral task, but not one with which
most college students are familiar. As noted earlier, in the absence of
explicit status or expertise information, men often presume that
women possess lower status and less knowledge than they do. Thus,
men presumably would be more inclined to use imperative verbs
when teaching a female peer how to perform a gender-neutral task like
the Heimlich maneuver. To investigate this possibility, Duval and
Ruscher (1994) taught the Heimlich maneuver to college-aged participants through a slide show. The slides portrayed a male and female actor who alternated performing different steps of the Heimlich maneuver on each other; male and female voices alternated descriptions of
the steps on the concurrent audiotape. The slide show also included information about recognizing the signs of choking and some background information on the Heimlich maneuver. After viewing the
slide presentation, participants were videotaped while they explained
the Heimlich maneuver to a same-sex or other-sex individual over
closed-captioned television. As seen in Figure 3, men used more imperative verbs when teaching the maneuver to a woman than any of
the other teacher–learner combinations. Use of other kinds of verbs did
not differ across the conditions. Future research needs to consider
whether women might "talk down" to men on tasks for which men
presumably are not knowledgeable. As seen with presumptuous behavior, the extent to which people use excessive detail also might depend on individual differences.

SUMMARY

The manner is which people talk to outgroup members can reflect their
lowered expectations of them. To members of certain lower-status
outgroups (e.g., groups of different gender or ethnicity) researchers
have found that speakers use controlling talk and are impolite, control-

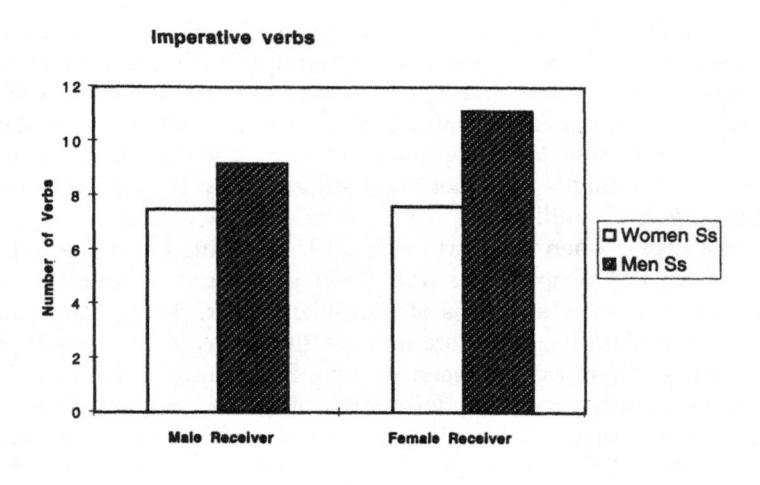

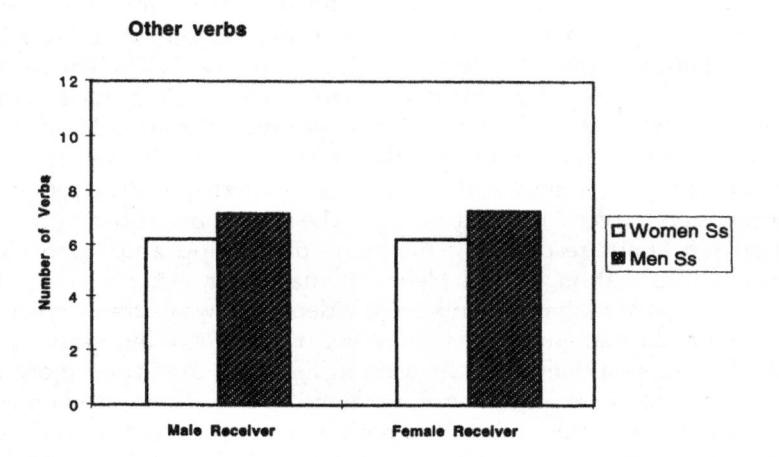

FIGURE 3. Use of imperative verbs versus other verbs by men and women teaching a task, as a function of receiver gender.

ling, or insultingly pedantic. To members of other lower-status out-groups (e.g., mentally retarded individuals, elderly adults), researchers have found that speakers use secondary baby talk, overaccomodating for the listeners' perceived lack of competence with a variety of baby-ish qualities such as simplistic lexical choices and higher pitch. In examining this literature, controlling talk appears to emerge most often when the speaker likely believes that the listener wants equal status.

Indeed, foreigner talk seems to be more directive than baby talk when the nonnative speaker is trying to equalize the playing field (Roberts et al., 1992). In like fashion, elderly individuals conceivably are more likely to receive nurturing baby talk than controlling talk when they cannot or do not attempt to assert their independence. One suspects that situational factors such as desire to retain or obtain status (or the certainty in retaining it) actually underlie which form of patronizing talk people adopt. The actual groups to which the people belong ultimately may prove immaterial.

The selection of a particular form of patronizing talk also could stem partially from individual differences. Among some individuals, the presumption of incompetence could be associated with a nurturing demeanor toward the group, whereas among other individuals the presumption of incompetence could be associated with conflict and hostility. Glick and Fiske's (1996) notion of ambivalent sexism fits well with this possibility. One might expect, for instance, that benevolent sexists would tend toward baby talk whereas hostile sexists would tend toward controlling talk when talking to women. Ambivalent sexists (i.e., individuals high on both dimensions) presumably would shift between baby talk and controlling talk, depending on the woman's efforts to assert or surrender status. An investigation of the role of individual difference into patronizing talk addressed toward women and other groups—foreigners, ethnic minorities, the elderly—could further clarify the motivations underlying these communication strategies.

PERFORMANCE FEEDBACK

The work on controlling talk and secondary baby talk primarily focuses on situations in which the allegedly lower-status individual is being instructed or supervised; these studies pay little attention to the content of these communications or to the effects that they have on the recipients (except that they may be experienced as patronizing). The delivery of performance feedback is another major arena in which allegedly lower-status individuals are the recipients of communication; the extent to which this feedback varies across demographic characteristics and what the recipients make of such feedback are considered in the remainder of this chapter.

Differential Feedback to Specific Groups

An impressive body of empirical literature shows differential performance evaluations as a function of group membership. For example, in a meta-analytic review (i.e., a systematic statistical integration of existing empirical studies), Huffcutt and Roth (1998) found a modest but consistent difference between white interviewers' performance ratings of white interviewees versus black or Hispanic interviewees (white–black $d = .25$; white–hispanic $d = .26$, respectively). These differences reflect a quarter of a standard deviation, which may be statistically modest but, in a practical sense, may matter a great deal. To get a sense of what this difference means, imagine being enrolled in a college course in which the grade cutoffs change exactly by this amount. The quarter standard deviation difference might mean the difference between obtaining a B- versus a B, a B+ versus an A-, and so forth. For many students, this difference is not inconsequential. And for potential employees, achieving this slightly lower interview rating can mean the difference between obtaining the job and looking elsewhere for employment, getting a decent raise or not, or receiving a promotion or staying in a dead-end job. Practical significance, at least, is in the eye of the beholder.

FORMAL FEEDBACK

Formal feedback typically is provided by someone in a superordinate role (e.g., teacher, employer, tutor) in a format sanctioned by a particular institution. Rather than being sought by the subordinate person at any time, formal feedback occurs routinely with changes in the calendar or with completion of substantial assignments. The type of formal verbal feedback that people receive varies across settings. Students, for example, typically receive comments on their written work, and usually receive letter grades as well. Many companies require their managers to discuss performance with their employees, and some companies require employee signatures verifying that they have seen and discussed an annual performance appraisal. One thing about performance feedback in general is pretty clear: Individuals in the supervisory role are reluctant to give negative feedback. When possible, supervisors delay the delivery of negative feedback, focus on specifics to avoid the appearance of capriciousness, and distort the feedback so that feedback is less negative than actual performance (Larson, 1986). While avoiding overtly negative comments, the supervisor instead may reduce the positive feedback and rely on more neutral comments. In addition, supervisors may use a contrite tone of voice and offer an apology for delivering the negative feedback, to help soften the blow (Baron, 1988, 1990).

Oddly enough, very few empirical studies examine formal feedback delivery as a function of recipient demographic characteristics.

Given a reluctance to communicate negative information in general, one might expect that negative feedback to outgroup subordinates is not extremely negative. Instead, supervisors from the ethnic majority should feel reluctant to provide negative feedback to minorities in order to minimize the appearance of racism. In one rare examination of this topic, Harber (1998) argued that whites' performance feedback to poorly performing subordinates would be more lenient when the subordinates were black rather than white. In this study, white college students read and rated a substandard essay, purportedly written by a black or a white college student. Acting as peer tutors with the task of editing the essay, these participants wrote comments in the margins and also corrected the mechanical aspects of the essay. Feedback along mechanical dimensions did not differ as a function of author race; concurring with other work on performance feedback, negative feedback did tend to be specific. In contrast to the specific feedback about mechanics, more global feedback about essay content did differ as a function of author race. Whereas general comments to the white author were negative (about 2.6 on a 7-point scale), general comments to the black author were more neutral in tone (close to the midpoint of the 7-point scale).

Given that white supervisors' performance evaluations typically are lower for black than for white subordinates (e.g., Huffcutt & Roth, 1998), the likelihood that the more favorable feedback to blacks in Harber's (1998) study is genuine seems unlikely. Instead, the more favorable feedback to the outgroup could derive from any number of causes, which are not necessarily mutually exclusive. First, people are motivated to appear nonprejudiced toward certain outgroups (e.g., European Americans generally do not wish to appear prejudiced toward African Americans), and they strategically use communication to serve this impression management function. Whereas specific negative feedback on the mechanics cannot readily be questioned, negative feedback on the more subjective dimension can easily be construed as racist. Another possibility is that people use different standards for evaluating allegedly high- and low-status group members (Biernat & Kobrynowicz, 1997). In this case, whites have lower expectations for blacks than for fellow whites and therefore are more lenient with blacks. In judging the substandard essay attributed to the black student, it is as if raters say to themselves, "This isn't so bad . . . for a black guy." If this shift in standards indeed is the case, though, one wonders why private performance evaluations consistently are more negative for minorities.

It bears mentioning that the comments made to the African American author in Harber's (1998) study tended to be supportive. Comments indicated, for example, how the reader enjoyed the essay or saw potential in it. Depending on how these were written, the comments conceivably might have been more patronizing than supportive, or at least strike the recipient as a backhanded compliment. For example, the addition of an emphasizer to a statement can imply anticipated disbelief on the part of the recipient. Compared to "I enjoyed your essay," for instance, "I *did* enjoy your essay" implies that the essay author needs reassurance and that other aspects of the essay were problematic. As discussed earlier in this chapter and in Chapter 2, the form and implication of a statement may matter as much as or more than its mere evaluative connotation. The limited work on differential feedback as a function of demographic characteristics could benefit substantially by an examination of the use of a patronizing speech register (or the written equivalent).

INFORMAL FEEDBACK

Informal feedback occurs during day-to-day interactions among individuals, and does not occur necessarily between supervisors and their subordinates. Peers and high-ranking individuals who do not have immediate power over an individual may provide feedback, and this feedback either may be solicited or provided without request. For instance, a first-year college student may ask his residence hall director for advice on a particular college course. Alternatively, one coworker may tell another that her boss seemed unhappy with the latter person's recent tardiness. Given that *useful* feedback is associated with higher performance (e.g., Becker & Klimoski, 1989), receiving feedback—formal or informal—can be helpful in obtaining the goals that are associated with desired outcomes.

As with formal feedback, few studies on informal verbal feedback have examined differential feedback to individuals from particular demographic groups. One exception is a study conducted by Rubovits and Maehr (1973) that considered how white women in a teacher training program treated black versus white junior high school students. Unbeknownst to the students or the teachers, these students randomly had been assigned an IQ score that designated them as gifted or not gifted. Observers noted teacher trainees' attention to the students' comments during an interactive discussion of television, as well as whether the students' comments were encouraged, ignored, praised, or criticized. The researchers found no difference in *amount* of attention as a function of label and race. However, teacher trainees praised the allegedly gifted white children more than they praised the allegedly gifted black students. No differences in criticism were detected as a function of student race.

Granted, this study is more than 25 years old, but it does offer an important counterpoint to Harber's more recent study in 1998. Harber's study focused on reactions to substandard performance, whereas Rubovits and Maehr (1973) focused on reactions to students presumed to be above standard (although the actual quality of comments was not assessed). Like judging overall essay content in Harber's study, reacting to students' opinions about television probably falls more along subjective than objective lines. Consequently, criticism—especially in this face-to-face setting—could seem prejudiced. Not surprisingly, the teachers avoided overt criticism. However, people may be less aware that a failure to praise outgroup successes could be seen as indicative of prejudice. The presence of a comment is much more salient than the absence of a comment. Consistent with this notion, M. C. Taylor (1979) also detected an attenuation of positive feedback: White teachers' positive feedback to bright black male students (and to bright white females) was considerably more brief than their feedback to other individuals. In a similar vein, failing to help may not be construed as prejudiced (Frey & Gaertner, 1986) or as aggressive (Schnake, Ruscher, Gratz, & O'Neal, 1997), even though research shows that people primarily fail to help people toward whom they harbor negative feelings. Given a general reluctance to deliver negative feedback, contemporary researchers interested in differential feedback as a function of demographic characteristics may wish to consider the attenuation of positive feedback more than the presence of negative feedback.

MENTORING

Mentors can be an important source of feedback, to the extent that the mentor role includes coaching (e.g., providing advice) and being a sounding board (Kram, 1985). Mentorship is associated with a variety of valued outcomes, such as salary attainment and advancement (Dreher & Cox, 1996). In many institutions, a high proportion of individuals with status and influence are both white and male. Compared to women and minorities, white men historically have had access to a wider influence network from which protégés might benefit (Dreher & Cox, 1996). Because mentors tend to adopt protégés who hail from similar ethnic, racial, or gender backgrounds (Kanter, 1977), women and minorities are less likely, on average, to have mentors possessing the most extensive networks and access to resources. Certainly, minorities and women might reap psychosocial benefits by having a similar mentor (Thomas, 1990), but tangible outcomes like salary—at least at present—often depend upon relationships with white men (Dreher & Cox, 1996).

Consider the feedback advantages of having a mentor who possesses high centrality in the institution, irrespective of the mentor's demographic characteristics. Such a mentor can provide the informational feedback that facilitates success by focusing on the processes needed to succeed: which courses to take, how to meet the "right" people to be a salient choice for a promotion, or how to mitigate conflicts with particular individuals. This type of feedback may be exactly what minorities and women are, all things being equal, likely to miss when they fail to include white men in their network of mentors. In addition to the importance of such informational or process feedback, men are more likely than women to provide negative feedback (N. Brewer, Socha, & Potter, 1996). If one assumes that at least some negative feedback is constructive, it does carry some advantages for improving performance. Failing to inform a person of correctable errors, just because it might appear prejudiced, ultimately does not help the person succeed. Obviously, it would be ludicrous to argue that having a white male mentor is the only route to success. *On average*, individuals with such mentors may do better, which does not mean that all individuals need a mentor or that the mentor needs to be white and male. Indeed, if the help is unsolicited and appears to be rendered on account of demographic characteristics, the benefits of help may backfire by implying to the target that she or he needs help (Schneider, Major, Luhtanen, & Crocker, 1996; cf. Steele, 1992).

SUMMARY

Although considerable research shows group differences in performance evaluations seen by third parties, little empirical work addresses verbal feedback delivered to the subject of the evaluation. Although recipients dislike receiving negative feedback, recipients typically consider negative feedback more informative than positive feedback. If negative feedback actually is more informative, then white supervisors' reluctance to criticize minority subordinates who are not performing well provides little opportunity to fix correctable problems. Even if not consciously intended, such communication patterns may function to maintain relative status differences among groups. Beyond evaluative feedback, women and minorities also may receive less useful informational feedback because they are less likely to receive mentoring from the most well-networked individuals. Because mentoring often is not sanctioned formally, both the organization and the mentor may view it as something extra given to an individual rather than as help that is intentionally withheld from another individual. Like failing to praise someone, failing to take on yet another protégé is less likely to be seen as prejudiced than actively performing a negative prejudiced behavior. And even if mentoring occurs, it may backfire if onlookers of the mentee infer that help is needed for success.

Clearly, more studies that consider the demographic characteristics of feedback recipients are needed. Although generalizing from only a few isolated studies is risky, feedback provided to members of traditionally disadvantaged groups simply may not be very informative. These individuals may be neither praised for their successes nor criticized for their failures. Instead, they may be treated in a neutral fashion. Indeed, this interpretation fits well with the attributional literature. Failure on intellectual endeavors from lower-status groups often is expected and is presumed to stem from stable internal deficiencies. Success, conversely, is explained at least partially by reasoning that the subordinate is atypical of his or her group or made an extraordinary effort. From the perspective of more powerful individuals, if most members of traditionally disadvantaged groups are incompetent and succeed only with luck or unusual effort, providing feedback or investing effort as a mentor is hardly worth the bother. The potential mentors may conclude that it is better to water, prune, and repot a plant that seems likely to grow (i.e., a similar other) than to "waste time" on a presumably incompetent woman or member of an ethnic minority.

Effects of Feedback

A larger body of research considers the effects of performance feedback. Two issues are considered here: the difficulty that members of traditionally disadvantaged groups may have in interpreting feedback from outgroup members and the impact of delivering feedback on the feedback provider.

ATTRIBUTIONAL AMBIGUITY

Having received feedback regarding success or failure, people often draw attributions regarding the cause of that feedback. They may, for example, decide that the feedback is deserved, given their level of aptitude or effort. Alternatively, they may determine that the feedback is a reflection of the feedback giver's own goals and biases. For example, feedback recipients may conclude that the person delivering the feedback is prejudiced toward the recipients' social group. Which attribution the recipient draws depends upon a variety of factors, including his or her own attributional style, knowledge about his or her own effort and ability, and knowledge about the feedback giver. Attributional ambiguity refers to a situation in which the reasons for the feedback (or other kind of treatment or outcome) is ambiguous, typically one in which the recipient's group membership is a salient potential reason for the feedback received. Attributional ambiguity can exist for both positive and negative outcomes, and makes it very difficult for the feedback recipient to know where, exactly, he or she stands.

For example, feedback recipients may have difficulty determining whether negative evaluation stems from the prejudices of the speaker or from their own inadequate performance. The effects of such attributional ambiguity is exemplified by two studies by Jennifer Crocker, Brenda Major, and their colleagues (both studies reported by Crocker, Voelkl, Testa, & Major, 1991). In the first study, college women wrote an essay that purportedly was evaluated negatively by a male peer. Previously, the male peer had expressed prejudiced attitudes toward women (e.g., "Women lack mathematical ability") or egalitarian attitudes toward women (e.g., "Women and men should share housework"). Negative feedback from the prejudiced man potentially could be attributed to poor performance or to his prejudice against women (i.e., a state of attributional ambiguity). In contrast, negative feedback from the egalitarian male peer more clearly would imply poor performance, because no other salient attribution is available. Compared to women who received feedback from the egalitarian man, the women who received negative feedback from the prejudiced man attributed the feedback to his prejudice and felt less depressed. At least in this case, then, prejudice was viewed as the more plausible explanation.

In their companion study, Crocker et al. (1991) examined attributional ambiguity and racial prejudice. This time, African American and European American students wrote self-descriptions regarding their strengths, weaknesses, and personal preferences. These self-descriptions then were evaluated by a same-sex white peer who purportedly could or could not see them through a one-way mirror. When black participants believed that the evaluator could see them, they attributed the feedback (negative or positive) to prejudice and tended to experience a less positive mood. Crocker and colleagues' second study (1991) therefore points out that positive feedback also may be mistrusted, when a salient alternative explanation is available. When receiving positive feedback, African American participants apparently reasoned that their white evaluator was bending over backward to avoid appearing prejudiced, rather than expressing true positive regard for the participants' personality. In similar fashion, physically attractive individuals discount positive feedback when they know that they can be seen (Major, Carrington, & Carnevale, 1984), presumably reasoning that the positive feedback is not genuine.

Attributional ambiguity presumably is exaggerated when the

feedback recipients are less certain of their performance quality or are relatively uncertain of their standing on a personality dimension. People typically believe feedback that confirms the self-views on which they are relatively certain but discount feedback the disconfirms those self-views (for a review see Swann, 1990). Uncertain self-views, in contrast, more easily are swayed by feedback. Indirect support for the notion that uncertainty exaggerates attributional ambiguity is found in the research on preferential selection. In one such study (Heilman, Lucas, & Kaplow, 1990), participants were led to believe that their appointment as a leader derived from (1) their superior score on an alleged selection test or (2) the need for more leaders of their gender. Among the participants selected on the basis of their gender, one-third received favorable feedback about their selection task score, one-third received unfavorable feedback, and the remaining third received negative feedback. Women who were preferentially selected but who also felt certain that they possessed the requisite skills evaluated themselves similarly to women selected on the basis of merit alone; the women provided with no information (i.e., who were less certain) or negative information derogated their abilities.

If traditionally disadvantaged groups indeed receive less informative feedback than their peers, they more often may find themselves in positions of uncertainty and, conceivably, heightened attributional ambiguity. This possibility underscores their need for access to objective information about their performance so that they can distinguish between a need for change in themselves (or, in the case of positive feedback, an opportunity to take on more challenging and potentially rewarding tasks) versus the prejudice of other people.

THE FEEDBACK PROVIDER

A recent meta-analysis (Georgesen & Harris, 1998) demonstrates that, as an evaluator's power increases, self-evaluations become more favorable whereas evaluations of subordinates become increasingly derogatory. This finding implies that the mere act of evaluating others can make subordinates seem less competent than they would seem otherwise. Support for the power–derogation relation is found in both experimental simulations (i.e., in which the researcher can assign a person to wield power on an entirely arbitrary basis; e.g., Sachdev & Bourhis, 1985) and also in field settings (which are more realistic even if certain researcher control is sacrificed; e.g., Ilgen, Peterson, Martin, & Boeschen, 1981).

Does the mere process of giving feedback—something people in power often must do—affect the feedback provider's impressions of the feedback recipient? Some indirect evidence suggests that it might. First, people often adopt the impressions that they convey to others. The increased elaboration that occurs during communication turns "saying" into "believing" (Higgins & Rholes, 1978). For example, despite somewhat similar precommunication impressions of a man with alcoholism or paraplegia, people who describe a target in a stereotypic fashion later tend to stereotype him more than people who describe him in a more individuated fashion (Ruscher & Duval, 1998). Praising or derogating one's subordinates, directly or to third parties, therefore may exaggerate the original impressions of them. What remains for researchers is to ascertain whether these impressions may generalize to other members of the feedback recipient's group. That is, once having provided feedback to an outgroup member that her or his performance was superb or suboptimal, does the feedback provider's impression bleed over into impressions of other outgroup members? Beliefs about negative behavior, at least, seem to generalize (Henderson-King & Nisbett, 1996). Second, formal feedback typically comes from a position of power and, in many respects, renders the supervisor–subordinate relationship quite salient. When people are speaking from a position of power and are using a powerful strategy to influence the recipients' beliefs or behaviors, the powerful individuals may conclude that the recipients are not particularly competent (O'Neal, Kipnis, & Craig, 1994). If, for example, a woman performs a task well after receiving detailed directions, the man who delivered the directions can attribute task success to his excellent directions. Alternatively, if a man engages in an applaudable behavior following a clever suggestion from a woman, the woman may credit her own manipulation tactics. By crediting their own directions and influence tactics, both communicators are, in effect, stripping the communication recipients of their potential competence. O'Neal et al. demonstrated this effect by showing that individuals who randomly were assigned to use a manipulative influence strategy derogated the influence recipient more than individuals assigned simply to reason with the person.

If using powerful strategies indeed reduces regard for the recipient, what might be said of the various patronizing strategies discussed earlier? Young people who think that the elderly are incompetent may speak baby talk to them, but speaking baby talk may reinforce and bolster that impression of incompetence. That is, the relation between patronizing speech and perceptions of target incompetence may be reciprocal. Caregivers new to an institution, for example, initially may hold relatively neutral (or, at least, less extreme) impressions of elderly competence but, after observing veteran caregivers use patronizing speech, may adopt that strategy themselves. Similarly, boys who observe adult men talking down to women may begin to conclude that women are indeed stupid; their own subsequent use of patronizing speech later may reinforce that view.

Summary

The limited work on the subject considers feedback delivered by whites and men to minorities and women, respectively, in academic or employment settings. Recognizing that prejudice partly may underlie the feedback they receive, these members of traditionally disadvantaged groups sometimes have a difficult time ascertaining the meaning of the feedback for their own performance. On the flip side, the mere act of evaluating others slants the evaluator toward negative impressions. In those instances in which negative feedback is given or controlling communication strategies employed, the speaker may bolster initial negative impressions. In the settings often studied by social, educational, and industrial psychologists, participants may be reticent to provide negative feedback to traditionally disadvantaged groups for fear of seeming prejudiced, but at least some managers and teachers must deliver such feedback. At least some evidence suggests that positive feedback is rare and that members of traditionally disadvantaged groups simply are treated in a neutral fashion. Such a communication strategy provides little opportunity for bolstering positive impressions.

Initial evidence suggests that feedback to traditionally disadvantaged groups is not particularly informative, so it is no wonder that feedback recipients sometimes have difficulty interpreting the meaning of that feedback. In the choice of targets, this research resembles the work on controlling talk more than the work on secondary baby talk. The patterns and effects of feedback on older individuals, at least, warrants attention. Increasing numbers of older individuals are returning to educational settings and the workplace and, like minorities, older workers are often evaluated less favorably than their counterparts (Finkelstein, Burke, & Raju, 1995). Unlike their concern about seeming prejudiced against minorities, however, most people may be less concerned about appearing prejudiced against older individuals and may be more willing to provide them with negative feedback. And, because being older is an acquired characteristic, an attribution to ageism may not occur as quickly to older workers as an attribution of sexism or racism.

CHAPTER SUMMARY

At least when the target's demographic or ascribed characteristics imply lower status, speakers from traditionally dominant groups tend to talk down to them. The higher-status speaker often patronizes the communication target and controls the conversation. The manner in which communicators speak to members of such groups contrasts with the content of their messages. Although communicators may often avoid negative feedback in order to avoid appearing prejudiced, they also may fail to provide positive feedback or mentoring. The conflict between the message content and its delivery partially may result in feedback recipients' experience of attributional ambiguity. Except when feedback cannot be attributed to prejudice, individuals from traditionally disadvantaged groups may find it difficult to determine where they stand.

The work on verbal communication directed toward members of traditionally disadvantaged groups almost exclusively considers situations in which the communication target implicitly or explicitly holds lower status. How members of historically powerful groups talk to high-status members of traditionally disadvantaged groups remains open to empirical investigation. When the status is clear, many speakers conceivably accord high-status persons with appropriate respect—avoiding presumptuousness and not interrupting, for example. Anecdotally, however, one does witness at least some members from historically powerful groups attempting to render the high-status person more of an equal. Older male college students, for example, might be more inclined to use titles such as "professor" or "doctor" when speaking to male instructors but substitute feminine titles devoid of such status such as "Ms." when speaking to female instructors. Alternatively, when the lower-status person hails from a historically powerful group, he or she may touch the higher-status person (which is a high-status behavior) or try to obtain an equal right to speaking turns. Indeed, high-status persons from traditionally disadvantaged groups implicitly may be punished for engaging in the powerful forms of speech used by other individuals in their station. They may be disliked and not accepted as easily as leaders if they seem to forget their "natural place."

FIVE

Preferred Cultural Patterns and Nonverbal Behavior

> When the dominant group has marked prejudice, it is favorable neither to cultural pluralism nor to assimilation. It says in effect, "We don't want you to be like us, but you must not be different."
>
> —ALLPORT (1954/1989, p. 240)

Nonverbal communication involves the interpersonal transmission and reception of messages, without relying upon words. Erect posture, a welcoming gesture, and a sour frown all communicate nonverbally, as do rapid speech rate and high pitch. Perceivers place great stock in nonverbal behaviors as signifying true attitudes and beliefs. For example, when trying to detect deception, people feel disadvantaged if restricted to a telephone conversation (DePaulo, Zuckerman, & Rosenthal, 1980). The telephone conversation, in turn, boasts some advantages over written communication formats such as electronic mail. The communicator's apparent conviction, sarcasm, or warmth often are not conveyed as easily in writing as orally, and message recipients may feel less able to gauge the genuineness of the communicator's intent when a message is written. Thus, people may use the nonverbal channel to ascertain the sincerity and warmth of their interaction partner, as well as the partner's implicit assumptions regarding their relative status and worth. The latter half of the present chapter considers these aspects of prejudice in nonverbal communication: how prejudices and stereotypes are transmitted nonverbally toward outgroup members.

Not only does nonverbal communication convey judgments of the other person's worth, status, or likability, it also is itself the subject of evaluation. The communication patterns of one's own group, by and large, are preferred. "They" sit too close or too far apart, speak with a dull tone or excessive variation, suspiciously avert their gaze or evidence a challenging stare. "We," in contrast, maintain just the right amount of distance, prosody, and gaze. As detailed in the next section of this chapter, many cultures have standard and nonstandard interaction patterns. The standard pattern typically is associated with higher status, and all other patterns are judged against it. Lower-status groups generally are penalized for not speaking with the allegedly appropriate dialect or accent and for displaying nonverbal behaviors that are construed as inappropriate or at least as confusing to persons who adhere to the standard. These evaluations of speech qualities and nonverbal behaviors, and the intergroup misunderstandings that they may engender, are considered first in this chapter.

"STANDARD" INTERACTION PATTERNS

In *My Fair Lady*, the musical adaptation of George Bernard Shaw's *Pygmalian*, cockney-accented Eliza Doolittle laments her inability to be hired in a flower shop because she "don't talk genteel." Her lessons, at the brusk hand of Professor Henry Higgins, involve learning the lexicon and prosody of upper-class English society. By the end of the musical, Eliza's speech lessons are so well learned that she is mistaken for a person of royal blood. The Pygmalian story and its variations often are invoked to illustrate expectancy confirmation effects in social psychology. But they also illustrate an intriguing type of prejudice in communication. Many societies possess standard and nonstandard versions of a language, the standard version typically being associated with prestige and status. Functioning to maintain the power of the dominant group as well as separation among groups, this bias against nonstandard patterns of communication is recognized as a form of prejudice and discrimination (Graumann & Wintermantel, 1989).

The standard version of a language may be distinguished by a particular prosody and accent, as well as by lexical choices. For example, during one of her lessons, Eliza Doolittle attempts to parrot Henry Higgins's pleasantry, "How *kind* of you, to let me come." Eliza's attempt gushes forth as "Ow koind of *you* to leh me come." She drops the "h" in "how," evidences a nonstandard pronunciation of the long-I in "kind," and emphasizes a different word in the sentence. Speakers of the allegedly superior standard dialect, like Professor Higgins and the persons from whom Eliza hopes to seek employment, regard her speech as an important factor that separates her from higher-status groups. The "haves" in part can tell the "have-nots" from the latters' speech, and can prevent them from acquiring a more financially rewarding position in life because they do not fit into genteel society. Moreover, speakers of the purportedly superior dialect regard the lower-class speech with distaste. Higgins brags that Eliza is butchering English, the beautiful language of Shakespeare and the Bible. Particularly in his inaccurate claim concerning the Bible, one sees that preference for the standard version of the language may serve a group-enhancing function, as well as the more easily recognized social and dominance maintaining ones.

The "Standard" Version of a Language

EVALUATION OF NONSTANDARD ACCENTS AND DIALECTS

A dialect of a spoken language is a variation that is particular to a specific region or social group, including both lexical idiosyncrasies and accent. Individuals who speak different dialects of the same language can, at least to some extent, understand one another. Different languages, in contrast, are considered mutually unintelligible. In many cultures, one dialect or accent is viewed as the "standard" dialect. For example, Standard American English (SAE) is the standard dialect in the United States, and Received Pronunciation English (RP) is the standard dialect in Great Britain. Although both nations comprise individuals who speak a variety of dialects (and languages), SAE and RP are viewed as their respective standards. The standard dominates commerce, educational instruction, and political dialogue so, not surprisingly, the standard often is associated with higher socioeconomic success. It bears mention that the standard is not necessarily spoken by the majority of people in a nation, but typically by the people with wealth and social status.

Even when lexical choices are identical, perceivers sometimes can distinguish among dialects and accents using other cues, such as prosody or speech rate. For instance, van Bezooijen and Gooskens (1999) examined how accurately residents of the United Kingdom could determine from which region (e.g., Glasgow or Newcastle) another British speaker hailed. In some conditions, listeners heard the speakers as they ordinarily would be heard, with all their varied pronunciations, prosody, and lexical choices. In other conditions, the speech was filtered to remove all but prosodic information. Recognition on the basis of prosody alone was well above chance, especially if the speech fragments included prosodic information unique to that dialect. The ability of prosodic information to contribute to recognition of regional dialects suggests that bias against nonstandard speakers can derive in part from their manner of speaking (not simply their choice of words).

Compared to speakers who use nonstandard accents or dialects, speakers who use the standard typically are viewed as more intelligent, as having higher status, and as being more dominant and competent (for a review see Bradac, 1990). This perceived intellectual superiority of speakers using standard dialects and accents is evidenced in a number of cultures. In the United States, speakers using a Mexican American accent, for example, are more likely to be assigned lower-status employment positions than speakers who use a standard accent (de la Zerda & Hopper, 1979). Similarly, in Great Britain, speakers with English accents are often viewed as more intelligent than speakers with Scottish accents (Cheyne, 1970). Exceptions to the standard-implies-competence rule occur when the culture from which the speaker hails is perceived as being higher or of equal status to the perceivers' culture. North Americans, for example, rate speakers with Japanese or British accents highly on status-related traits (e.g., A. C. Cargile & H. Giles, 1996, cited in Cargile, 1997; Stewart, Ryan, & Giles, 1985), even though these speakers evidence a nonstandard accent. Similarly, to North American perceivers, speakers using a Mandarin Chinese accent are rated as equally qualified for various employment positions as speakers with a standard North American accent (Cargile, 1997). In the aforementioned studies concerning Asian accents, however, all evaluated individuals spoke fluent English, so only the accent varied across evaluation conditions. One might surmise that individuals with Asian accents who do not speak fluent English are less likely to be viewed as possessing high status or high intellect by European American raters. Rather than evoking stereotypes of Asians who are experts in technology or other highly valued industries, an Asian accent with nonfluent English instead probably evokes stereotypes of Asians in lower-status positions of North American society, such as servers in a Chinese restaurant.

Speakers using dialects and accents associated with lower social status are not derogated across the board, however. Nonstandard dialects, in contrast to standard ones, often are associated with perceptions of interpersonal attractiveness. To British listeners, the Scottish accent, for example, conveys a more likable and friendly impression of the speaker than does the standard English accent (Cheyne, 1970). Similarly, at least to Welsh participants, a fellow Welshman who speaks English or Welsh with a Welsh accent is viewed as more friendly and sociable than a fellow Welshman who speaks English with RP accent

(Bourhis, Giles, & Tajfel, 1973). Again, the apparent status seems to underlie these perceptions. In fact, when socioeconomic indicators of status are used, resulting evaluations are similar to those produced with accent cues (Stewart et al., 1985). The higher-status group is competent but dislikable, whereas the lower-status group is likable but incompetent. Additional evidence of the importance of apparent status derives from work on variation in the degree of accent. If the accent is subtle, listeners sometimes misidentify the speaker's actual group; the misidentification in turn leads to ratings according to the group to which listeners believe that the speaker belongs (R. J. Sebastian, E. B. Ryan, & L. Corso, in press, cited in Ryan, Hewstone, & Giles, 1984).

Why are standard-accented individuals viewed as more competent but less likable than nonstandard accented individuals, and vice versa? One possibility is that perceivers are threatened by high-status outgroups yet want to assert differences between their own group and the high-status outgroup (Fiske, 1998). Derogating a higher-status outgroup on its successes is difficult, because the successes and traits that presumably produced them are (at least to the perceiver) blatantly obvious. Unless people wish to derogate their own ingroup, competence-related traits are not useful dimensions for intergroup differentiation. Group differentiation from higher-status groups can, however, be maintained along likability dimensions. Perhaps the higher-status group cannot be denigrated for its self-confidence and intelligence, but it can be perceived as unfriendly, aloof, and uncaring. Conversely, lower-status outgroups are not threatening, because perceived intergroup differentiation along competence dimensions already exists. Consequently, lower-status outgroups need not be derogated along likability dimensions. Thus, compared to high-status outgroups, they are perceived as relatively likable.

At least among college students from a predominantly white sample, these two kinds of outgroups are perceived to exist (Fiske, Xu, Cuddy, & Glick, 1999). College students in this study rated 17 social groups on various competence- and likability-related traits, and their ratings of the groups were submitted to cluster analysis. The social groups tended to cluster into two types of people: one with high competence and low likablity; the other with low competence and high likability. Groups perceived as incompetent but likable included Latinos, disabled individuals, housewives, migrant workers, and retarded individuals. Groups perceived as competent but dislikable included feminists, Jews, Asians, rich people, and businesswomen. These findings, when considered alongside the speech evaluation literature, corroborate the notion that perceived status drives competence versus likability perceptions of outgroups.

THE CASE OF BLACK ENGLISH

Black English is a common dialect used in the United States and has a variety of features that currently distinguish it from SAE. For example, these features include the occasional absence of an "s" on third person singular verbs (e.g., "John sing at church"), the use of "be" to signify ongoing actions (e.g., "Mary be heading to the store now"), and the omission of tense markers when other cues about the time are present (e.g., "Yesterday, I go to the store"). Pronunciation also may differ from SAE. For example, r may be deleted unless it appears before a vowel, allowing words like "court" and "caught," or "guard" and "god" to sound similar. In some variations, r is not pronounced between vowels (e.g., "Paris" and "pass" are homophones) or l is deleted when it is not the first letter of a word (e.g., "help" is pronounced "hep") (for discussion see Fromkin & Rodman, 1988).

White Americans historically have regarded black English with disdain, and have used it to illustrate an alleged incompetence of blacks. Whites' written discourse on black English from the late-19th and early-20th centuries included arguments that the dialect was an inevitable product of black inferiority. For example, white discourse about black English included references to African American speech as "an ingenious distortion of words" or "baby talk." The slight variations in grammar and word choice were construed as deriving from the "confusing of persons" or from "characteristic laziness" (see Smitherman-Donaldson, 1988, for additional examples). Later commentaries, following on the heels of the civil rights movement, argued that black English stemmed from living in impoverished environments. Individuals in such environments purportedly were verbally deprived because of their limited exposure to SAE. Black English therefore became viewed as an underdeveloped type of SAE, caused not by innate inferiority of African Americans but instead caused by a deficit in learning and exposure. Smitherman-Donaldson argues that the solution implied by these deficit models is for speakers of black English to change their style of speech, rather than recognizing black English as an alternative language or dialect spoken alongside SAE in the United States. The reaction to an Oakland, California, school district's proposition to recognize black English as a language—Ebonics—in its own right generally met with negative reactions. But, at the same time, courses, journals, and books devoted to Ebonics have been on the rise. Then again, within African American communities, there continues to be avid debate concerning whether Black English should be embraced as a culturally viable dialect or abolished as the residual language of slavery. Tracking this debate through the coming decades of the 21st century certainly will prove interesting.

Regardless of where one stands on the Ebonics issue, the current evidence points to negative evaluation of and discrimination against speakers of black English in the United States. A provocative examination of housing discrimination (Purnell, Idsardi & Baugh, 1999) nicely illustrates this point. Purnell et al. noted that ethnic accent alone—without accompanying visual cues to ethnicity—may be sufficient to prompt discrimination. Citing the 1994 case of *HUD v. Ross*, these researchers note that judge's recognition that Ross, the defendant, never provided an opportunity for two separate Hispanic women to complete rental applications. With one woman, Ross purportedly hung up the phone prematurely; with the second woman, Ross failed to return her phone call after a message was left with his secretary. The accent of these women, according to the judge, was sufficient to identify their ethnic background (and therefore sufficient to allow discrimination on the basis of race or ethnicity).

Purnell et al. (1999) therefore devised a study in which phone calls were placed to landlords who listed vacancies in their rental properties. The caller used one of three linguistic guises: African American Vernacular English, SAE, and Chicano English. The landlords' properties were listed in the greater San Francisco area, whose neighborhoods vary distinctly in ethnic composition. For example, the 1990 U.S. Census indicated that Palo Alto and Woodside respectively comprised 84.9% and 95% European American individuals. African American individuals were best represented in the Oakland area (43.9%), and Latino individuals were best represented in East Palo Alto (36.4%). Securing a confirmed appointment to view the property served as a measure of discrimination. Results indicated that nonstandard dialects could prompt discrimination and that discrimination was most pronounced when the geographic area's ethnic composition was highly skewed toward whites. In Woodside, for example, 70% of the phone calls placed in SAE resulted in a confirmed appointment, whereas about 22% and 29% of the phone calls placed in Chicano English and African American Vernacular English resulted in a confirmed appointment. In contrast, in the more diverse Oakland area, the percentages respectively were 69%, 58%, and 72%. A subsequent study by the same authors showed that even the single word "Hello" allowed perceivers to identify a dialect over 70% of the time. Very early in a conversation, then, perceivers may have the information necessary to categorize the speaker's race or ethnic group, and this categorization conceivably can prompt discrimination.

Earlier studies by Gaertner (1973; also Gaertner & Bickman, 1971) using the wrong number technique are consistent with Purnell and colleague's more recent findings (above). In such studies, a black or white confederate telephones a local resident, alleges that his car broke down, and says that he was trying to phone the garage for help. Given that he reached the wrong number and is allegedly out of change, the confederate attempts to persuade the call recipient to make the call on his behalf. Whites were less likely to help the caller who used a Southern black accent than the speaker who used a standard white accent (Gaertner & Bickman, 1971). A later study showed that this type of discrimination was more likely among political conservatives, although political liberals often hung up the phone before the entire appeal could be made (Gaertner, 1973). The scripts were identical, pointing to black English pronunciation as the source of discrimination.

Another early study (Bishop, 1979) suggests that speaking black English itself, not its cuing of race per se, in part can underlie discrimination by whites. In this study, white female undergraduates and black female confederates simulated an employment interview. The black confederates always played the role of the interviewee and spoke either in standard white English or black English. White participants reported feeling more relaxed and agreeable when the black confederate spoke white English, expressed a greater willingness to work with her, and considered her more responsible than when she spoke black English (see Jussim, Fleming, Coleman, & Kohberger, 1996). When the confederate spoke black English, interviewers rated the interview as more informative and the speaker as more honest than when she spoke white English. Overall, then, the white participants were more at ease and inclined more favorably toward the speaker of white English. Congruent with Purnell and colleague's (1999) findings, the behavioriod measures in Bishop's study (i.e., willingness to work or become friends with the confederate) again linked the nonstandard accent with discrimination.

Bishop's (1979) study also varied the apparent attitudinal similarity of the confederate to the participant. When an attitudinally dissimilar black speaker spoke white English, she was evaluated more harshly than when she spoke black English. Bishop suggested that the black speaker of white English may have been viewed as an appropriate person for comparison, whereas the speaker of black English was not so viewed. Because a black person speaking standard white English is an appropriate comparison, attitudinal dissimilarity would encourage participants to reevaluate their own beliefs. The ensuing threat to beliefs may have lead to negative evaluation. (From this social comparison perspective, the speaker of black English simply could be ignored.) An alternative way to interpret these findings is in terms of social status and threat. Participants initially may have accorded some degree of social status to the black speaker of white English, because she spoke the standard dialect. When she was attitudinally dissimilar, however, participants may have felt threatened or uncomfortable. A prejudiced person certainly would not want to interact with an articulate out-group member who disagrees with her! Indeed, such a person potentially threatens the cultural worldview (see Schimel et al., 1999).

A related alternative is that each of the four black individuals evoked a different subtype. For example, an attitudinally dissimilar speaker of black English might evoke a stereotype of impoverished blacks who hold low-status jobs, viewed as incompetent but not necessarily dislikable. In contrast, an attitudinally dissimilar speaker of white English might evoke a stereotype of articulate black leaders and professionals whose views do not necessarily coincide with the white majority; individuals perceived as belonging to this subtype probably are seen by many whites as competent but perhaps as dislikable. Blacks, rated as an entire group by whites, do not easily emerge as one of the two types of outgroups, perhaps because of these disparate subtypes (Fiske et al., 1999).

GROUP IDENTIFICATION

Like Professor Higgins in *My Fair Lady*, proponents of the deficit models essentially presume that nonstandard dialects must be "fixed" or even eradicated. More recent movements propose that native speakers of nonstandard dialects may wish to become bidialectal, switching between dialects as situation and context dictate. (Note that the focus rarely involves teaching speakers of the standard dialect to become bidialectal themselves—or at least to value linguistic diversity.) The reticence to surrender one's native tongue may stem in part from ingroup pride: Language sometimes may be a symbol of group identity. For example, residents of Wales who speak Welsh or are learning Welsh view themselves as "more Welsh" than nonspeakers, and also are dissatisfied with British handling of Welsh demands for autonomy (Bourhis et al., 1973). The Ebonics movement in the United States and the push for using Breton in the French region (and former province) of Brittany may serve a similar group-enhancing function. These individuals may desire to change standard speakers' disdainful views of the nonstandard dialect or language and, by extension, change views of their culture as well.

Rather than surrender their native dialect or language entirely if they learn the standard language, many individuals become multi-dialectal or multilingual. Such individuals possess the rudimentary skills to "code switch," that is, to select the dialect or language that seems appropriate to the situation. For example, early research on code switching showed that people reverted to the native dialect or language when discussing culturally relevant topics or emotional issues (for a review see Sachdev & Bourhis, 1990); presumably these topics could be discussed more efficiently in the native dialect or language. People also might code switch when they have more to gain by doing so. For example, when seeking employment, multilingual or multidialectal individuals presumably select the language or dialect used by (or presumably desired by) the potential employer. The failure to do so may cost the applicant a decent job, whereas the employer simply can shrug and reexamine an ample-sized applicant pool.

More germane to present purposes, multidialectal speakers also might use a native nonstandard dialect when they expect communication partners to initiate ingroup solidarity or to encourage interpersonal liking. The more formal standard dialect might be interpreted as stilted or creating distance unless it is interpreted as humorously intended (Smitherman-Donaldson, 1988). Even when unilingual or unidialectal speakers want to be liked, their speech converges to that of their communication partners (e.g., language intensity; accent and prosody mimicry; for a review see Street, 1990), so speakers do appear to use language to create a feeling of solidarity. Of course, the recognition of the relation between language and solidarity is not new or even unique to social science. Several of Shakespeare's heroes (e.g., Henry V) effortlessly switch from spouting formal iambic pentameter with high-status characters or in soliloquy in some scenes to speaking colorful but less formal prose with the "rustic" characters in other scenes. Presumably, this flexibility promotes understanding and liking across status groups.

Conversely, people may use language to emphasize intergroup differences (Bourhis, Giles, Leyens, & Tajfel, 1979; for a review, see Street, 1990). Bourhis and colleagues' study (1979) in Belgium provides a clear example of the use of language for intergroup differentiation and ingroup identification. The native language of Flemish individuals in Belgium is a dialect of Dutch; for Walloon Belgians, the native language is French. For trilingual Belgians, English can serve as a neutral compromise. In Bourhis and colleagues' study, Flemish participants interacted with a Walloon confederate; the Flemish participants used English until the Walloon's questions became ethnically threatening. At that point, the Flemish participants switched to Dutch. Although the trilingual Walloon interviewers presumably could understand Dutch, the switch could represent an assertion of ingroup identification and function as a mechanism for defending the group's self-esteem. Related research suggests that people expect speech divergence during conflict. For example, accent convergence, compared to divergence, seems unnatural during a competitive interaction between members of two regionally distinct Swiss individuals (Doise, Sinclair, & Bourhis, 1976). Thus, although code switching sometimes occurs in the service of communication efficiency, it also is used—and expected to be used—to accentuate or attenuate social distance.

SUMMARY

The standard accent or dialect typically is presumed to reflect intelligence and competence, whereas the nonstandard dialect typically is presumed to reflect superior interpersonal qualities. The group status implied by the standard form appears to underlie these differential ratings. Analyses in terms of status also is informative in understanding European Americans' contemporary evaluation of African Americans. Black English currently may evoke stereotypes of African Americans in lower-status positions of society, say, ghetto-dwelling television characters or friendly but underpaid janitors. White English, instead, may evoke historically newer African American subtypes: black professionals or political figures. Although the standard form may open doors, dialect and language may be a source of ingroup pride to multidialectal and multilingual individuals. Rather than abandon the nonstandard form in favor of the standard, such individuals may adopt the strategy of code switching. Code switching may be used to generate and maintain ingroup solidarity, as well as to provide a mechanism for intergroup distancing.

"Standard" Nonverbal Patterns

Although the focus of Eliza's lessons in *My Fair Lady* primarily concerns accent and prosody, the audience also witnesses a transformation in other aspects of her nonverbal communication patterns. The highly animated young woman develops the stiff and slow movements of upper-class ladies, deigns to smile delicately on occasion, and learns to withhold her challenging glare. Like paralanguage and prosody, other nonverbal behaviors, including those not central to spoken language, vary across cultural and social groups. For example, patterns of eye contact, use of personal space, and the degree of peripheral body movements all may vary across cultures (e.g., for a review see Dew & Ward, 1993). Similarly, rules for displaying feelings and emotions vary across cultural groups (Matsumoto, 1998) and occupational groups (Willson & Lloyd, 1990). Such differences in the communication of emotion (e.g., Albas, McCluskey, & Albas, 1976), in expressing challenge to authority (Hanna, 1984; Kochman, 1981), or simply in the degree of gazes exchanged (Vrij, Dragt, & Koppelaar, 1992) can contribute to intergroup misunderstanding. What one group views as rude, another might view as polite. What one group views as arrogant, another group might view as self-confident. The interactional patterns of one's own culture are preferred and are used as a lens through which the patterns of other cultures are interpreted and judged.

DIFFERENCE AND DISCOMFORT

Most research on nonverbal interaction patterns has focused on dyadic interactions, particularly patterns of compensation and reciprocation (Patterson, 1996). Compensatory behaviors occur in order to offset a partner's behavior. If a disliked person draws too near, for example, an individual might take a step back or aside, or might avert his or her gaze and fold the arms. Reciprocal behaviors attempt to match the partner's behavior. Individuals who like one another may mirror each other's degree of forward leaning or smiling, for example. Both compensatory and reciprocal behaviors may be reactive and spontaneous (i.e., driven by an affective response to the partner) or strategic and relatively deliberate.

Although people place considerable credence on the honesty of nonverbal behavior (DePaolo, 1998), the possibility that nonverbal interaction patterns may be deliberate affords some degree of complexity to interpreting nonverbal behavior. At least some of our behaviors are intentional—or at least may be inferred to be intentional. Intergroup settings add another layer of complexity to the equation, because of differences in nonverbal behaviors across cultural and social groups. For example, in New Zealand, compared to the majority Anglo-Europeans (2.6 million, called *Pakeha* by the half-million indigenous Maori and called *Palagi* by some 100,000 settlers from Samoa), the Samoans maintain less direct eye contact, touch others more often, and maintain smaller interpersonal space. Samoans also seem more comfortable with silence than do Palagi, although silence does not imply consent. Imagine the possibilities for misunderstanding: The Samoan sits too close for Palagi comfort, and compensatory Palagi behavior is to turn away; the Palagi individual maintains a high direct gaze, but this behavior is not reciprocated by the Samoan. The results can be miscommunication and general discomfort.

Examining these two groups in particular, Dew and Ward (1993) arranged dyadic interactions between Palagi and Samoan women. Four Palagi and four Samoan college-aged confederates, all fluent in English, were trained to display the nonverbal communication styles of each group. Differences included posture, chair orientation, spatial distance, and eye gaze. One confederate then interacted with a female

Palagi college student, using either a Samoan or Palagi nonverbal style. Participants' interpersonal attraction ratings (e.g., liking for the confederate; level of comfort) only were influenced by nonverbal style: If the confederate evidenced a Palagi interaction pattern, she was liked significantly more than if she evidenced a Samoan interaction pattern. With respect to their failure to detect an effect of confederate ethnicity, the authors caution against concluding nonverbal patterns are more important than ethnicity. The confederates (and participants) all were college students at the same university, fluent in English, the majority language, and engaged in an equal-status interaction; ethnicity might be more important when interaction partners cannot be construed easily as part of an ingroup, when interaction partners are not fluent in each other's language, or when contact is asymmetrical. Moreover, in light of the research discussed previously, it is conceivable that the Samoan women mimicked Palagi prosody, speech rate, and other linguistic features while mimicking their other nonverbal behaviors. If so, these features of their spoken language might have contributed to the Palagi participants preferring Samoans who evidenced a Palagi interaction style.

Discomfort during cross-cultural interaction also may arise due to differences in how different groups typically regulate the flow of conversation. For example, people might obtain the floor by interrupting or noticeably shifting their body position in one culture or situation but use an explicit signal (e.g., a raised hand) in another situation. Among European Americans, for example, the surrendering of a speaking turn often is signified by disengaging eye contact briefly while still talking, then returning eye contact as the utterance is finished. This pattern may not hold across cultural groups. Back-channel indicators also control the flow of conversation, by signaling understanding or agreement, or even conveying exasperation at unnecessary verbosity. Shaking the head from side to side may mean "I am listening" in one culture but "Your argument makes no sense at all" in another. Simply knowing whether one is expected to speak or what each nonverbal back-channel indicator signifies can be complicated.

Interruptions, for example, sometimes are perceived as an assertion of status or reflecting a lack of discipline or social skills. Pre-adolescent Native American individuals (e.g., Choctaw students) are likely to interrupt instructors in school settings (Greenbaum, 1985), which is frustrating for European American teachers. These teachers typically adhere to a "switchboard" system of communication in which the instructor controls which students speak, when they speak, and how much speaking time is allotted to them. This unilateral style is just as frustrating for Choctaw students, who favor a choral-response system in which many individuals simultaneously answer a question. Choctaw students' interruptions seem to reflect unfamiliarity with the switchboard system, rather than rudeness or "lack of discipline," despite its interpretation as such. Efforts to enforce the switchboard system seem to lead to embarrassment and, eventually, to a reticence of the students to speak in the classroom setting (for a discussion, see Greenbaum, 1985).

DIFFERENCE AND MISTRUST

In a variety of professions, individuals who hold the superordinate position sometimes are in the position of accusing a subordinate of an inappropriate action. A teacher alleges that a student cheated, a store manager accuses a clerk of stealing, a father believes that his son destroyed the beloved toy of a younger sibling, or a business executive questions whether her secretary leaked confidential information to a coworker. To European Americans, at least, nonverbal behaviors such as gaze aversion and increased peripheral body movements are expected to betray guilt. Ironically, both nonverbal behavioral patterns are seen more commonly in African American than European American individuals. Compared to European Americans, African Americans exhibit more gaze aversion and, indeed, apparently interpret prolonged eye contact as arrogant and rude. African Americans also may exhibit more frequent peripheral nonverbal changes than European Americans, which may perpetuate their being stereotypically perceived by European Americans as less "mechanical" or "rigid" (for a discussion see Majors, 1991, or Vrij et al., 1992). The main issue, though, is that the very behaviors that are typical among one group may be interpreted to mean something very different in another cultural group.

Somewhat similar patterns are observed in the Netherlands, when white Dutch individuals are compared to Surinamese immigrants. Surinamese individuals gesture more and exhibit more trunk movements, but maintain less eye contact than do members of the Dutch majority (see Winkel & Vrij, 1990). In one study examining these two groups, Surinamese or Dutch individuals viewed a video in which a Dutch or Surinamese citizen was being questioned by a police officer. The police officer was off-camera and the sound was omitted. Consequently, only the ethnicity of the citizen and his nonverbal behaviors provided an obvious basis for impressions of suspicious, tense, or cooperative behavior patterns. The Dutch participants' impressions of citizens who averted gaze were negative, even after the results were statistically controlled for the citizen's ethnic origin. The Surinanese participants, in contrast, only evaluated gaze aversion in a negative fashion if they were well integrated into Dutch society; less-integrated Surinamers viewed the extended eye contact typical of the Dutch in a negative fashion. Conceivably, then, the suspiciousness with which Dutch police officers regard Surinamese suspects derives in part from the latter's nonverbal behaviors.

Other ethnic minorities in the Netherlands (e.g., Turks, Moroccans) also exhibit less direct eye contact than the white Dutch majority (Vrij et al., 1992). Moreover, Turks, Moroccans, and Surinamers also speak more slowly, more quietly, and with less pitch variation than do the Dutch. Vrij and his colleagues argue that these different nonverbal patterns may in part explain the high rate of unemployment among ethnic minorities in the Netherlands; the nonverbal differences create a negative impression on the Dutch individuals who, more often than not, are responsible for hiring and promotion decisions. Examining this issue, Vrij et al. asked Dutch veteran police officers to observe standardized interviews with Dutch versus ethnic minority police candidates. Participants viewed the tape either with sound or without sound, or they simply read a transcript of the interview. In both video versions, impressions of ethnic minority candidates were more negative than impressions of Dutch candidates. In addition, ethnic minorities faired better when only a transcript rather than a video was examined. Again, the different nonverbal behaviors displayed by ethnic minorities in part may contribute to the discrimination that they often experience. They therefore remain separated from the mainstream society and remain in lower-status positions.

SUMMARY

The nonverbal behaviors of outgroup members may seem suspicious, rude, or simply disquieting. Sitting with the legs outstretched is a relaxed posture for many people from Western nations, but the posture may offend individuals from Nepal if the feet are pointed in their direction (Moghaddam, Taylor, & Wright, 1993). Similarly, North American heterosexuals sometimes feel uneasy when they witness two adult males kiss, though such behavior is common in Turkey (Moghaddam et al., 1993). "They" make "us" uncomfortable by not maintaining the right amount of eye contact, by sitting too stiffly or fidgeting too much, by talking out of turn or unilaterally controlling the conversation. As with using nonstandard accents and dialects, evidencing nonverbal behaviors that are different from those of the traditionally more powerful group can carry negative consequences. Such individuals generally may be considered difficult interaction partners, be held in greater suspicion of wrongdoing, or have difficulty obtaining satisfactory employment.

THE NONVERBAL COMMUNICATION OF PREJUDICE

Paralinguistic information, patterns of eye contact, personal spacing, and other nonverbal forms of communication vary across cultures. Individuals from the dominant culture, at least, seem to prefer other people who adopt or successfully mimic the nonverbal communication patterns of the dominant culture. Thus, one aspect of prejudice in nonverbal communication concerns the (usually negative) evaluation of the nonverbal interaction patterns of other cultures. That is, nonverbal communication serves as a predictor of evaluation. The other major aspect is more traditionally examined in mainstream social psychology: During communication, nonverbal indicators may convey prejudiced feelings or assertions of higher status. The behaviors associated with these apparent prejudiced feelings then either are examined as dependent variables or as factors that produce negative thoughts, feelings, or behaviors in targets.

Facial Expressions

In the absence of contradictory contextual information, most people will infer that a frowning person with a clenched jaw is annoyed or angry, that a smiling person is happy, or that a person who wrinkles up the nose and squints the eyes is disgusted. Matching such emotional experiences with corresponding facial expressions is reliable across cultures. Even if the number of core emotions remains debatable, there is little doubt that facial expressions can reflect affective experience (for a review see Fiske & Taylor, 1991). The challenge for researchers interested in prejudice is that people in contemporary society often attempt to mask their affective reactions toward disliked outgroups. Because communication in intergroup settings can serve self-presentational functions, the validity of examined facial expressions sometimes may be limited. If, however, people are unaware that they are being watched or are otherwise unconcerned about self-presentation, facial expressions may be useful in studying prejudiced reactions.

Schemes for assessing facial expressions range from highly detailed classification schemes and physiological measures to gross ratings of affect. One detailed visually oriented scheme is the Facial Action Coding System (FACS; Ekman & Friesen, 1978), which requires coders to ascertain which muscles have been contracted to produce a particular expression. Although this method requires highly trained coders, it allows the precise specification of a particular affect. For example, the Duchenne smile includes action in the orbicularis oculi muscle. This action most noticeably produces wrinkling at the corners of the eyes (crow's feet) and is associated with genuine enjoyment. The non-Duchenne (fake) smile includes other actions associated with smiling such as activity in the zygomatic major muscle (the cheek muscle which draws the face into a smile), but fails to include the crow's feet-producing Duchenne marker. Recent work on smiles using this coding scheme detects different affective experiences associated with smiling as a function of the type of relationship between the interacting individuals (Hecht & LaFrance, 1998). Both Duchenne and non-Duchenne smiles are correlated directly with the reported experience of positive affect, but only when people interact with equal- or lower-status others. When people interact with higher-status others, the affect–smiling relation disappears and even becomes slightly negative. Interacting with higher-status others apparently elicits obligatory smiles, regardless of how one actually feels. Thus, the smiles of one's subordinates should not be taken as necessarily reflecting their liking or pleasure. Conversely, reduced smiling may lead to inferences of higher status, and when smiling by high-status persons occurs, it perhaps is seen as reflecting genuine pleasure. One might hazard a guess that other types of obligatory smiles also might show little relation to experienced pleasure. For example, people might smile obligatorily at an outgroup member if they were afraid of being labeled prejudiced, but they might not necessarily like the outgroup member.

A quicker but less detailed method of assessing emotion in the face, used more by researchers with secondary interests in affect, involves the assignment of gross ratings of affect. Raters assess the extent to which the person's face implies a more or less pleasant feeling state. Such gross ratings of facial affect can discriminate between liked and disliked significant others (Andersen, Reznik, & Manzella, 1996), and presumably should distinguish between liked and disliked outgroups as well. Neuberg and Fiske (1987), for example, showed that gross ratings of change in behavior distinguish people expecting to interact with heart patients versus schizophrenics. Although the behavioral markers were not exclusively facial expressions, the findings do support the notion that gross ratings can be useful. On the other hand, gross ratings may not always distinguish among distinct varieties of negative affect. Unabashedly prejudiced individuals might display facial expressions of disgust or contempt when interacting with outgroup members, whereas "modern" prejudiced individuals may display facial expressions of embarrassment or fear, as they worry about leaking their prejudices during a conversation (Devine, Evett, & Vasquez-Suson, 1996). A rating of degree of mere negativity would not distinguish these different affective reactions.

An alternative to coders' assessments of facial affect is to go directly to the muscles themselves. Electromyographic (EMG) recording allows researchers to measure the specific muscle contractions in the face that are associated with affective experience. Lowering of the brow (by contraction of the corrugator supercillii muscle) is linearly associated with exposure to unpleasant stimuli. Activity in this muscle increases during exposure to unpleasant stimuli but decreases during exposure to pleasant stimuli. In contrast, the zygomaticus major muscle tends to produce a J-shaped pattern. For pleasant stimuli, activity is high. For neutral stimuli, activity is low. For unpleasant stimuli, activity is moderate (for a brief review see Guglielmi, 1999). Numerous studies with various types of stimuli evidence the utility of EMG activity to indicate affective experience. An advantage of EMG recording is that microexpressions may be recorded before they subsequently are masked by socially acceptable facial expressions.

Vanman, Paul, Ito, and Miller (1997) used EMG recording specifically to examine racial prejudice. In one of their experiments, white participants imagined cooperating with a black or white partner. EMG activity was recorded during the imagination exercises, along with activity from locations other than the face. Results showed that self-report measures were at variance with the EMG measures: Participants' reported more positive affect when imagining a black rather than a white partner, but EMG measures indicated that participants experienced less positive affect when imagining a black partner. Vanman et al. also showed that such EMG activity may be moderated by the degree of prejudice. In this subsequent study, white participants who were high versus low in modern racism toward blacks viewed slides portraying black or white target individuals (for a discussion of modern racism, see Chapter 2). Low modern racists' brow (corrugator supercillii) and cheek (zygomaticus major) activity were unaffected by target race. High modern racists, in contrast, evidenced greater brow activity and lower cheek activity when viewing slides of black versus white targets, suggesting greater negative affect. Thus, subtle microexpressions apparently can reflect negative attitudes toward outgroup members.

SUMMARY

EMG recording and FACS-type coding both indicate that the face can provide information regarding how people feel about others. Both procedures also render it obvious that true affect may be expressed subtly or quickly masked for self-presentational reasons. Individuals who wish to avoid the public appearance of prejudice are unlikely to sneer or frown at outgroup members in highly public settings. Presumably, they present fake smiles or create a seemingly neutral blank look on their faces. If a genuine expression did appear, masking might occur too quickly for detection. In one study of smiling toward authority figures, for example, Japanese participants smiled more than American participants. Replays of the videos in slow motion, however, showed that smiling among the Japanese participants was superimposed upon initial expressions of fear or disgust (W. V. Friesen, 1972, cited in Ekman & O'Sullivan, 1991). Given that facial expressions can be faked or masked, how well facial expressions can be relied upon in daily life for information about the prejudices of others remains to be seen.

At least two venues for exploration might help delineate the usefulness of facial expressions as indicators of prejudiced affect in daily interactions. First, in determining how others feel about them, perceivers may try to collect base-rate and comparison information, just as social scientists do. As a general rule, people tend to think that another person will perceive them as they perceive themselves, but this tendency would not necessarily hold when people suspect others of prejudice against them. For instance, an African American individual who wonders if a particular European American colleague is prejudiced against him might note the facial expressions that his colleague exhibits toward his peers. He also might note how this colleague's facial expressions compare to those of other colleagues. If the colleague typically smiles at everyone but gives him only an acknowledging but blank-faced nod, the African American individual might infer prejudice. Contrarily, if an exaggerated smile greets him and him alone, he might conclude that the person was trying (too hard) to appear unprejudiced. And if the colleague smiles at no one, prejudice might not be the most likely inference. A second possible venue for research stems from the fact that managing a nonprejudiced social image involves deliberate conscious strategies. Intention and extra effort may be necessary to mask a genuine but socially inappropriate facial expression or to present a fake expression. Thus, in the busyness of daily interaction, people might leak their facial affect more than one might imagine at first blush.

Nonverbal Vocalizations

"Um. I was wondering if, er, I could maybe ask for some help on my um, homework assignment?" The inclusion of *ums* and *ers* into this petitioning student's request probably encourages the inference that the student is anxious. Intuitively appealing as that sounds, empirical research does not support that assumption in a straightforward manner. Instead, recent work suggests that such pause fillers increase when speakers are closely monitoring their own speech (Christenfeld & Creager, 1996) or when they can select among alternative ways to craft a similar message (Schacter, Christenfeld, Ravina, & Bilous, 1991). For example, speakers who believe that they are being evaluated on the quality of their message produce more pause fillers than do control participants. Similarly, speakers who feel self-conscious about their speaking produce more pause-fillers than do controls. In contrast, intoxicated individuals produce few pause fillers, presumably because they care little about their manner of speaking (Christenfeld & Creager, 1996). For researchers interested in prejudiced communication, these results suggest that speakers who produce ums and ers when speaking to outgroup members probably are monitoring their own speech and are hesitating while they try to identify the "right" words. Ruffled by impression management concerns, these speakers may become so concerned that observers or the targets themselves will interpret some comment as prejudiced that they simultaneously become hyperattentive to their own speech. Alternatively, these speakers may be trying to sound "normal," so that their prejudice does not leak through vocal affect. Although focusing on low-level behaviors such as the particular words selected often can help achieve a difficult goal (Vallacher, Wegner, McMahan, Cotter, & Larsen, 1992), the strategy ironically might backfire by encouraging the very inferences that the speaker wishes to avoid. While the speaker is hesitating in deciding what to say, his or her speech is littered with extraneous noise and listeners may infer that the speaker is nervous (Christenfeld, 1995). As discussed further below, given that speech disfluencies in general can be associated with intergroup prejudice (Word et al., 1974), a link between the hesitation-producing fear of appearing prejudiced and increased pause fillers seems feasible.

Related work directly links nonverbal vocalizations to hesitation in intergroup settings, though in regard to communication *about* targets rather than communication directed to targets. Blascovich, Wyer, Swart, and Kibler (1997) asked participants verbally to categorize projected slides of faces that were unambiguously white, unambiguously black, or ambiguous with respect to race. Compared to individuals low in prejudice, individuals high in prejudice against blacks required considerably longer to categorize ambiguous faces; presumably, more prejudiced individuals would be more concerned about making a mistake in classification than would less prejudiced individuals. In addition, more prejudiced individuals produced a greater number of nonverbal vocalizations while making their decision. Similar effects were not observed with nonsocial stimuli (gray, white, and black ovals), suggesting that prejudice rather than differences in perception, compliance with the experimenter, or degree of comfort with ambiguity underlay the results.

The nonverbal vocalizations examined by Blascovich et al. (1997) were those that activated the sound-sensitive taperecorder and prefaced participants' decision regarding the appropriate category for each slide. Presumably, these nonverbal vocalizations included *ums* and *hmmms*, as well as other sounds such as throat clearing, clicking the tongue against the roof of the mouth, and loud sighs. Whereas the *ums* that are interjected throughout speech probably are unintentional, the *ums* and other nonverbal vocalizations that preface an utterance may have a conscious communicative purpose. Casual observation hints that people preface their messages with these sounds in order to hint that they are attending to someone's query or comment but still are in the process of constructing a response. Combined with other nonverbal cues, these sounds could act as back-channel indicators that the other person's comment is confusing (i.e., the sounds are paired with a puzzled look) or is worthy of careful consideration (i.e., the sounds are paired with thoughtful nods). Hesitation per se may not always reflect negativity.

Immediacy Behaviors and Expectancy Confirmation

Immediacy behaviors are a class of behaviors that enhance psychological closeness among individuals. Someone who behaves in an immediate fashion is liked by her interaction partner partly because she conveys her own liking for the interaction partner. Immediacy behaviors also include decreased interpersonal distance, increased smiling, shoulder and body orientation, and forward lean. If a conversation is underway, nonverbal immediacy behaviors also can include increased time listening to the partner without interrupting, as well as nodding and providing other back-channel indicators of understanding or encouragement. Although not part of Mehrabian's (1968) original indices of immediacy, speech disfluencies also may be examined. Given the research noted above, speech disfluencies suggest that the speaker is paying close attention to message construction, as though worried about the impression being made; undergraduate students, at least, interpret speech disfluencies as reflecting nervousness (Christenfeld, 1995). In the studies discussed below, less immediate behaviors typically are thought to reflect dislike of, and even prejudice toward, the communication target. Theoretically, these behaviors can encourage expectancy confirmation, in which the target's behavior confirms the negative expectations held by the communicating perceiver.

In the now-classic study of nonverbal immediacy in interethnic settings, Word et al. (1974) required white college students to serve as employment interviewers. The interviewees were white versus black high school students, naive to the hypothesis but trained to respond verbally and nonverbally in a uniform fashion across interviewers. Each participant interviewed both a white applicant and a black applicant; order of applicant race was counterbalanced across participants. Interviewers positioned a wheeled office chair at their own discretion, allowing the measurement of physical distance between interviewer and interviewee. Hidden observers also recorded the interviewer's degree of forward lean, degree of shoulder orientation, and percentage of time looking directly into the interviewee's eyes. In addition to these four immediacy behaviors, observers also measured the length of the interview and the speech error rate of the interviewer. Speech errors included *ums*, stutters, and sentence incompletions.

Overall, the white interviewers evidenced greater nonverbal immediacy toward fellow whites than toward blacks, and this difference largely derived from differences in physical distance. In addition, the white interviewers produced fewer speech errors and allowed a longer interview with the white interviewees than with the black interviewees. Thus, overall, white participants' nonverbal cues seemed to leak negative feelings toward the black interviewees. The next step was to ascertain how interviewer immediacy affected the interviewees. Consequently, in the companion study, white interviewees served as participants who interacted with confederate interviewers. The researchers trained the interviewers to behave with high or low immediacy toward participant interviewees; the high immediacy interviewers maintained smaller physical distance, evidenced fewer speech errors, and allowed longer interviews than did the low immediacy interviewers. Ratings by hidden observers indicated that interviewees exposed to nonimmediate interviewers were less calm and composed, as well as judged to be less qualified for the alleged job. Moreover, these participants themselves reported feeling inadequate, felt that the interviewer was unfriendly, and tended to reciprocate the nonimmediate behaviors of the interviewer. Nonverbal immediacy behaviors therefore may have contributed to expectancy confirmation effects.

A number of empirical studies since that of Word et al. (1974) have further examined immediacy behaviors in interethnic interactions, particularly between black and white individuals (e.g., Babad, Bernieri, & Rosenthal, 1989; Feldman & Donohoe, 1978; Feldman & Orchowsky,

1979; Simpson & Erickson, 1983). For example, a series of studies by Feldman and his colleagues focused on interactions in educational settings. In these studies, college students participated, playing the role of teacher to either a black or white confederate student. The researchers somewhat constrained the verbal feedback of the teacher participants by requiring them to say "Right—that's good" in response to correct answers; for incorrect answers, they were required to explain why the answer was wrong. The question was whether unconstrained nonverbal feedback might leak a degree of prejudice. To examine this possibility, additional college students viewed silent video segments that showed only the teacher, then rated how pleased the teacher appeared to be with the (off-camera) student. In one of the studies (Feldman & Donohoe, 1978, experiment 1), black or white college-aged confederates responded correctly on 84% of the trials presented by a white teacher, so most of the time the teacher verbally was praising the student's performance. Without the sound available or knowing the students' race, raters detected that the highly prejudiced teachers seemed less pleased with black students than with white students. The less prejudiced teachers, in contrast, did not appear to discriminate nonverbally across race. A subsequent study (Feldman & Orchowsky, 1979) showed similar nonverbal bias among white participant teachers toward black students irrespective of whether the students' performance was excellent or substandard. As in the Word et al. (1974) study, the nonverbal behavior of white participants leaked some measure of negative affect toward black interaction partners.

CAVEAT 1: HOW IS NONVERBAL BEHAVIOR INTERPRETED?

Are these nonverbal behaviors necessarily interpreted as indicative of displeasure by the targets themselves? Given cross-cultural differences in the display and interpretation of nonverbal behavior, what constitutes "low immediacy" for European American individuals may not be interpreted as negative by recipients of other ethnic backgrounds. For example, patterns of eye contact vary across cultures (Dew & Ward, 1993; Feldman, 1985; Greenbaum, 1985; Winkel & Vrij, 1990); African Americans, at least, sometimes view extended eye contact by whites as arrogant or rude. The "right" amount of eye contact, personal distance, or body orientation is needed to create psychological warmth and closeness, and the "right" amount differs across cultures. Even in Word and colleagues' (1974) study, the participants who performed poorly when treated in the manner that whites treated blacks were themselves white. How black participants would have responded to these particular magnitudes of increased distance, reduced eye contact, or shorter interviews is unclear. Supporting this notion, extended eye contact (at least from a white teacher) is not as closely associated with successful outcomes for African American students as it is for European American students (M. J. Collier & R. G. Powell, 1986, cited in Sanders & Wiseman, 1990; cf. Bishop, 1979). Again, the meaning of extended eye contact seems to be different across groups.

Along a similar vein, what members of each culture interpret as indicative of displeasure or as nonverbally immediate may vary considerably. In one study of the Feldman series (Feldman & Donohoe, 1978, experiment 2), for example, white judges recognized the greater nonverbal displeasure of white teachers directed toward black over white students, but black judges failed to detect this nonverbal discrimination. To the black judges, the white teachers appeared equally pleased with both (off-camera) students. Conversely, black judges recognized greater nonverbal displeasure of black teachers directed toward white over black students, but white judges failed to detect nonverbal discrimination. Thus, the differential nonverbal behaviors may leak negative attitude, but it may not always be interpreted that way by members of other cultures (for additional evidence of differential immediacy in Japan see McGinley, Blau, & Takai, 1984; Neuliep, 1997).

To consider how behaviors are interpreted is not to challenge evidence that expectancy confirmation effects emerge in cross-cultural or interethnic settings. Indeed, these settings might produce some of the strongest expectancy effects (for a discussion see Jussim, Eccles, & Madon, 1996). Instead, it is important to emphasize that the contribution of nonverbal immediacy presumably depends more upon how it is understood than its sheer magnitude. For example, students may come to interpret certain teacher behaviors as encouraging ones, regardless of the teacher's cultural background, and may use that information to interpret behavior toward the self and other students. Moreover, most real-life interactions in which nonverbal behavior would be evident also include verbal behaviors that can encourage or discourage feelings of immediacy. For example, a coworker who inquires after the health of one's infirm grandparent, someone who extends a greeting to a new student, or a member of the clergy who occasionally makes personal disclosures may encourage psychological closeness through verbal means. Teachers who remember the names of their students or provide feedback that is nonthreatening and constructive also may encourage psychological closeness. Again, how these behaviors are understood presumably matters more than their sheer frequency, but verbal immediacy also would contribute to expectancy confirmation effects.

Finally, not all interactions among people of different groups are as complex as interethnic or cross-cultural interactions. In many cases, interactants hail from the same basic culture or at least are highly familiar with the other group's interaction style. College students from different fraternities or sororities, overweight women versus women of normal body weight, or executives and their secretaries may have sufficient similarity in their cultural backgrounds to understand each other's nonverbal behavior. Interactions between members of different genders is another good example. Men and women exhibit different nonverbal behaviors and even may differ in their ability to decode nonverbal messages. But, at least in relatively gender-integrated societies, people regularly interact with spouses, siblings, schoolmates, and parents of the other gender. The genders arguably might be better at reading each other's nonverbal messages than those produced by members of unfamiliar cultures or ethnic groups (although this admittedly is an empirical question). The point is that interpretation of what a nonverbal behavior actually implies probably is more accurate with members of familiar outgroups than with less familiar outgroups.

CAVEAT 2: TARGETS ARE NOT PASSIVE

The majority of work on immediacy and expectancy confirmation has focused primarily on the behaviors of the perceiver and their subsequent effect on the target. Targets obviously are not passive recipients of a perceiver's behavior. Instead, they typically care about the impression that they appear to be making, and also are in the process of forming their own impressions. (Indeed, the perception is mutual, and who is labeled as the "target" often is a function of the experimental paradigm.) If targets are trying to learn about the perceiver, rather than simply trying to create a smooth interaction, their behaviors do not confirm the perceiver's expectancies (Snyder & Haugen, 1995). Alternatively, if targets recognize that a perceiver holds a highly inaccurate impression of them, they accordingly may attempt to adjust the impression. For example, women who are overweight appear to recognize the stigma associated with their physical appearance. These women apparently learn to compensate by developing social skills that they especially employ when they feel it is necessary. Social skills ratings of overweight women are similar to those of normal-weight women, but only if they believe that their interaction partner can see them (Miller, Rothblum, Felicio, & Brand, 1995). At least in these equal-status interactions, the target need not fall prey to the negative expectancies conveyed by others.

SUMMARY

Immediacy behaviors such as decreased interpersonal distance and smiling can convey liking for one's interaction partner. Some evidence suggests that people treated in a less immediate fashion feel uncomfortable, and ultimately appear less competent than people treated in an immediate fashion. These targets may fulfill the negative expectancies that perceivers hold of them. At the extreme, what constitutes immediacy, however, varies across culture. At the very least, the "right" amount of these behaviors—if the behaviors themselves are the same across cultures—may vary. For example, a consistently smiling person with folded arms is more likable to Japanese participants than to American participants, whereas Americans prefer a little less smiling with an open body position (McGinley et al., 1984). What is perceived as immediate may be more important than the behaviors per se. If this is indeed the case, one probably would observe multicultural individuals code switching to the appropriate type of immediacy, just as multidialectal individuals code switch along verbal channels.

Status Behaviors

Immediacy behaviors produce the sense of psychological closeness and liking, but many of these same behaviors can engender a sense of status differences between interacting individuals. According to Henley (1995), absence of mutuality is what differentiates immediacy behaviors from status displays: caressing from pawing, moving closer from invading space, gazing from staring. With status behaviors, one of the parties involved in the interaction does not welcome the behavior. Moreover, the recipient may feel powerless to fend off the behavior (i.e., compensation) or to produce a dominant behavior of his or her own (i.e., reciprocation). Individuals who wish to retain or magnify their status may draw upon a variety of behaviors to display their dominance or status. These behaviors include the use of territory and social touch.

TERRITORY FORMALITY

Individuals who hold either white-collar or clerical positions are often allocated spaces that, for all intents and purposes, are considered their own. The clerk or secretary has a cubicle, the professor has an office, the dean or chief executive officer (CEO) has a suite. Although the organization may transmit explicit or implicit rules about appropriate decor, and the size and shape of the space may constrain variation, individuals still may try to personalize the space. Personalization of these surroundings may include cues to the occupant's preference for hierarchical interactions versus interactions that minimize unequal status, for maintaining a formal relationship with visitors versus for developing friendly rapport, or for highlighting competence and efficiency versus highlighting warmth. On average, higher-status individuals occupy larger spaces, enjoy greater access to potential variation among furnishings, and possess the idiosyncrasy credits to diverge from implicit norms. Thus, conceivably, a larger amount of variation exists for the territories of higher-status individuals than for those of lower-status individuals.

Consider variation between the offices of two hypothetical college professors. One professor places her desk as a barrier between herself and visitors. The soft visitor's chair initially creates the illusion of being inviting, until the visitor sinks just below the professor's eye level once seated. The professional portrait of the professor stiffly posing with her husband and children seems to lend an air of personalization, but it is dwarfed by the imposing diplomas on the otherwise stark eggshell walls. With nary a gesture, the professor apparently communicates how she prefers to be portrayed to the world, who will be in charge of the conversation, and that formal interactions are deemed appropriate. In contrast, another professor arranges his desk so that it faces the entrance and places an inviting chair catty-corner from his own to allow a casual conversation. The colors are soft grays with burgundy accents, a couple of plants grace the filing cabinets, and several candid snapshots are taped haphazardly on the computer monitor. A tranquil framed print completes the arrangement. Visitors are welcome here, and they infer immediately that the occupant is warm and accessible. Thus, the arrangement of the occupant's territory can share or protect his or her power.

These settings probably are not equal in the behavioral flexibility that they provide for the occupant. The formal setting of the first professor can be cast aside by drawing close another chair, by bringing the visitor on her side of the desk (where some more candid photos may reside), or by suggesting a walk to the coffee shop or other neutral ground. She can share management of the conversation or retain the control for herself. She can convey negative feedback, but a warm disclosure would not seem amiss. Someone who possesses the trappings of status can set them aside. In contrast, the second professor might be hard pressed to regain the control already surrendered by the arrangement of his office. Already inferring a warm informal occupant, a visitor might be more presumptuous than the occupant actually desires. Conveying negative feedback in a cozy setting might be more difficult than it otherwise would be, and even be unexpected by the visitor. Once the setting of equality has been created—even if more illusory than real—lower-status others may resent efforts to reestablish asymmetry.

Higher-status individuals also enjoy greater license to invade the territories of lower-status individuals, to restrict access to their territories, and to touch the possessions of lower-status individuals. The supervisor enters the clerk's cubicle and thinks nothing of rifling through the files, the parent enters the child's room, and the instructor "borrows" a pen off a student's desk. Although the clerk, child, and student may be irritated at the invasion, obvious compensation for the gesture may not be worth retaliation at the higher-status person's hand. Moreover, marked asymmetry typically characterizes the perceived liberty to touch possessions or invade territory. Clerks who enter the supervisor's office without permission and who "borrow" office supplies from the desk may be reprimanded by the supervisor or, at the very least, generate surprise from fellow clerks. The student who curiously pulls down a book from the professor's shelf is apt to seem presumptuous; obtaining explicit or implicit permission to touch the professor's possessions is necessary for maintaining a positive impression.

TOUCH

Invading the territory and touching the belongings of lower-status individuals is an aspect of the "touching privileges" of higher-status individuals. Henley (1973) proposed that initiating touch could express status and that higher-status individuals are perceived as possessing a greater right to initiate touch than are lower-status individuals. Consistent with this view, initiators of touch are seen as possessing more power and higher status (for a review see Major, 1981). Henley further indicated that men, by virtue of their implicitly higher status, initiate touch with women more than women initiate touch with men. Empirical evidence supports this pattern, but largely in public nonintimate settings where touch is clearly intentional (Major, Schmidlin, & Williams, 1990). For example, people who intentionally touch in airports or at parties are more likely to be closely affiliated than not, so touch initiation often expresses intimacy rather than dominance. Henley (1995) notes that studies failing to account for whether touch occurs intentionally or in which settings it occurs may fail to detect gender differences or even find reversed patterns (e.g., Stier & Hall, 1984). Certainly, not every touch is intended or interpreted as an assertion of dominance.

In addition to intentionality and setting, the type of touch may be important as to whether it is likely to be seen as dominant. For example, hand-holding is seen as intimate and mutual, and therefore is unlikely to be seen as dominant. Touching the arm or shoulder, in contrast, is more likely to be interpreted as an assertion of dominance (Burgoon, 1991). Consistent with the notion that the type of touch is important, Hall (1996) found no status differences in the sheer amount of touch at professional meetings but did find status differences in the type of touch. Lower-status individuals, as implied by factors such as institutional prestige and membership status, usually initiated formal nondominant touches such as handshakes with higher-status individuals. Higher-status individuals, in contrast, typically touched the arm or shoulder of lower-status individuals. Interestingly, these latter touches were judged to be both presumptuous and more affectionate. This finding perhaps reflects the occasional difficulty of differentiating dominance from immediacy when initiators' intent and recipients' subjective response are unclear.

The apparent status or group membership of the touch initiator also may influence the meaning or evaluation of the touch. For example, compared to touch by men, touch by women may be more likely to be perceived as indicating sexual interest than dominance (Henley & Harmons, 1985). Moreover, women's efforts to assert dominance through touch may backfire in other ways. In an experimental study of gender, status, and touch, Storrs and Kleinke (1990) found that low-status females who initiated touch were evaluated in a negative fashion. In their study, participants interacted with male or female interviewers who were portrayed as low- or high-status interviewers. Low-status interviewers wearing jeans and tennis shoes were introduced as sophomore undergraduates; high-status interviewers wearing suitcoats or dresses with semiformal shoes were introduced as graduate students. Both at the beginning and at the end of the interview, the interviewer either touched the participant on the arm or did not initiate any touch. Low-status female interviewers received a negative evaluation if they initiated touch, compared to those females who did not initiate touch or female interviewers who held high status. For male interviewers, touching did not moderate the effect of status on evaluation.

The implications of this experiment are important for members of other implicitly lower-status outgroups who initiate social touches that are deemed inappropriate for persons of their status. Conceivably, such individuals are viewed as presumptuous or arrogant, as overly familiar, or as interpreting the boundaries between status groups as relatively permeable. If the higher-status individual reasserts dominance, the lower-status person may be embarrassed at the mistake. A display of embarrassment presumably will appease the higher-status individual and reestablish the interaction norm. For instance, the higher-status person might stiffen upon being touched and the lower-status person might smile sheepishly, then shift to a tentative speech style or use the higher-status person's title. In contrast, the failure to display embarrassment could have long-term repercussions, even though failure to display embarrassment could derive from cultural differences rather than from a desire for status or from poor interpersonal skills. Failing to notice the higher-status person's stiffened posture and averted gaze, the lower-status person might continue the conversation without adjustment or, worse, make additional "errors."

SUMMARY

A multitude of nonverbal behaviors can assert or imply status. For example, high-status individuals may display more visual dominance, defined as the ratio of looking-while-speaking to looking-while-listening (e.g., Dovidio, Ellyson, Keating, Heltman, & Brown, 1988). High-status persons apparently have the implicit right to avert their gaze when people are speaking to them. Similarly, high-status individuals may have "touching privileges," experiencing more license to touch lower-status individuals, as well as to touch their belongings and invade their territories. Lack of mutuality can help distinguish immediacy behaviors from status behaviors, but even this factor is not a perfect indicator: Higher status individuals who initiate nonmutual touch may be seen as warm as well as powerful.

Most of the aforementioned studies of touch comprised U.S. samples, in which people who are members of ethnic minorities groups are, arguably, less likely to be represented. How touch is interpreted as reflecting dominance versus immediacy, which particular types of touch are used to express dominance, and similar questions, all may pan out differently among less studied groups. For example, which parts of the body are (and are not) touched varies across nationalities (McDaniel & Andersen, 1998) and, within each nation, which touches are appropriate within even familial situations may well differ across ethnic groups (Harrison-Speake & Willis, 1995). Future research would be well served to extend the study of status behaviors beyond the typically studied white populations.

CHAPTER SUMMARY

Judgments of and feelings about others often are influenced by factors that, theoretically, are independent of those persons' personality characteristics. In the arena of communication, each person's accent, dialect, pattern of eye contact, or patterns of peripheral body movements may be used to infer whether the person is competent, confrontational, lazy, suspicious, or friendly. Members of traditionally higher-status groups use the "standard" versions of the dialect and nonverbal repertoire, and seem to prefer individuals whose patterns are similar to their own. This preference may encourage members of traditionally lower-status groups to adopt these standard interaction patterns, at least in mixed-group interactions.

The judgments of and feelings about others that are produced by factors such as differences in dialect and nonverbal style may be leaked through nonverbal channels. Work on nonverbal immediacy implies that prejudice against others may be betrayed in various ways: gaze is averted, forward lean is absent or unreciprocated, interpersonal distance is maintained, and speech errors abound. These nonverbal signs, at least among whites, seem to reflect discomfort and preoccupation with the specifics of the verbal message. Because nonverbal behaviors vary across cultural groups, only recipients familiar with the meaning of such behaviors may interpret them as implying prejudice or discomfort. Individuals with the opportunity to compare the communicator across time and targets, multicultural individuals, or individuals with access to both verbal and nonverbal channels presumably may infer what the behaviors signify. They may infer that they are judged unlikable, uninteresting, unintelligent, or simply unworthy of warmth and consideration.

Nonverbal channels also can convey beliefs that the other person implicitly or explicitly has lower status than the communicator. Communicators may convey higher status through use of territory and through touch. Communicators also may convey status by not producing obligatory smiles, by averting gaze when the other person is speaking, or by failing to shift to a less formal dialect or communication style. If the recipients of these cues understand them, they presumably infer that they are perceived as nonequals. At least in some settings, this perception may seem appropriate and even be welcomed (not all students *want* a first-name comfy-cozy interaction with their profes-sors!!). But especially where status differences should be minimized, status displays may be offensive and counterproductive. As school and work settings become increasingly diverse, encompassing people of various ethnicities, degrees of physical disability, and representa-tives of each gender, the need to understand how other groups' non-verbal behaviors are interpreted will become critical. To paraphrase the ancient prophecy, we will live in interesting times.

SIX

❧

The News Media

Freedom of the press is guaranteed only to those who own one.
—ARTHUR MILLER

Although some researchers do report contemporary differences in the sheer amount of news allocated to traditionally lower-status groups (e.g., Butler & Paisley, 1978; Kahn & Goldberg, 1991; van Dijk, 1988; but see Wann, Schrader, Allison, & McGeorge, 1998), qualitative differences between portrayals of higher- and lower-status groups appear to be the more common distinguishing characteristic in research findings. Because these portrayals disproportionately are negative, they possess the capacity to perpetuate the negative stereotypes that more powerful groups implicitly hold about less powerful groups. This chapter first presents empirical studies, largely drawn from the communication literature, on these differential portrayals. These differential portrayals include distortions via visual depictions and linguistic devices. With these differential portrayals as a backdrop, the chapter next explores several theories concerning why the media may portray traditionally disadvantaged groups in negative and stereotypic ways, including the media as a cultural mirror and as a vehicle by which the privileged position of dominant social groups is preserved. Finally, the chapter considers whether and through which social cognitive mechanisms news media portrayals might influence the impressions of media consumers.

PORTRAYAL OF OUTGROUPS
BY THE NEWS MEDIA

Before considering why news media portrayals might be biased and what effect those biased portrayals might have, it first should be established that news media portrayals are, in fact, biased. Bias may involve portraying members of the dominant group more favorably than members of another group, when all else appears to be equal. Alternatively, bias may comprise the subtle laying of blame on the nondominant group while exonerating the dominant group. As discussed later, bias need not be consciously intentional at the individual level to exist. Instead, bias may have been built into the system long ago and derive from long-standing patterns of not questioning the potential biases of sources. Moreover, news organization managers may fail to examine the possibility of bias built into established practices, not considering carefully the diversity of the audience (and truly understanding the cultural aspects of diversity), and fail to consider their own biases and those of their subordinates who contribute to the communication.

Visual and Audio Portrayals

Previous chapters dealt primarily with interpersonal communication, in which communicators differentiate among members of different groups along both verbal and nonverbal channels. Mass communication presents additional layers of complexity, including an increased reliance on audiovisual aids for storytelling and disseminating information. Newspapers and news magazines include photographs and charts; broadcast news includes background video, soundbites, and still photographs. These technologies have become an integral part of contemporary communication by the mass media. Images in particular serve the function of economical expression, as they can be presented simultaneously with verbal information. At the same time, they can efficiently evoke the emotions and memories that are intertwined with particular stereotypes. The welfare queen, the baby-kissing politician, and the marijuana-smoking Latino are familiar media images, conveying particular messages to those consumers who subscribe to such stereotypes. The empirical work that addresses use of audiovisual information by the news media suggests that these technologies generally depict traditionally disadvantaged groups in both stereotypic and negative ways.

STILL PHOTOGRAPHS

Open a newspaper or news magazine to a story about the problem of poverty in the United States. Odds are that the accompanying photographs prominently feature African American individuals, or at least nonwhites. According to the 1990 U.S. Census, 29% of individuals at the poverty level in the United States are African American, but that is not the image held by middle-class America. Instead, when asked to hazard a guess, respondents estimate that 50% of the poor are African American. Apparently, our culture views poverty as a "black" problem, and images in the news media corroborate and reflect this cultural belief.

Examining this distorted estimate in the media, Gilens (1996) examined major news magazines (e.g., *Time*), and coded over 600 pictures of the poor in the United States. In these articles, 62% of the depictions portrayed African American individuals, well above the objective statistical estimate. Objective data also estimate that 42% of the African American poor are employed; these news magazines portrayed only about 12% of poor African Americans as working. Such portrayals are entirely consistent with middle-class whites' view of African Americans as poor, as not wanting to work, and as exhausting the social resources provided by the taxes of hardworking whites. These image distortions are especially notable when cast against the lack of distortion along other demographic dimensions. Gilens (1996) found, for example, that news magazines were relatively accurate in the representing the distribution of various age groups among the poor. Thus, distortions are not across the board but only along specific dimensions. Finally, the print media are not unique in their overestimation of the relation between poverty and being of African descent. Gilens also conducted an analysis of major network television news stations during the same period and found that discussions of poverty overwhelmingly (65% of the time) focused upon or presented images of African Americans. Thus, the reality provided by statistics (which few people examine) and the view of reality provided by the news media (which people witness daily) are often at odds. The representation of impoverished Americans as black, then, may well be reinforced by the news media.

Systematic variation in the selection of backdrops or camera angles also may convey different perspectives on the target. K. Ross and Sreberny-Mohammadi (1997) claim, for example, that female members of the British Parliament are photographed in relatively feminine domains (e.g., sipping tea on a comfortable sofa) whereas male members are photographed with backdrops that clearly signify their professional status (e.g., on the street outside the houses of Parliament). Although the authors do not provide statistical analyses to support this claim, bias is not unlikely given that women hold fewer than 10% of the seats in Parliament. When underrepresented in a traditionally masculine profession, women are especially at risk of being stereotyped (e.g., Fiske, Bersoff, Borgida, Deaux, & Heilman, 1991). The interviewed women members of Parliament seemed none too happy about their visual depictions by the media, which suggests that the choice of photograph settings may not have been entirely their own.

Empirical evidence that the media publish different types of photographic "shots" for men versus women derives from work on Goffman's (1976) "face-ism" index. Goffman proposed that the face predominantly is seen as depicting who a man is, whereas the entire body is featured more prominently in defining a woman. Variation in a woman's figure or clothing style, for example, help perceivers subtype what kind of woman she is; as well as conveying these physical attributes, the full-body depiction also conveys emotional qualities. The face, in contrast, conveys competencies associated with the head, such as ambition and intelligence. To quantify this distinction, Goffman proposed the "face-ism index," which is defined as the distance from the top of the head to the lower part of the chin, divided by the top of the head to the lowest visible part of the body.

Using this index, Archer, Iritani, Kimes, and Barrios (1983) showed that photographs of men printed in U.S. periodicals evidenced a higher face-ism index than photographs of women. But the degree of face-ism apparently depends, in part, on who is responsible for creating and publishing it. In a conceptual replication, Zuckerman (1986) distinguished between pictures published in periodicals that identified with women's issues (e.g., *Working Woman*) versus more traditional periodicals (e.g., *Newsweek*). The face-ism index was attenuated in the former type of periodical; a reanalysis of the Archer et al. (1983) data corroborated this pattern. Given that individuals are rated as more intelligent and assertive when their pictures depict a larger proportion of the face (Schwarz & Kurz, 1989), the portrayal of women in more traditional periodicals as less dominant supports gender stereotypes. One wonders whether media that predate photography (e.g., oil painting, sculpture) similarly would show the gender–face-ism relation, and whether that relation varies with the status of women across cultures and across the centuries.

In the dominant U.S. culture, both women and blacks are viewed stereotypically as being more emotional and as possessing less intellectual competence than their white male counterparts. Given this stereotypic low dominance, Zuckerman and Kieffer (1994) reasoned that media depictions of blacks also might evidence a lower face-ism index than that of whites. Drawing upon issues of *Time, Life, U.S. News & World Report*, and *Newsweek*, they matched photographs of blacks and whites for their appearance in advertisements versus articles and indicated in which section (e.g., sports) the photograph appeared. In addition to finding the usual gender difference, Zuckerman and Kieffer detected higher facial dominance for whites than for blacks; the difference between whites and blacks marginally was more pronounced for photographs of men. Finally, to demonstrate the generality of the effect, they replicated the finding of higher facial dominance of whites over blacks when examining European periodicals, and in portraits and postage stamps created by white artists. To the extent that facial dominance conveys greater dominance in reality (Schwarz & Kurz, 1989; Zuckerman & Kieffer, 1994), then, women and blacks are portrayed by the media as less powerful than their male or white counterparts.

VIDEO IMAGES

Visual images also accompany the news reports of broadcast journalists. For many stories, video images are presented during the reporter's voice-over. These background images must correspond roughly to the topic at hand, but they need not have been recorded on the same day or even the same year. Instead, broadcast journalists often rely upon "b-roll," which are libraries of film footage. Faria Chideya, an African American network news correspondent, recently discussed the use and misuse of b-roll by the news media in a talk delivered at Smith College in Northampton, Massachusetts (recorded by C-SPAN in 1998). Chideya pointed out that access to b-roll is a handy technology when broadcast journalists are under time pressure. She then related a personal experience in which she received about 2 hours to pull together a story about shelters for homeless persons. Under time pressure, she and her staff relied upon b-roll that happened to portray African American individuals utilizing the shelters, rather than persons of diverse ethnic and racial backgrounds. In another example, Chideya argued that although drug abuse in American society cuts across ethnic and socioeconomic lines, the news media typically obtain footage that features drug use among nonwhites or persons from lower-status socioeconomic groups. Why? Television news organizations in urban areas, Chideya claimed, are typically near the heart of the city rather than in or near the suburban areas populated by whites. She argued that obtaining footage of whites in suburbia abusing drugs in their private residences simply is more difficult than utilizing existing footage of individuals abusing drugs on inner-city street corners.

Chideya asserted that use of footage that repeatedly pairs stories about negative attributes with nonwhite faces is not responsible journalism, but she also noted that this pattern unfortunately does emerge under time pressure. Interestingly, time pressure and distraction also encourages a reliance upon stereotypes among individual perceivers (Pendry & Macrae, 1994) and interpersonal communicators (Webster et al., 1997). With individuals, stereotypes are applied to the target of perception especially under time pressure or in the absence of special motivation to avoid relying on mere stereotypes (Fiske, 1998). Thus, stereotypes operate as a cognitive default for individuals perceivers. Analogously, on-hand stereotypic images apparently serve as a default for news stories. They provide efficient, accessible, and economical forms of expression . . . and if b-roll is unavailable, the crew relies on the most efficient way to make the deadline. To the extent that the use of on-hand stereotypic images is analogous to using a cognitive default, increasing motivation in response to public pressure to avoid relying on such negative images conceivably might encourage efforts by responsible journalists and editors to avoid their use.

It bears mentioning, though, that motivations to be accurate might not always produce accuracy per se. With individual perceivers, for example, efforts to be accurate may encourage greater complexity and reduced stereotypicness, but these outcomes need not be *objectively* accurate. For example, an interpersonal communicator who feels accountable to her audience may interject some counterstereotypic information into her description of an outgroup target, but the overall message may remain stereotypic. Analogously, a journalist or broadcasting network publicly criticized for presenting too few positive images of minorities may sprinkle stories with the trappings of diversity. Doing so does not mean that the proportion is accurate or that these positive portrayals represent qualities valued by the targeted minority community. At least, however, these images reflect efforts to dilute the usual stereotypic depictions. The point is that, without an internal or external motivation to be accurate, dilution of stereotypic images is unlikely to occur.

In addition to relying upon existing video footage or photographs to accompany general stories, journalists also obtain new video footage that corresponds to stories concerning particular individuals. In such cases, the visual depictions that actually appear on television could reflect subtle bias in selecting images. Alternatively, they could be relatively accurate representations of existing reality. For example, Entman (1992) examined the video footage of specific white versus black individuals being arrested for crimes in the Chicago area. Before analysis, he equated the crimes according to whether they were violent (e.g., rape) or nonviolent (e.g., fraud). Regardless of crime type, in the visual depictions, white persons accused of a crime were generally better dressed than black persons accused of a crime, and arresting officers were more likely to be shown physically restraining accused blacks than accused whites. Conceivably, the police indeed may use more physical restraint when arresting black individuals than when arresting whites. The question is, in the minds of the audience, whether these images convey the possibility of police brutality against blacks or do these images reinforce stereotypic images of blacks as violent and as "needing to be managed." Conceivably, the existing prejudices of the audience influence how the images are interpreted, with prejudiced individuals obtaining validation of the stereotype and less prejudiced individuals (and members of the targeted group) experiencing anger at the portrayals. Entman (1994) argues that the cumulative effect of these repeated images eventually may work to distort social reality, a point considered later in this chapter.

More interesting perhaps than the visual images of the arrests, Entman (1992) also examined the soundbites that accompanied these news stories. Soundbites are accompanying audio sequences which, in the case of Entman's study, were quotes provided in the arrested individuals' own words. Entman found that whites accused of a crime typically were heard to utter one or two statements in their own defense, whereas accused blacks typically were heard to utter no such statements. As with the video footage, one cannot be certain whether the Chicago news media elected not to provide soundbites when blacks were arrested or whether arrested blacks generally do not offer statements in their own defense. The net effect on receivers, of course, may be the same. The audience is exposed to the possibility that accused whites are not guilty of their alleged crime or is provided with mitigating circumstances that potentially could reduce the apparent severity of the crime. The soundbites also may help portray the arrested person as an individual, rather than as a member of a particular ethnic group. When a black individual commits (or merely is alleged to commit) a negative behavior, many whites interpret this behavior as reflecting the behavioral tendencies of the entire group (Henderson-King & Nisbett, 1996). The long-term effect of exposure to such images, as a function of the audience's own biases and group membership, warrants careful investigation.

SUMMARY

The news media's video and audio depictions of less powerful groups, namely, women and minorities, seem largely consistent with cultural stereotypes. Women subtly are portrayed as weak objects compared to their male counterparts; blacks are often portrayed as criminals or as draining the resources of social services. Which visual depictions are recorded or published may reflect a subtle but insidious form of bias. Media consumers who strive to avoid a prejudiced self-image may quickly take umbrage at explicit verbal expressions of prejudice and try mentally to counteract the affects of such messages. They may not, however, recognize subtle but consistent differences in visual images or audio selections. Without realizing it, even the most well-intentioned media consumer may be processing prejudiced messages.

Skewed Coverage

In the contemporary politically correct climate of the United States, the use of blatantly prejudiced language in major periodicals, major newspapers, and network television news arguably is becoming less common than in previous decades. As evident with materials accompanying the story, prejudice or bias in the stories themselves instead can be subtle. Certainly, some portion of the news contains factual information, but that information may be framed in ways that are more or less beneficial to dominant versus nondominant groups. The decision regarding which sources to consult also can put a particular spin on a story. Indeed, decisions as to whether an issue receives media attention at all or is ignored may derive from bias and help perpetuate certain skewed viewpoints.

WHAT IS NEWSWORTHY?

Although responsible members of the news media strive to communicate the facts, they also are part of a business. To sell newspapers or obtain good TV ratings, news personnel need to cover issues that they believe are of interest to news consumers. Some issues or stories, consequently, will receive little coverage. For example, mainstream U.S. newspapers may elect not to publish announcements or stories of same-sex weddings or life commitments (Jensen, 1996), presumably because many individuals—both members of the news media and media consumers—object to homosexual relationships. The failure to print such announcements maintains the notion that stable homosexual relationships are both rare and deviant. Indeed, some researchers suggest that, when homosexuality receives news coverage, it often is linked to AIDS rather than gay sexual identity or romantic desires (Alali, 1991; Myrick, 1998). The repeated pairing of homosexuality with a serious health threat such as AIDS may perpetuate the marginalization of the gay community (Myrick, 1998). In contrast, stories that potentially dispel myths or fears concerning the gay community, such as the markedly similar outcomes among children of homosexual versus heterosexual parents (e.g., Bailey, Bobrow, Wolfe, & Mikach, 1995; Patterson, 1992) receive little attention.

Thus, mainstream news media may be at odds with minority groups in their determination of what is newsworthy or centrally important to communicate to the general public. For example, an analysis by Daniel and Allen (1988) examined the disparity between the published agenda of the National Urban League versus the actual coverage of issues relevant to race relations during the 1980s. At that time, the National Urban League's agenda concerned civil rights, the relief of poverty, and the promotion of economic policies that would not penalize (and ideally would help) the poor. Publications of the National Urban League clearly reflected this agenda, and the agenda clearly required consciousness of race and ethnicity (e.g., civil rights issues). Not only did major news magazines fail to report on the priorities of black leaders, they focused instead on the elimination of affirmative action and the desire for a color-blind society (rather than consciousness of race and diversity). True, the news media were devoting attention to race relations and to issues theoretically interesting to some African Americans. On the other hand, what many black leaders deemed most important failed to obtain mainstream attention.

In another interesting example of the selection of "newsworthy" issues, Kahn and Goldberg (1991) examined 26 U.S. senatorial races that included women candidates during 1984 and 1986. These researchers distinguished among competitive, somewhat competitive, and noncompetitive senatorial races, then examined the type and amount of coverage allocated to female versus male candidates in their local newspapers. Women candidates received marginally less media coverage, but—more important—the type of coverage differed. Specifically, media coverage devoted most of its focus on women's chances of winning, irrespective of the competitiveness of the race. In addition, women generally earned less favorable assessments regarding their viability. When the media *did* consider the stance of female candidates on issues, they tended to focus on stereotypic "women's issues." These candidates therefore were portrayed more as candidates for other women than as candidates for the general population, and they were also portrayed as candidates whose chances of winning must be questioned.

As with visual information, however, in many cases one must bear in mind the question of whether the reported story mirrors reality or actually reflects some implicit choice on the part of the editors, producers, or journalists. For example, Entman (1994) examined news portrayals of African American leaders which, after stories about blacks alleged to have committed crimes, was the second most common reported topic during 1990 and 1991 on network news programs. He found that approximately 30% of the stories concerned the black leader being accused of a crime, about 10% concerned the leader alleging racial discrimination, and about 14% concerned the leader criticizing government policy. Black leaders never were portrayed as praising or supporting government. On the one hand, this portrayal is consistent with the tenets of modern racism, which alleges that blacks are pushing too hard for change when discrimination is no longer a problem. On the other hand, black leaders indeed may at times tend to be more critical of government than leaders from other groups, in which case some portion of the portrayal could be accurate. Because the study failed to report an explicit comparison with white leaders (e.g., if white leaders are accused in the media of crimes at a similar rate; if white leaders rarely are portrayed as supporting government policy), whether the finding reflects partial reality, clear media bias, or some combination thereof is thus inconclusive.

SOURCES

The sources to which the news media turn for a story also may be selective and provide a particular slant on an issue. For example, in her analysis of *The New York Times*'s coverage of the breast implant controversy, Darling-Wolf (1997) argues that the *Times*'s preference for official sources lead to a male-oriented perspective. She reports that one journalist relied on 83 sources to write his 21 articles on the breast implant debate. Only two of these sources were women, both of whom previously had undergone mastectomies. In contrast, the male sources included 18 plastic surgeons, 15 other medical doctors, 20 officials from the implant manufacturing companies, and 17 Food and Drug Administration (FDA) officials. Darling-Wolf further argues that the quotes provided by the male officials implied that women cannot bear the thought of life without a breast and that the availability of silicone implants would increase the likelihood that women will take pains to detect breast cancer early. She further remarks that no data were presented, however, to support these stereotypic claims. The claims indeed may not be well founded. Primary factors that influence early detection measures such as mammography include family history and worry about developing breast cancer (McCaul, Branstetter, Schroeder, & Glasgow, 1996), doctor recommendations (Caplan, Wells, & Haynes, 1992), and not needing to be concerned about financial cost (Fajardo, Saint-Germain, Meakem, Rose, & Hillman, 1992). More telling, many women prefer mastectomy to less radical procedures because they fear cancer reoccurrence (Wilson, Hart, & Dawes, 1988), which calls into question whether women value their breasts more than their lives. Darling-Wolf (1997) further argues that the reliance upon official sources largely represented the position of the breast implant industry and therefore provided more thorough coverage of one side of the issue than the other. Although not a quantitative analysis, this paper raises the issue that the media's selection of particular sources may place a unique spin on a story.

In many cases, reliance upon official and expert sources strikes one as a reasonable approach to telling a story. The official source often represents a group of individuals who presumably have access to factual, statistical, and historical information. In contrast, the person-on-the-street appears to represent her or his opinion alone. In addition, official and expert sources are easily identifiable as such, so they may be easier to contact than less official sources (e.g., ad hoc groups of concerned or directly affected citizens). On the other hand, not all expert sources necessarily represent the same side of an issue. With respect to the breast implant issue, for instance, social scientists who study women's recovery from breast cancer or leaders of survival groups presumably could better represent the issue than a handful of people on the street. Nearly a half century of research attests that credible sources typically are more persuasive than less credible sources (for a review see Petty & Wegener, 1998), so relying upon experts and official sources is an obvious choice. The risk of bias arises when too few experts or official sources represent the side of the story reflecting the position of traditionally disadvantaged individuals. The extent to which the average consumer is able to weigh the validity of a source of information for a news story remains an open question for empirical investigation.

FRAMING OF RISK

Another way of putting a particular spin on a story involves how the information is framed. For example, news stories commonly report various social and health risks to which people are exposed. The risk can be presented in terms of loss or gains, but—even if everything else holds constant—slight variations in the presentation can influence decisions (Tversky & Kahneman, 1981). Imagine, for example, a nation's decision to adopt one of two programs to combat an impending disease outbreak. Consider these two different frames:

> If the nation does nothing, 600 people are projected to die. With the first program, 200 people can be saved. With the second program, there is a one-third probability that all 600 people will be saved but a two-thirds probability that no one will be saved.

> If the nation does nothing, 600 people are projected to die. With the first program, 400 people will die. With the second program, there is a one-third probability that no one will die but a two-third probability that all 600 people will die.

When the issue is framed in terms of lives saved, nearly three-fourths of the participants favor the first program. Framed in terms of lives lost, in the latter way, over three-fourths of the participants favor the second program. The information is identical, but the frame changes the ways people think about the risk.

In their stories about risk, the news media often compare the risks of ethnic minorities or women compared to majority groups or men. Women, for example, are more likely to suffer from depression than are men (note that this statistic rarely is expressed as "Men are less likely to suffer from depression than are women"). As another example, during 1993, African Americans were more likely to be laid off than their white counterparts. The latter example could be framed as (1) African Americans are more likely to be laid off, (2) African Americans are less likely to keep their jobs, (3) European Americans are less likely to be laid off, or (4) European American are more likely to keep their jobs. The first two frames focus upon the risk of black losses, whereas the second two frames focus on potential gains for whites. Under what conditions do the media frame messages in terms of black loss rather than white gain, and vice versa?

Gandy (1996) showed that preferred framing can depend, at least in part, on the anticipated target audience. He first identified four major stories concerning black–white comparative risk that were reported nationwide in 54 newspapers. These stories included a report that whites were more likely to receive aggressive cardiac care (e.g., bypass surgery) than their black counterparts and a report that blacks were less likely than their white counterparts to receive disability benefits. Overwhelmingly, news articles framed these reports in terms of black loss (about 75% of the 411 phrases examined). More interesting, however, was the moderation of this pattern by the estimated proportion of blacks in each paper's metropolitan area. With two of the stories (and marginally with a third), a greater proportion of blacks living in the particular metropolitan area predicted framing in terms of black loss. The greater proportion of blacks also modestly predicted the story's mention of discrimination or bias.

The increased use of the black loss frame in cities with a larger black population suggest an implicit recognition of the difference among these possible frames. According to work on decision frames, losses loom larger than gains and usually encourage people to adopt a course of action that will minimize the loss. Presumably, cities with a higher proportion of blacks would be sympathetic to actions that would minimize the loss; these frames therefore may reflect an effort to match the perceived audience attitude (Higgins & Rholes, 1978), or they may reflect the possibility that members of the media in more ethnically diverse cities may be sympathetic to policies that equalize the playing field. As with a large proportion of work on the news media, the actual impact of the frames on audiences currently is unknown. On the one hand, framing in terms of black loss could encourage support for corrective legislation and government policy from media consumers (Gandy, Kopp, Hands, Frazer, & Phillips, 1997). On the other hand, such framing could be viewed by prejudiced whites through the lens of modern racism, as an example of blacks allegedly demanding too much too fast. Indeed, biased readers easily could scrutinize news articles for weaknesses or generate reasons why the risk factor somehow is the fault of blacks. For example, to counter the allegation of bias in the medical system, a white reader could point to a specific black acquaintance who suffered a heart attack but who smoked like a fiend and who refused to have routine medical checkups. In general, people ignore or counterargue the messages that contradict their preferred beliefs (e.g., Liberman & Chaiken, 1992), so potentially beneficial messages ultimately may fail to have impact on all members of the audience.

ALLEGED RESPONSIBILITY

Another common type of news story describes civil disputes or criminal charges in which attributions regarding responsibility can be drawn. As discussed in Chapter 2, the selection of particular words or a specific sentence structure can convey subtly different slants on the same basic event. Use of the passive voice, for example, can attenuate attributions of responsibility by implying the role of larger unspecified forces. With the passive voice, the object of the sentence is implicated as playing a causal role. For example, in the sentence, "Bill was hit by Jane," Bill seems to get in the way of Jane, and Jane's responsibility for the event is somewhat mitigated. In contrast, the active voice clearly implicates the subject of the sentence as the primary perpetrator. "Jane hit Bill," for example, vividly conveys Jane's agency, and her behavior strikes the reader as much more intentional.

In many—but not all—cases involving interpersonal actions, causal agency is assigned to the grammatical subject of the sentence (R. Brown & Fish, 1983; Rudolph, 1997). Being ascribed agency obviously is a good thing if the action is positive, such as volunteering at a homeless shelter or winning a 5K race. Agency even for more neutral actions conveys the image of a viable group or individual. Being ascribed agency for negative actions, in contrast, conveys a negative impression. Work by van Dijk (1988) suggests that outgroups may be accorded agency primarily when they are associated with negative outcomes and actions. In an analysis of Dutch news headlines, he found that non-Dutch residents were the grammatical subject only about 8% of the time. The implication, then, is that non-Dutch minorities depend upon the agency of others rather than acting as agents themselves. When non-Dutch individuals were the grammatical subject of the headline, the actions typically were undesirable (e.g., "Surinamese Criticize Arrest" or "Turks Battle for Seat"; van Dijk, 1988, p. 253).

A number of studies demonstrate that the passive voice directs the reader's attention to the object of the sentence (see Henley, Miller, & Beazley, 1995). Consistent with that notion, people who read a sentence in the passive voice more easily act out the role of the object, and also evidence better recall if the object is used as the recall cue. A statement such as "the woman was raped by her assailant," for example, reduces the perceived responsibility of the rapist and encourages the reader instead to focus on the woman's role in the event. The phrasing prompts questions such as "What did the woman do to fend off her attacker?" or, worse, "Did her manner of dress or risk-taking behavior elicit the attack?" Henley et al. found that U.S. newspapers overwhelmingly used the passive voice to describe both sexual and nonsexual violence. Suffering of victims essentially is delegitimized and allows communicators to cordon victims off into a group that somehow "deserves" to suffer. Doing so serves a social function by prescribing a way to deal with victims, but it also may serve an ego-defensive function. If victims appear to deserve their fate but belong to a group of people separate from one's own group, one's personal safety seems assured.

What possible effect might such usage have on media consumers? Henley et al. (1995) also created news reports of sexual and nonsexual violence, and varied the use of the passive versus the active voice in the reports. College-aged participants then read the reports and indicated their perceptions of harm to the victim, perceptions of perpetrator responsibility, and their overall acceptance of sexual violence. Among male participants, perceptions of harm to the victim of sexual violence attenuated with the use of the passive voice; however, voice exerted little effect on perceptions of other victims or on female participants' ratings. Attributions of responsibility to the perpetrator mimicked this pattern, again tending to exonerate the perpetrator. Finally, both male and female participants reported greater acceptance of sexual violence following exposure to the passive voice. The news media's use of the passive voice in describing sexual violence therefore may do little to combat myths regarding sexual violence or to increase sympathy for victims of sexual violence. Instead, the passive voice may decrease sympathy, at least among individuals unlikely to directly experience that type of violence.

In contrast to Henley and colleagues' (1995) findings, Lamb and Keon (1995) detected no difference in the effects of the passive voice versus the active voice on attributions of responsibility for wife battering (e.g., "Mr. Jones beat his wife" vs. "Mrs. Jones was subjected to beatings"), but—as the authors note—perceivers might have construed their created articles in significantly different ways. For example, the use of evaluative and abstract terms like "subjected" implicitly might have attributed more responsibility to the husband, even though the sentence was written in the passive voice. Lamb and Keon did find that articles which alleged shared responsibility (e.g., referring to "the abusive relationship") encouraged greater leniency toward the male batterer. Interestingly, expressions such as "the abusive relationship" involves the transformation of a verb (i.e., "to beat") into a noun ("the abusive relationship"). This nominalization masks who is doing what to whom, which also can affect attributions of responsibility (see the subsequent section on *linguistic masking*). Both Henley and colleagues' (1995) study and Lamb and Keon's (1995) study are important in that they provide experimental evidence that readers can be affected by how newspapers subtly convey responsibility, whether in terms of the passive voice, nominalization, or other subtle differences in wording. Conceivably, these disparate interpretations of events could encourage discrimination against victims of sexual violence.

USE OF SPECIFIC EXEMPLARS

Even when statistics and official sources are available and used by the news media, the presentation of specific exemplars seems to be a common device. A New Orleans newspaper article on welfare reform (*Times-Picayune*, January 10, 1998), for example, allocated 25% of its lines to a specific individual. This single mother of three, formerly on the welfare roll, now held a job that earned about twice what she received on welfare. Another 25% of the lines were allocated to another single mother who was somewhat worse off financially for taking a job but who was seeking a better job in order to avoid returning to welfare. The photograph of the latter individual clearly portrayed an African American woman. These particular exemplars are at once a double-edged sword. On the one hand, the exemplars counterstereotypically insist that welfare recipients do want to work and do not want to rely on welfare. (Such a counterstereotypic portrayal, especially of an African American woman, may be more common in cities like New Orleans whose racial composition includes many black citizens.) On the other hand, these portraits also uphold the Protestant work ethic of mainstream American culture, implying that people who are willing to work hard can escape poverty. Sometimes, the very same example easily can be interpreted in different ways, depending on the lens through which the audience views it.

The news media also may present their audience with exemplars who unambiguously violate the prevailing stereotype for the group. The existence of female or black leaders (e.g., Lady Margaret Thatcher, Gen. Colin Powell) is proof that women or blacks can possess leadership ability. Ironically, however, these extreme exemplars may bolster the very stereotype that they personally appear to defy, because they are not seen as representative members of the group. Work by Kunda and Oleson (1995, 1997) indicates that perceivers cordon off these extreme exemplars into subtypes; once subtyped as atypical of the overall group, the perception of variability within the larger group need not change and the overall view of the group remains intact. An exemplar whose violation of the stereotype is somewhat more modest, however, can influence the overall perception of the group. Women or black individuals who run small companies, graduate law school, or teach math certainly are more common and representative of their groups (albeit less dramatic!) than individuals who run countries or major divisions of the government.

To demonstrate the differential effect of extreme versus moderate exemplars, Kunda and Oleson's participants read about a moderately unassertive or extremely unassertive feminist, or a feminist whose assertiveness was not explicitly described. Assertiveness stereotypically is associated with feminism, so an unassertive feminist violates the stereotype. Participants who read about the moderately unassertive feminist later judged feminists as a group as less assertive than did controls or participants who read about an extremely unassertive feminist. Thus, when the news media, in good faith, present counterstereotypic exemplars in efforts to increase perceptions of diversity, they sometimes may be shooting themselves in the foot if the exemplars too extremely violate the stereotype.

SUMMARY

Differential portrayals of women and minorities by the news media begin, first and foremost, with what aspects of these groups receive media attention. Homosexual individuals may receive media attention with respect to AIDS, as may women political candidates with respect to their viability or stance on feminine issues; what black leaders define as important may not be represented adequately in the mainstream news media. What does receive media attention may be subject to a particular slant, depending on the sources consulted, examples used, audience targeted, or particular frame and wording. Empirical research into these methods of bias, with appropriate control conditions, are necessary to help tease apart further when these potential mechanisms for slant reflect true bias or underlying social reality.

Headlines

In the print media, one of the first things to grab a reader's attention is the headline; in the arena of broadcast journalism, the opening statement made by the reporter or the "teaser" provided just before the commercial break often is the initial bit of information about the story. From a social cognitive standpoint, the earliness of the headline renders it extremely important. The headline can provide a schema or frame through which the remainder of the story is interpreted. That is, whether the subsequent information receives attention at all and how that information is encoded into memory should depend considerably on a perceiver's use of initial information (Fiske & Neuberg, 1990)—in this case, the headline. Take, for example, the headline "Teens See Less Racism," from a CBS news poll reported on the CBS website on January 19, 1999. The story itself presents some information that is consistent with the headline's claim, such as teens viewing race relations "as better than do adults." At closer inspection, however, some information is inconsistent with the claim. For instance, over half of teens and adults expect prejudice to remain a problem in America (i.e., teens see as much racism as adults, and see quite a bit). Finally, some information is ambiguous with respect to the claim. For example, most teens think affirmative action programs are necessary; support of such programs typically is associated with less prejudice, but also implies that the programs are needed because prejudice is a problem. Applying schema theory, the lens of the headline "Teens See Less Racism" may make readers generally less attentive to the inconsistent information. Moreover, ambiguous information like supporting affirmative action should be interpreted as meaning that teens are less prejudiced than adults, rather than as meaning teens recognize that prejudice and discrimination continue to exist and require external constraints to hold them in check. A headline, then, presumably influences how readers interpret subsequently encountered information.

Headlines also are important because they contain a brief but highly abstract representation of the article. In this regard, headlines are for mass communication what group epithets are for interpersonal communication: an economical portrait. But in the case of headlines they provide a schema of an event or situation rather than a schema of a group. This abstract representation conceivably is the best-recalled information from the story, long after the details fade from memory (van Dijk, 1988). As noted earlier, van Dijk's (1988) analysis of Dutch headlines showed that they portray non-Dutch individuals as initiating little agency, and primarily as perpetrators of negative actions when they are portrayed as agents. In his sample, more than 50% of the headlines dealt with an "ethnic" topic of some variety. Typically, the topics were those in which ethnic minorities are a source of some problem, such as immigration issues or accusations of criminal activity and deviance. van Dijk argues that most majority members' everyday discourse about ethnic minorities derives from the mass media. To the extent that this is the case, this discourse may be based primarily on the highly abstract summary judgments provided by the headlines, rather than on specific details.

LINGUISTIC MASKING

In a more recent examination of headlines, T. Cole and Leets (1998) examined the differential use of linguistic masking devices as a function of the ethnicity of the readers and of the subject of the story. Linguistic masking devices are used by powerful individuals in order to de-emphasize or accentuate particular aspects of their subject matter. These devices help camouflage the control that powerful individuals wield over others. According to Ng and Bradac (1993), these devices are truncation, generalization, permutation, and nominalization. Truncation deletes the agent. This device obfuscates who is doing what to whom, rendering the exercise of power ambiguous. For example, "Bill criticized Jim" fingers Bill as the critic, whereas "Jim was criticized" points to no clear critic; the reader is left wondering what Jim did to deserve the criticism. Henley et al. (1995), for example, found that newspapers truncated sentences describing sexual violence (e.g., "The woman was raped"), drawing attention to the woman and not to her assailant. Also masking the use of power, nominalization involves the transformation of verbs into nouns. For example, "The teaching assistant will appraise performance on the laboratory exercises using a 10-point grading system" clearly points to the teaching assistant's power to reward or punish. "Laboratory exercises will be assessed with a 10-point grading system" fails to name the particular person who holds power. In a sense, the latter type of sentence implies that larger or distal forces are at work and that those unnamed distal forces will stand behind decisions made by a proximal force like the teaching assistant. Power—in this case, evaluation—is institutionalized.

In the Ng and Bradac (1993) scheme, generalization uses an abstract rather than concrete style to refer to people and their behavior. An example of a generalization would be "People dislike Mary," rather than "José and Jim dislike Mary." Verb transformations also can create generalizations, such as "Mary is unkind," rather than "Mary spoke harshly to an employee yesterday." Although this last example is reminiscent of the linguistic category model (Semin & Fiedler, 1988) described in Chapter 2, Ng and Bradac's (1993) classification scheme allows abstraction with both verbs and nouns, whereas the linguistic category model only examines abstraction in verbs. Finally, permutation involves the assignment of responsibility for the action or outcome. As previously discussed, responsibility ordinarily is assigned to the individual named earliest in the utterance. For example, "Bill visited Jim" suggests that Bill is responsible for the visit, whereas "Jim was visited by Bill" implies that something about Jim elicited the visit from Bill.

Applying this classification scheme to headlines, T. Cole and Leets (1998) required participants to generate a headline for a news story as an overall interpretation of an event. They reasoned that these generated headlines therefore might reflect intergroup biases in preferences to mask certain aspects of the news story. The news story that they selected as a stimulus described, in relatively concrete language, an impending trial of a white police officer. This officer was accused of beating a black man while fellow officers restrained the black man's companions at gunpoint. In one study, European American police officers and African American college students served as research participants. On the whole, the black students were more likely to use abstract language in creating their headlines for the story. Moreover, the black students were more likely to nominalize the event (e.g., "Injustice to Black Citizen"), whereas the white police officers typically retained the verb phrases that portrayed the event as a isolated incident (e.g., "Officer Claims Innocence"). Put another way, the black students seemed to see the incident as indicative of problems with white police officers and the larger system, whereas white officers seemed to focus on the situation as an exception to the rule.

The confounding of ethnicity and status in this study (i.e., white officer versus black private citizen) leaves ambiguous which intergroup membership primarily influenced respondents' perspectives. Partially addressing this problem in a subsequent study in their article, T. Cole and Leets (1998) retained the interracial aspect of the incident, but varied the ethnicity of the officer and citizen (i.e., white officer–black victim; black officer–white victim). Only African American students participated. On the whole, black students used more specific language when the police officer was black but used more abstract language to describe the behavior of the white police officer. That is, the African American students characterized the behavior of the black officer as reflecting an isolated incident, whereas the behavior of the white officer seemed more stable. This finding suggests that intergroup biases can affect the headlines created in the media; presumably, those biases also slant the story details as well.

INNUENDO

Although not examined explicitly with respect to intergroup differences, work on innuendo effects is relevant to understanding the importance of headlines. An innuendo comprises both a *direct statement* that associates the attribute with the particular individual, as well as a *qualifier* that seemingly reduces the probability of that statement (R. J. Harris & Monaco, 1978; Wegner, Wenzlaff, Kerker, & Beattie, 1981). For example, headline-like statements such as "Jamal Jackson may have murdered his girlfriend," "Do women have poor spatial skills?," or "Can Sarah Thompson win the Senate race?" (see Kahn & Goldberg, 1991) all are innuendos. Such innuendos may do more harm than if the issue simply was ignored.

Wegner and his colleagues (1981) argue that the direct statement typically carries more weight than the qualifier, for two reasons. First, direct statements should be more salient than the qualifiers because they are more imageable, concrete, and encourage confirmatory hypothesis testing. For example, the headline "Do women have poor spatial skills? "should encourage media consumers to imagine or recall instances in which particular women have evidenced poor spatial skills, but it is less likely to encourage thoughts about men with poor spatial skills or women with good spatial skills. Later work by D. T. Gilbert (1991) also points to increased weight to the direct statement. Gilbert argues that the mind essentially requires two steps in understanding statements in which the direct statement is negated or whose truth is questioned. Simply to comprehend the sentence "Do women have poor spatial skills?," the reader first thinks "Women have poor spatial skills" and then as a second step thinks "This may or may not be true." Anything intervening between these two steps, such as a distraction or lack of motivation, can reduce the probability that the reader can correct the initial thought. How often are individuals distracted when reading the newspaper or web-reported news or when watching the television news? Second, innuendo effects depend on listeners' expectations that speakers adhere to implicit communication rules; these expectations are called pragmatics. Following these implicit communication rules, listeners expect, among other things, that communication sources be truthful and relevant. They recognize, of course, variation in the credibility and underlying motivations of certain sources. For example, headlines appearing in a tabloid may be enjoyed with a grain of salt, with inferences that the editor and writers are sensationalizing the topic in order to sell papers. In contrast, headlines appearing in an internationally renowned daily newspaper more likely engender inferences that the paper seeks to ferret out the truth or to provide thoughtful commentary on an issue. With pragmatics in mind, Wegner et al. (1981) exposed undergraduates to headlines about political candidates that were attributed to a highly credible paper (e.g., *The New York Times*) or a rather less credible paper (e.g., the *National Enquirer*). Compared to control headlines, headlines that directly asserted, questioned, or denied nefarious activity significantly marred impressions, reflecting the power of innuendo. However, the credibility of the news source moderated the relation between type of headline and impression judgment. Direct assertion damaged impressions of the candidates much more when the source was credible, indicating that readers did question the truthfulness of the lower-credibility source. However, source credibility did not influence the effect of innuendo. Questioning or denying the negative behavior damaged impressions regardless of the paper's credibility. Insinuating the incompetence, moral depravity, or insufferable rudeness of an outgroup member therefore may be an effective way to transmit the intended message, regardless of source credibility.

Summary

As a whole, two things may be said about the work on differential portrayals in the media. First and foremost, additional empirical work with proper control groups and comparisons to objective reality is needed. Second, the empirical work that is published does provide some evidence of differential portrayals. African Americans are often portrayed as poor or as criminals, and demanding of additional rights and social resources. Homosexual individuals seem to receive little attention, except in connection to AIDS (and perhaps in insisting for gay rights). Visual depictions of women are stereotypic (indeed, most pictures of women in newspapers are brides!), and their competence for traditionally male jobs is questioned. Although women are not blamed directly for being victims of sexual assault, neither are their assailants.

Overall, there is evidence to suggest that the news media do little to undercut stereotypes and prejudice, and subtly may support those stereotypes and prejudices. Why this may be the case is the topic of the next section.

WHENCE THE DIFFERENTIAL PORTRAYALS?

Although more empirical research clearly is required, the existing literature points to the possibility that portrayals of traditionally disadvantaged groups are negative, stereotypic, or at least nonrepresentative. To the extent that differential portrayals do exist, they exist for underlying reasons. The literature that addresses reasons for differential portrayals is largely theoretical, and direct empirical investigations to test the underlying reasons are rare. Several explanations for differential portrayals are discussed next, with the caution that the explanations are neither exhaustive nor mutually exclusive. These explanations are (1) the historically limited access of traditionally advantaged groups to the news media, (2) the group dominance perspective, (3) adherence to communication rules, and (4) the notion that the media mirror existing objective reality versus mirror implicit cultural beliefs.

History of Limited Access

Who controls the news? Although this question carries the ominous connotations of a society envisioned by George Orwell or Margaret Atwood, some groups and individuals arguably do wield more influence over what appears in the news than do other groups and individuals. For example, an examination of 1986 data from the Associated Press Managing Editors showed that African American print journalists comprised only 1% of journalists in the United States; blacks comprised about 4% of the professionals in broadcast journalism (Mazingo, 1988). A more recent report by the American Society of Newspaper Editors indicates that members of minorities also are unlikely to hold high-level positions in the news industry. For example, only 9% of supervisors and 10% of copy and layout editors belong to minorities, which seriously curtails the influence that minorities can exert on the news (St. John, 1998). Whites, in contrast, predominate as both owners of newspapers and as the journalists who report the news.

To the extent that it exists, minority access to the mainstream news media grew, in part, out of the Kerner Commission Report in 1968 (Mazingo, 1988). During the 1960s, civil unrest, especially in the arena of race relations, was at a peak. Dr. Martin Luther King, Jr., was assassinated, the riots in Watts and other areas of the country burned out of control, and government authorities used physical aggression to counter nonviolent protests by black citizens working toward civil rights. The Kerner Commission Report criticized the media for its role in perpetuating the "black–white schism." The report suggested that the media failed to educate the white audience regarding the frustrations that blacks experienced in the United States. To whit, the Kerner Commission called for increased numbers of blacks to be recruited into the media. Presumably as an immediate consequence, minority representation in the media reached a height between 1972 and 1978, although minority representation later failed to keep pace with the industry growth (Mazingo, 1988).

What might increased access of women and minorities to the news media accomplish? First, diversity within the workforce should increase the likelihood of diverse coverage of issues. Social scientists, for example, strive toward the use of unbiased methods for conducting research but generally recognize that values influence the topics that they pursue and what topics of research currently merit publication. Concurrent to the influx of women and minorities into the field of social psychology, for example, was an increase in the empirical investigation of topics of interest to these groups, including increased study of sexual violence and of ethnic identity. With respect to the news, Mazingo (1988) argues that reporters implicitly learn the unwritten policies of news organizations regarding acceptable publication topics. In her survey, black reporters and editors recognized unwritten policies for covering black issues, particularly implicit pressures to downplay those issues. The black news personnel also felt that violating policy carried repercussions such as reduced story length or unfavorable positioning of their stories. However, black news personnel also indicated that their presence in the organization coincided with increased sensitivity toward publishing stories of concern to blacks and that they occasionally lobbied for or directly initiated such stories. Thus, the presence of women and minorities in the newsroom conceivably increases coverage of issues important to those groups.

In addition to influence *what* is reported in the news, the presence of women and minorities also could influence how information is reported. For example, Gandy's (1996) study showed that the presence of minorities on the news staff correlated with a more race-sensitive framing of risk. Similarly, T. Cole and Leets's (1998) experiment showed that participants generated qualitatively different headlines for stories concerning an interracial incident, depending on the ingroup versus outgroup membership of the apparent perpetrator of the violence. As a final example, Zuckerman and Kieffer (1994) found no difference in black versus white facial prominence when artists were black, similar to Zuckerman's (1986) finding that differences in female versus male facial prominence were smaller in magazines devoted to women's issues than in traditional news magazines. Thus, an increased presence of members of traditionally disadvantaged groups may increase the diversity in the perspectives reported. Conceivably, their presence also increases the sense of accountability among news personnel who belong to groups that traditionally have enjoyed media access. That is, the presence of women and minorities whose opinions matter—star reporters, news anchors, producers, editors—may engender efforts among men and whites to appear less biased. When people believe that their communicated judgments or impressions will be scrutinized by important others, they are more careful and try to think about the issues in a less biased fashion (e.g., Tetlock & Kim, 1987). Admittedly, accountability does not always result in more accuracy (e.g., Tetlock & Boettger, 1989), but its encouragement of more careful processes may be a step in a less biased direction. People may not be consciously aware of their initial slants on a story, biases, or linguistic patterns, but a sense of accountability can increase attention to previously unconsidered sides of the issue and consequently may attenuate bias (see Ruscher & Duval, 1998).

The General Group Dominance Perspective

Historically, both money and power have dwelt with dominant groups, which has allowed them privileged access to the media. The absolute gap perhaps may narrow over time, but some social scientists are not sanguine about an elimination of the gap altogether. Proponents of the general group dominance approach likely would argue that, even if the gap narrows, inequity will remain. An essential assumption of the general group dominance approach is that most societies are hierarchical. In these hierarchically arranged societies, positively valued outcomes (e.g., wealth, education) are possessed disproportionately by at least one dominant group. Conversely, negatively valued outcomes (e.g., low-status occupations) are possessed disproportionately by at least one nondominant group (Sidanius, Pratto, & Bobo, 1996). Moreover, dominant groups use available means to maintain inequity among groups and to preserve the lion's share for their ingroup. Thus, by this logic, dominant groups who possess privileged media access should try, at least implicitly, to protect media access for their ingroup (see van Dijk, 1988).

Much of the recent empirical research on the general group dominance approach specifically has examined social dominance orientation (e.g., Sidanius et al., 1996). Social dominance orientation is an individual difference that reflects the drive toward maintaining group-based inequalities. Individuals high in social dominance believe, for example, that it sometimes is necessary to use force against other groups, that problems are caused by certain groups not staying in their place, and that efforts to equalize income and living conditions are inappropriate. Given these beliefs, people high in social dominance orientation endorse legitimizing myths that perpetuate hierarchies or inequalities, such as opposing gay and lesbian rights and affirmative action (Pratto, Sidanius, Stallworth, & Malle, 1994) or opposing interracial marriage (Fang, Sidanius, & Pratto, 1998).

Researchers interested in social dominance orientation argue that, on average, men should have a higher social dominance orientation than should women (Sidanius, Pratto, & Bobo, 1994). They argue that men are more likely to hold positions that facilitate the acquisition or maintenance of power than are women. Moreover, they argue that aggression is more likely to be taught and modeled to men, and men form coalitions in order to perpetrate violence against other groups in order to acquire outgroup possessions, territory, and labor. Both by holding positions of power and using aggression, men presumably protect and acquire valued resources. These researchers also contend that gender differences in social dominance orientation holds across ethnic groups. A survey of nearly 2,000 individuals in the greater Los Angeles area found consistent gender differences in social dominance irrespective of age, political party, income, religion, ethnicity, and education (Sidanius, Pratto, & Bobo, 1994). Approximately 33% of the respondents in this sample were white–non-hispanic, 25% were Hispanic, 25% were black, and 15% were of Asian descent. Note that the consistent detection of gender differences does not preclude average differences when comparing among people of different ages, religions, and so forth. Jewish individuals, for example, evidenced relatively low social dominance orientation whereas Catholic individuals evidenced relatively high social dominance orientation. But social dominance in both groups was higher for men. Note also that the magnitude of the gender difference across ethnic groups and cultures may not be invariant. For example, in Australia and the United States, the gender difference is less pronounced than in Russia and Sweden (Sidanius, Pratto, & Brief, 1995).

But given that men appear to be higher in social dominance orientation, on average, they also should prefer occupations that perpetuate the hierarchy. And, indeed, people who are high in social dominance orientation do prefer jobs that enhance rather than attenuate the hierarchy (Pratto, Stallworth, Sidanius, & Siers, 1997). In their study, Pratto et al. created hierarchy-enhancing and hierarchy-attenuating versions of 10 different jobs. For instance, the hierarchy-enhancing version of a paralegal position involved assisting corporations in combating suits filed by injured laborers; in the hierarchy-attenuating version, the paralegal assisted the poor, immigrants, and children. Although none of the jobs included news personnel per se, several positions did involve mass communication. For example, one job involved being an advertising agent for an elite corporation versus a national charity; another job involved a public relations position with a company then known to supply goods to the (formerly) apartheid military in South Africa versus supplying goods to the United Way. As expected, men preferred the hierarchy-enhancing type of position, although controlling for social dominance orientation attenuated the relation between gender and preference for certain types of jobs. Similarly working in the news industry presumably includes variation in the types of jobs available: the news media can work for or against change in existing hierarchies, and people may gravitate toward broadcast and cable networks, newspapers, and news magazines that match their own social dominance orientation.

Theorists (e.g., van Dijk, 1988) have argued that privileged access to the mainstream media perpetuates hegemony, and that males and whites are most likely to "control" the mainstream media. Indeed, van Dijk reports that in the Netherlands, non-Dutch minorities—even those with Dutch citizenship—do not own periodicals and news journals. In the United States, in contrast, several cable television stations are devoted to programming for women or minorities, and a number of magazines are published primarily for and by members of those groups. Whether these venues present mainstream news or are consumed regularly by outgroup members is unknown. The general group dominance perspective would predict that men, especially those high in social dominance orientation, would select the types of news media jobs that would perpetuate inequality among demographic groups. Analogously, to the extent that European Americans have higher social dominance orientation than African Americans or Latinos (Sidanius, Liu, Shaw, & Pratto, 1994), European Americans also may gravitate toward such media positions. Thus, the positions of such individuals in the mainstream news industry may in part underlie differential and nonrepresentative portrayals of women, minorities, and perhaps homosexual individuals in the media.

Communication Goals

Implicit communication rules enjoin communicators to take into account the characteristics of their audience (Higgins, 1981). Communicators who believe that their audience has a particular viewpoint, for example, tailor their messages to be more acceptable to that audience (Higgins & Rholes, 1978). With the mass media, the communicator is faced with a multiple-audience problem, that is, one in which the communicator may wish to convey different impressions or information to different subsets of the audience; in this case, the communicator may rely upon "hidden" messages to various groups (Fleming, 1994). That requires, of course, that the communicator be cognizant of diversity among the audience and cares about addressing that diversity. Without evidence to the contrary, people typically assume that other people share their own viewpoints (i.e., the false consensus effect; Marks & Miller, 1987). The male or white individuals who have greater access to the media may not, as a rule, think about targeting the female or minority members of their audience (unless the topic deals with classic female or minority issues). When potentially faced with a multiple audience, falling back on one's own perspective or catering to the salient subgroup of the audience may be default options, adopted without much thought. If these defaults exist in multiple-audience situations, the news media certainly would not be alone in relying upon them. For example, college-level introductory psychology textbooks written by women cover diversity issues to a greater extent than do textbooks by mixed-gender coauthors or male authors (Hogben & Waterman, 1997). Perhaps the female authors examined by Hogben and Waterman more deeply considered audience composition—or their editors did! In a similar fashion, it is possible that differential portrayals of women and minorities in the media could derive, in part, from an insensitivity to audience diversity.

When communicators feel accountable to their audience, they try to be more evenhanded with their messages (e.g., Tetlock, 1983). With the mass media, the sense of accountability might be heightened by the anticipation of negative letters to the editor, public criticism, or reduced sales if the interests of various groups are not represented. Gandy's (1996) finding concerning the relation between framing of risks to blacks and the proportion of blacks in the metropolitan areas is consistent with this notion. Also addressing this issue, Henley, Miller, Beazley, Nguyen, and Kaminsky (1997) examined the differences in reporting of crimes against gay victims versus victims of unspecified sexual orientation, as a function of newspaper. The researchers collected reports of both murders and nonlethal violent crimes, and examined the extent to which the crimes were nominalized (e.g., using neutral nouns such as "the incident" rather than verbs such as "was stabbed"). They found that a newspaper that traditionally was sensitive to the rights of gay individuals (*San Francisco Chronicle*) did not differentially nominalize crimes against gay victims versus victims of unspecified sexual orientation. The other mainstream newspaper examined (*The Washington Post*) used more nominalization in stories concerning gay victims, rendering the stories less violent. Although only two newspapers were examined in this study, these findings support the notion that news personnel can and do take audience characteristics into account, and that efforts to adhere to this implicit communication rule may play a role in the news media's depictions of various groups.

Cultural Mirror versus Objective Reality

The stereotypic and negative portrayals evidenced in the mainstream news media may be a reflection of the dominant social culture. That is, like their audiences, news personnel are members of their culture and therefore may possess the same stereotypes that exist in the general culture. For instance, if U.S. culture believes, on average, that poverty is a "black problem," then the media's overrepresentation of blacks in photographs of impoverished citizens (Gilens, 1996) could result from shared cultural beliefs. Americans also might believe, on average, that women have little chance of winning in political races; they also might believe that most women are not as capable leaders as are men. If the overall culture holds such beliefs, news media representations that question the viability of women candidates (Kahn & Goldberg, 1991) simply may be tangible reflections of those beliefs.

Another alternative is that the news media may be providing a relatively accurate reflection of reality. Perhaps police officers do use more force when arresting African American suspects (see Entman, 1992), and news media are simply capturing this pattern. Perhaps the only issues of interest to women candidates are stereotypically feminine issues, and perhaps women encourage full-body photographs of themselves in lieu of portraits. Perhaps. The differential linguistic representations (e.g., Gandy, 1996; Henley et al., 1997) suggests that, in some cases at least, interpretation of reality rather than reality per se is communicated. But even if the news sometimes accurately reflects reality, it highlights certain aspects and omits other aspects. The portrait over time, then, may be quite skewed (Entman, 1994).

Summary

As noted earlier, these explanations—a history of limited access, general group dominance, implicit communication goals, and mirroring culture or reality—are not mutually exclusive. The history of limited access, for example, helps perpetuate general group dominance and feeds perceptions of who comprise the most important subgroups of the audience. Similarly, individuals who are high in general group dominance may influence which slices of reality are presented and subtly may discourage other news personnel from thinking about how they cast various stories.

    None of these explanations explicitly requires that differential portrayals of nondominant groups stem from a devious sort of scheming, conscious intent. Instead, the failure to portray nondominant groups in a unfavorable light may operate as a sort of default option, executed without really thinking much about it. Note that this interpretation does not absolve the news media—or any communicator—from taking the more effortful route and trying to be more accurate. If communicators possess the flexibility to portray targets in more or less biased ways, they may be held responsible if they consistently are biased against a particular group (see Fiske, 1989). Thus, at a minimum, biased portrayals could derive from an unwillingness to think about diversity of the audience, the biases of one's sources, or how one's own biases can affect subtle wording or framing. At the extreme, biased portrayals could derive from the influence exerted by powerful individuals, individuals who decide which stories receive airtime or premium print locations, who receives an entry-level job in the newsroom or is promoted into editorial positions, and which photographs or headlines "best" represent the gist of a story. How these cognitive versus motivational factors influence news reporting and, in turn, influence audiences remains an interesting empirical question.

POTENTIAL IMPACT OF THE NEWS MEDIA

Few empirical studies directly address how differential portrayals of nondominant groups by the news media affect media consumers (e.g., Henley et al., 1995, 1997). This paucity of studies does not necessarily reflect a failure to find such influence, but instead may reflect researchers' recognition of the difficulty in finding a balance between internal and external validity (i.e., wanting control over the factors studied without sacrificing realism), their placing top priority on establishing differential portrayals, or any number of other reasons. This final section of the chapter considers the social psychological mechanisms by which the news media conceivably could influence the audience and illustrates with several empirical studies.

The Power of Negative Information

Evaluatively negative information grabs attention. The disclosure of a public figure's indiscretions, a hurricane's devastation, the rumor of a coworker's impending termination, or the gory details of a murder-suicide capture attention. Bad news is news. Admittedly, people sometimes allocate attention to positive information, but they typically do so only when that positive information is extreme (e.g., neighbor rescues elderly person from a burning building; couple wins $7 million in state lottery). Because extreme or negative information receives more attention, such information also receives more weight in the judgments that people make (Fiske, 1980). Thus, to the extent that media portrayals of nondominant groups tend to be negative, impression judgments concerning those groups by and large will become (or remain) negative.

DIAGNOSITICITY

When the negative information is in the form of behavior (i.e., as opposed to an event such as a natural disaster), perceivers in Western cultures tend to infer that the behavior corresponds to an underlying dispositional quality of the actor (E. E. Jones & Davis, 1965). This tendency variously has been termed the correspondence bias, the over-attribution bias, and the fundamental attribution error. Negative behaviors vary in their ability to evoke the correspondence bias. Some traits almost exclusively are presumed to produce directly corresponding behaviors, whereas other traits can produce both the directly corresponding behavior and its opposite (Rothbart & Park, 1986). For example, an honest person should exhibit primarily honest behaviors, whereas a dishonest person can exhibit both honest and dishonest behaviors. Thus, a few honest behaviors do not necessarily lead to the inference that the actor is honest, whereas a few dishonest behaviors quickly imply a dishonest person. According to Rothbart and Park's analysis of 150 traits, traits that are difficult to disconfirm but easy to confirm (e.g., dishonesty) overwhelmingly are negative traits. Consequently, once an audience believes that people from a particular group are dishonest or lazy, a few examples of honest or hardworking behavior hardly can override that belief about the group as a whole. That apparently honest or hardworking individual could, in fact, be "proved" dishonest or lazy later. And even if perceivers were to conclude that a specific individual in a group probably was honest or hardworking, people generally accept variability among group members. Thus, overall negative perceptions of the group would be unlikely to change. Conversely, a few negative behaviors by members of a cohesive group remain diagnostic of an overall negative group impression (Coovert & Reeder, 1990; cf. Henderson-King & Nisbett, 1996).

Visual allegations in background video or photographs that blacks or Latinos are violent, lazily reliant upon social services, or hopeless drug abusers essentially convey just this sort of information. Such traits are difficult to disconfirm at both the individual and group level. Just because a person currently is not using drugs, for example, does not convince others that the person will remain drug-free. Similarly, one or two individuals who no longer are dependent on the welfare system does not negate the perception that the group as a whole is poor and unwilling to work. When this person belongs to a disliked outgroup, the generalization is easy. For example, Dutch residents who read a news article in which a Turk raped a woman would tend to presume that another Turk might well do likewise, but would not make such a generalizing inference were the perpetrator Dutch (Winkel, 1990). Innuendos also may raise the question of whether a person or group possesses a negative disconfirmable trait and lead audiences to find negative confirming information. Thus, although not explicitly examined in news settings, these underlying features of the information could help perpetuate or create negative beliefs.

Both Fiske's (1980) and Rothbart and Park's (1986) research primarily considered negative traits that correspond to what Skowronski and Carlston (1987) term *morality* dimensions. Morality traits imply that the person theoretically could choose to exhibit either end of the dimension, that is, to be honest rather than dishonest, hardworking rather than lazy, or polite rather than rude. Because they implicate free will, negative morality behaviors clearly imply that the actor possesses the underlying trait. Positive behaviors, however, do not disconfirm the negative morality trait. As a contrast, Skowronski and Carlston denote another class of traits as reflecting *ability* dimensions. Negative behavior along ability dimensions essentially corresponds to failure, which can be caused by fatigue, reduced motivation, or any number of other factors. Here, a negative behavior does not necessarily imply the apparent corresponding trait. The fact that an honor student has received a D on an exam need not lead to the conclusion that she is stupid, nor does the fact that an 11–5 professional football team has lost a playoff game necessarily lead to the conclusion that the team lacks athletic prowess or good coaching. Positive behavior, in contrast, is much more diagnostic. Acceptance at a selective doctoral program implies intelligence, just as winning the playoff game implies athletic ability and good strategy. Of course, where outgroup members are concerned, perceivers often search for causes of success in lieu of or at least in addition to ability (Hewstone et al., 1990; Jackson et al., 1993), attributionally robbing outgroup members of their achievements. The outgroup member's successful admission to a selective institution or organization may be attributed to an aggressive or quota-based affirmative action program (see Heilman et al., 1990). Similarly, the outgroup team's success can be attributed to biased or inept officiating, or to underhanded tactics (Hastorf & Cantril, 1954/1990). The electoral viability of a female senatorial candidate (Kahn & Goldberg, 1991) therefore may be played down in the media without even considering her capability to fulfill the role (i.e., an ability dimension). Male candidates generally are presumed to possess leadership and "vote-getting" qualities, but female candidates' abilities often stereotypically are deemed questionable.

APPARENT COVARIATION

Media perpetuation of stereotypic (and generally negative) impressions of nondominant groups also may be compounded by repeatedly covarying certain qualities with certain groups. For example, some evidence suggests that increased exposure to news about race relations may exaggerate perceptions of black poverty (Armstrong, Neuendorg, & Brentar, 1992; Gandy & Baron, 1998), perhaps because these stories keep the image of poor blacks salient and accessible (as opposed to blacks in other situations or roles). Once such an association is created, research suggests that it may generalize to related targets (see Henderson-King & Nisbett, 1996). One study on this topic (M. C. Hamilton, 1988) found that major news magazines (e.g., *Time*) and newspapers (e.g., *The New York Times*) typically used the generic term "homosexual" rather than gay men and lesbian women. The study also showed that the use of the generic rather than gender-specific terms exaggerated perception of lesbians being at risk for AIDS, although lesbians historically have remained a very-low-risk group. Repeated media exposure presumably perpetuates perception of AIDS as a homosexual disease, of blacks as poor, of women's primary role as romantic partners or mothers.

Repeated covarying of a group with a given quality could, over time, produce an illusory correlation. An illusory correlation is a tendency to overestimate the covariation of events that are meaningfully associated or share a unique feature, such as being statistically rare.

This latter account, paired distinctiveness, partly may underlie negative stereotypes about certain outgroups (E. L. Hamilton & Gifford, 1976). Hamilton and Gifford argue that, on the average, people know more about and interact more often with members of their ingroup than with outgroup members. In addition, negative behaviors are encountered with less frequency than positive or neutral behaviors. Outgroup members and negative behaviors thus share the distinct quality of being rare. This combination therefore may engender the erroneous conclusion that outgroups exhibit negative behaviors.

To demonstrate that illusory correlation may underlie stereotype formation per se, rather than simply reflecting existing stereotypic beliefs, experimental studies of illusory correlation typically pair positive or negative attributes with members of neutrally labeled groups. For example, 16 positive and 8 negative behaviors are attributed to members of group A and 8 positive and 4 negative behaviors are attributed to members of group B. Despite the equivalent proportions, people tend to overestimate the covariance of negative behaviors with group B. A meta-analytic review of studies on the paired distinctiveness account for illusory correlations shows that the affect is quite robust (Mullen & Johnson, 1990).

The news media's continual pairing of negative attributes with minorities or traditionally low-status groups may reflect a real-world instance of the illusory correlation. Winkel (1990), for instance, presented Dutch individuals with headlines concerning various crimes. Half of the time, the perpetrator was Dutch, and half of the time the perpetrator was Surinamese. Whereas 38% of the Dutch participants overestimated the number of Surinamese criminals, only 9% overestimated the number of Dutch criminals. These overestimates may stem, in part, from the Dutch media's frequent attention to the criminal activity of foreigners (van Dijk, 1990). Similarly, but using a different methodology, Galliker (1996) provided evidence congruent with the notion that illusory correlations can be created in the media. Galliker examined all issues of the major daily newspaper in Germany, published over a 3-year period, looking for instances in which ingroup words (e.g., "German," "resident") versus outgroup words (e.g., "immigrant," "refugee") co-occurred together with words reporting allegations of criminal behavior (e.g., "was arrested"). His data showed a more frequent co-occurrence of outgroup words and allegations of criminal behavior than other possible pairings; this increased frequency exceeded actual crime statistics. The reported covariation of negative behaviors with nondominant groups, then, may help maintain the association in the minds of media consumers.

Biased Information Sampling

Perhaps one of the most significant ways that the news media can influence perceptions is by conveying only a select subset of the available information. Consumers of the news do not and cannot be exposed to all sources, opinions, camera angles, or slants on a particular story. To the extent that these form a pattern over time, the information stored in the minds of the audience is not representative of underlying social reality. Instead, people store heuristics or summary representations through which they think about outgroups, based in part on media exposure.

CONSENSUAL REALITY

Exposure to the news also may provide consumers with a biased sample of public opinion. Although people infer public opinion from their own interpretation of the media (i.e., the false consensus effect), they also infer public opinion from the particular slant placed on the news (Gunther, 1998). The role of perceived consensus on attitudes is far from trivial. When individuals are not deeply involved with the issue at hand, consensus information drives their opinions (Darke et al., 1998). In a word, what "everybody believes" may come in part from news exposure. Admittedly, the news media are not the only sources of consensual information upon which perceivers rely. Conversations with peers, overheard conversations, or the stance transmitted during an organized religious service or social meeting, for instance, also can provide consensual information. Moreover, individuals may gravitate toward magazines or newspapers that are generally sympathetic to their own preexisting views. Just how much relative impact the news media have on impressions remains unclear, but one mechanism by which they conceivably could influence individuals is by helping create and maintain consensual reality.

DIRECT EXPERIENCE

Reading or hearing about something is quite different from actually experiencing it oneself. On average, direct experience with an attitude object, such as a member of an ethnic outgroup, creates an attitude that is more accessible than an attitude formed through indirect means (e.g., reading about it; Fazio, 1986). Attitudes and beliefs that are accessible are more likely to be used in making judgments—and used with greater speed and efficiency—compared to less accessible attitudes. At first blush, then, news media effects really should be quite trivial. After all, people only are reading about or viewing stories about outgroups, not actually interacting with them.

True, an extreme or negative encounter with an outgroup member probably does have more impact than reading about such an encounter in the news. But many people do not have direct negative or extreme experiences with outgroups. For them, the news may be the primary source of information about certain outgroups. In certain parts of the United States, for instance, European Americans may have few or no opportunities to interact with ethnic minorities. Even in less homogeneous settings, the kind of stereotypic information provided in the news may outweigh the information obtained through personal experience. In one day, news about ethnic minorities could comprise a report of an upcoming trial, an award received, an arrest, and a poster depicting a wanted suspect. In that same day, an average white person might encounter the same number of minorities or even more; odds are that these encounters are relatively nonextreme—say, a bank teller, a person sitting on the bus, or a speaker at a conference. Extreme information weights more heavily in judgments, and news is more likely to be extreme than mundane.

Accessibility also is not created by direct experience alone. An attitude (e.g., toward a group) may be accessible because it is expressed often or because it has a strong evaluative connotation (for a discussion see Fazio, 1990). Ethnic outgroups may be associated with clearly negative affects such as fear, hatred, or anger (Dijker, 1987). Similarly, some heterosexual individuals regard homosexual or bisexual individuals with disgust or fear. To the extent that the media help create these associations between group membership and certain feelings, or at least fail to contradict existing affective associations, the news may help prejudiced attitudes remain accessible.

Summary

To the extent that the news media influence the stereotypes and prejudices of media consumers, well-known psychological factors should underlie these effects. Information that is negative, extreme, or diagnostic typically exerts considerable influence on impressions; this sort of information may be the typical ways that outgroups are portrayed in the news. Although unlikely to be as powerful as direct experience with outgroup targets, the mass media may be the primary source of information about them for many perceivers. The extent to which these effects are cumulative and nontrivial requires further investigation.

CHAPTER SUMMARY

Members of the news media are themselves members of the culture that they portray, and differential portrayals need not reflect intentional conscious bias. Instead, like many communicators, news personnel may fall back upon their cognitive defaults: stereotypes, heuristics, and false consensus about audience beliefs. Although few studies have examined the actual impact of the news media on creating and perpetuating stereotypes, the ingredients for impact certainly seem to be present. Headlines, story frames, and linguistic devices provide differential slants on ingroup versus outgroup members. Visual information, integral to contemporary mass communication, also may create stereotypic portrayals. Perhaps most important, the inclusion versus exclusion of particular issues potentially influences news consumers. The repeated exposure to some issues and images potentially keeps them accessible and alive in the culture.

SEVEN

The Culture of Prejudice

... that personal disrespect and mockery,
the ridicule and systematic humiliation,
the distortion of fact and wanton license of fancy. . . .
        —W. E. B. DuBois (1897/1970, p. 24)

In his essay, "Strivings of the Negro People," W. E. B. DuBois indicates that prejudice involves such indignities as "mockery," "systematic humiliation," and the "wanton license of fancy." He hits upon several aspects of the culture of prejudice that constitute the topics for this penultimate chapter. Images in advertising, for example, have become less blatantly prejudiced than in earlier decades. However, they still distort rather than accurately reflect social reality. African American models, especially women, typically are light-skinned with "Caucasian" features. Women are svelte, men have well-toned physiques and full heads of hair. Elderly individuals and certain ethnic minorities (e.g., Latinas) appear on relatively rare occasions, certainly not in proportion to their actual numbers in society. Similarly, fictional portrayals in television and film include mockery and wanton license of fancy, varying considerably in their subtlety. Although the frequency and extremity of blatant stereotypic portrayals perhaps have declined in recent years, the popularity of cable reruns and video rentals keep many such images cognitively accessible.

More blatant than contemporary advertising and fictional video, group-targeted humor helps keeps prejudice alive and kicking. Jokes told among the ingroup or transmitted along the Internet target the foibles of outgroup members. Stand-up comics poke fun at ingroup and

ily as doctors and business personnel, now do laundry and other domestic tasks. The stereotypic gender roles have not changed entirely, however. Still, compared to men, women are seen shopping and cooking, whereas men purchase computers and other electronics. Women appearing with children typically are inside the house, whereas men are outside the house playing or reading with (usually male) children (Kaufmann, 1999). An examination of commercials sorted according to their time of appearance also seems to suggest prescriptive cultural support for traditional gender roles. For example, prime-time commercials are more likely than weekend and daytime commercials to show women working outside the home and in positions of authority. Advertisements during daytime television, whose audience is primarily female, typically show stereotypic domestic images. Overall, male characters are seen as more dominant than female characters (Craig, 1992). The conception of males as important and dominant even extends to commercials with animated spokes-characters: most animated characters are male in gender, and indeed are better remembered if they are male (Peirce & McBride, 1999).

Other Systematic Variations

Like the evolution of Aunt Jemima, images of blacks used in advertising also have evolved. Several interest groups (e.g., the National Black Media Coalition) monitor how ethnic minorities are represented in advertisements. And certainly representation, in terms of sheer numbers, appears to have increased in recent decades. Whether that representation adequately reflects the population, especially of television viewers, remains to be questioned. For example, a study conducted during the autumn of 1984 (Wilkes & Valencia, 1989) examined television commercials that appeared on the three major networks during prime time (i.e., 7:00–10:00 P.M., Central Time). In commercials that included minority individuals, these individuals typically were part of the background. The study distinguished among three types of roles in a televised ad. A "major role" was defined as talking about or touching the product, a "minor role" was defined as a role that was central to the theme but did not included talking about or touching the product, and a "background role" was a role not central to the theme. In ads that included minority characters, African Americans played background roles 47% of the time but major roles 31% of the time and minor roles 22% of the time. The rates were slightly more unbalanced for Hispanic individuals: 59%, 25%, and 17%, respectively, but again show a preponderance of background roles. A more recent analysis showed that Asian Americans also typically play background roles, almost exclusively roles that place them in business rather than social settings (emphasizing perhaps their stereotypic work ethic; C. R. Taylor & Stern, 1997). (Note: These are only ads that include minority characters. These data do not speak to which percentage of all ads contain minority characters.)

The different rates in role type raise an interesting point that merits further investigation: Although organizations and industries clearly are responding to pressures toward diversity in general, they may not be increasing diversity equally across levels. Having a few nonwhite members in the background of a commercial, as minor characters in a television program, or as the token newscaster of color on the weekend still relegates little prominence to nonwhite individuals. One interesting trend toward equalizing the apparent importance of the advertising characters is to use a serial montage or choral approach. In such televised ads, a series of diverse speakers or characters provide thoughts about the product or service. An ad for the employment finder monster.com, for example, features a somewhat lost young woman in a large city. Ethnically diverse individuals pass by her, each speaking a snippet of Robert Frost's poem "The Road Less Traveled." Similarly, a serial montage approach by Cox Cable features people of various ages and ethnic backgrounds who all benefit from cable television and WebTV. By portraying an apparent awareness of a diverse clientele, a favorable, nonprejudiced impression presumably is conveyed. It would be interesting to see whether ads such as these are more or less successful marketing strategies than more traditional ads, at least with members of historically underrepresented groups.

In its creation of not-quite-real worlds, the advertising industry also takes advantage of what seem to be cultural ideals or prescriptions. As discussed further below, for example, advertised women are typically attractive and thin, which may cause viewers to feel inadequate by comparison. With African American advertising characters, the industry may help perpetuate a long-standing bias with respect to skin complexion. In earlier decades, membership in churches and admission to certain social gatherings for blacks could depend upon meeting criteria such as the "paper bag" test, which required skin tone no darker than a standard brown paper bag. Alternatively, the "ceiling fan" or "comb" test, required hair that was sufficiently straight to move under the fan and that would respond easily to a fine-toothed comb. The bias for lighter complexion, both from inside and outside African American communities, has had clear outcome implications. For instance, lighter complexioned African Americans tend to enjoy higher incomes, higher-status occupations, and greater educational attainment (Keith & Herring, 1991).

Black models—especially female models—who appear in print advertisements have distinct characteristics, namely, they have lighter complexions than blacks who appear in other print sources. During the years 1989–1994, Keenan (1997) compared editorial photographs from the business magazines *Fortune* and *Black Enterprise* (whose primary readerships are white and black, respectively) to print advertisements from the fashion magazines *Glamour* and *Essence* (whose primary readerships are white and black, respectively). Keenan reasoned that editorial photographs would be more likely to reflect a fuller range of complexions and facial characteristics. As expected, compared to black individuals in editorial photographs, blacks in ads had lighter skin and lighter eyes (blue, green, or hazel as opposed to black or brown). Gender comparisons within the ads alone showed that black female models had lighter skin, lighter eyes, and more narrow noses than did black men in ads. The only discernible difference between ads from *Glamour* versus those from *Essence* was that black models in the latter magazine were more likely to have dark eyes. As with speech and nonverbal patterns, the prescription is for adopting the qualities of the higher-status cultural group. Not only should women be beautiful, but beauty is defined largely by possession of fair skin and other "Caucasian" features.

Effects of Character Group Membership in Advertising

At least to some consumers, attributes of the characters in print and video ads do matter. Manring (1998) reports that economist Paul Edwards surveyed blacks in 1932 concerning their feelings about an Aunt Jemima ad. Blacks objected to the notion of a magical black mammy who spoke exaggeratedly poor English, and especially took issue with her wearing a bandanna, a sign of ignorance and servitude. But he also surveyed their opinions about an ad in which a black laundress was speaking to a higher-status white woman about a laundry detergent. Despite the status difference, the surveyed blacks liked the ad, because the laundress was neatly attired, did not have stereotypically exaggerated physical features, and spoke well (P. Edwards, 1932, reported in Manring, 1998). More contemporarily (e.g., Qualls & Moore, 1990), other researchers report that people evaluate same-race characters in advertisements more favorably than other-race characters. This effect of perceived similarity is sufficiently well known in advertising, so much so that magazines that cater primarily to readerships of a particular ethnic or racial group create parallel print ads that differ only with respect to model race.

Character race also may affect memory for attributes of the product or service, as well as interest in obtaining more information about it. Remembering the name of a product in particular is important if sales, the ultimate bottom line, are to be affected by advertising. In one investigation of this possibility, Whittler (1991) created print ads for a word processor and for a laundry detergent; parallel forms of each ad were created with a black and a white actor. White college student raters perceived the white actor as more similar to themselves, and highly prejudiced whites were uninterested in receiving additional information about the product if the actor was black. In a follow-up study using a noncollege sample of adults from the southeastern United States, highly prejudiced whites differentiated between the ads with black versus white actors. With a white actor, they were better able to recall the brand name of the product, showed more interest in obtaining additional information, and expressed more willingness to purchase the product. The black college students from the initial sample, in contrast, saw the black actor as more similar only if they also reported a strong ethnic identification. They did, however, claim that they would be more likely to purchase the product when the actor was black (see also Whittler & Dimes, 1991).

Targeting an ad for a certain audience therefore seems to make sense if one has an accurate representation of the audience. Advertisements also may have unintended effects, however. Images of women that perpetuate sex-role stereotypes, for example, may undermine women's self-confidence (Jennings-Walstedt, Geis, & Brown, 1980), which presumably is not the primary intent of such ads. Advertisements vary in their stereotypicness, of course. For example, from more to less sexist, women may be portrayed as mere decorations, in traditionally female occupations, or as professionals whose primary place is the home; they also may be portrayed in a nonsexist fashion, as equals to men or in way that transcends sex role stereotypes (Pingree, Hawkins, Butler, & Paisley, 1976). Lafky et al. (1996) demonstrated that exposure to the more sexist types of advertisements affected subsequent perceptions of a woman in a neutral setting. Participants viewed print advertisements that were either sex role stereotypic (e.g., women using cleaning products; engaged in child care; pouring coffee at a party) or nonstereotypic (e.g., women as doctors or wearing business suits). Participants who had viewed stereotypic ads rated the woman in the neutral setting as more likely to solicit permission from her husband before taking on volunteer work, as doing most of the household chores, and as preferring someone other than herself to chair committees. Thus, it appears that ads can elicit stereotypes and encourage their use.

The prescriptive aspects of ads—that women should be beautiful, young, and svelte—also affect consumers, both male and female. Most individuals arguably cannot live up to the standard of beauty from the ideal world of advertising. Lavine, Sweeney, and Wagner (1999) argue that images of beautiful, sexy young women activate a discrepancy between an actual and an ideal body image. For female viewers, such ads tend to make them feel fat and cause them to judge their own bodies to be larger than they otherwise would. Interestingly, Lavine et al. argued that these images would affect male viewers as well. For men, they argue that the cultural ideal is to possess a larger muscular build so images of beautiful, desirable women should cause men to feel smaller (i.e., less muscular) than they otherwise would; put another way, beautiful, svelte women may make them feel wimpy or scrawny, when they would prefer to feel powerful and muscular. The authors tested this hypothesis by exposing participants to women in either sexy or nonsexy ads, then asking participants to circle which of nine sketches best depicted them. (Obviously, a different set of pictures were presented to participants of different genders.) The primary hypotheses, that exposure to ads with sexy female models would encourage self-image discrepancies, was supported: men selected less muscular sketches of men as self-descriptive whereas women selected less lean sketches of women as self-descriptive. Perhaps more interesting, although participants who were sensitive to feminist perspectives consciously rejected the ads, their self-perceptions nonetheless were affected by those same ads. Awareness of and rejection of stereotypes therefore may be insufficient protection against the effects of stereotypic images in the media.

Summary

The goal of an advertisement is to encourage consumers to purchase products and services, to vote for specific people, or to contribute to initiatives. To do so, ads highlight the discrepancies between who people are and who they wish to be, between the existing world and a more ideal one. Images related to prescriptive gender roles in particular seem to highlight discrepancies, hinting at a way to reduce the discrepancies through the advertised product or service. As suggested by the above Lavine et al. (1999) study, simply being on guard against stereotypes or impossible standards may not be an adequate defense against adverse effects. Further research should examine the cumulative effects of descriptive and prescriptive stereotypic images on self-perceptions, self-definition, and group identification.

In the interest of brevity, advertisements may rely upon stereotypes as a communication shorthand. Fashion magazines, for example, often portray white women in submissive poses, highlighting a prescriptive stereotype that femininity should involve submissive seduc-

tion (McLaughlin & Goulet, 1999). The recent paucity of empirical research into advertising stereotypes does not necessarily mean those
stereotypes are gone. A cursory look at ads during prime-time television hours suggests that stereotypes of older adults, for example, continue to be perpetuated. Older adults in the world of advertising primarily seem interested in buying insurance and medications; they
apparently travel only to casinos and places in Florida; they buy products for dentures and bladder control, but do not seem to use deodor-
ants, shaving razors, and microwave dinners. Admittedly, these images may not be as blatantly stereotypic as the black mammy Aunt
Jemima, the Chinese laundryman in the Calgon ad, and the devilishly
thieving Frito Bandito. Still, the continual pairing of older adults primarily with products that link declining health with age may reinforce
the view that elders are weak and sickly. The impact of such images on
the development and maintenance of stereotypes merits further attention.

VISUAL ENTERTAINMENT: TELEVISION AND FILM

Contemporary people, Americans especially, watch a tremendous
amount of television and home videos, as well as attending movies at
the theaters. Whereas few people watch TV or read magazines explicitly for the advertisements (Super Bowl commercials aside), people intentionally devote attention to TV and film. But certainly there are similarities between advertising and video fiction. For example, some of
the same groups are underrepresented. Hispanic characters and adults
over 65 are as rare as 3% during prime time (B. S. Greenberg &
Baptista-Fernandez, 1980; Robinson & Skill, 1995). Game show hosts,
even of recently launched TV shows such as "Rock and Roll Jeopardy"
and "Who Wants to Be a Millionaire?" invariably are male (and white).
This role seems to reinforce the role of white men as holders and dis-
tributors of valued resources, as well as solidifying inferences that men
are uniquely competent and knowledgeable (see L. Ross, Amabile, &
Steinmetz, 1977).

Television and films with significant minority representation also
may not receive the same kind of public attention as other programs
and films. For example, in the past 20 years, the only film to win the
Academy Award as best picture that had a minority actor, Morgan
Freeman, in a primary role was Driving Miss Daisy. Although several
members of minorities have won best *supporting* actor or actress in the
past 20 years (e.g., Denzel Washington, Whoopi Goldberg), winning
best actor or actress has been noticeably absent, despite nominations

received (The notable exception is Sidney Poitier, who won the Academy Award for best actor in 1963 for *Lilies of the Field*; see also the website of the Academy of Motion Picture Arts and Sciences, 2000). Minority members fare little better with the Emmy awards. Winners of best dramas or comedies rarely have significant minority representation. (The notable exception here is "The Cosby Show" in 1985, ironically one of the few comedies to win only once.) Emmy winners of best actor or actress, again, typically are white (see the website of the Academy of Television Arts and Sciences, 2000), although the best supporting actor or actress occasionally is from a minority. Although the congratulatory culture of the United States boasts many additional award shows, the Emmys and Oscars are among the oldest and most prestigious. Why performers from minorities have been infrequent nominees and winners is unclear, with possibilities ranging from underrepresentation in the industry to failure to obtain the best roles. But at least subjectively they do not seem to receive as much mainstream public attention for success in the entertainment industries as do whites. The inception of awards such as the Essence Awards and recent Grammy categories such as rap may, in part, be a response to real or perceived inequities with respect to public recognition for superior work.

Stereotypes in Television and Film

Try to imagine video fiction without any stereotypes whatsoever. Not only no black mammies, dumb blondes, flaming gay men, and hard-working Asians, but also no nerds, snitches, evil scientists, and over-controlling school principals. The ease with which an audience understands characters, especially those who appear briefly or who are peripheral to the story line, is aided considerably by stereotypes. The audience knows immediately how to feel about the character and how the main character feels about that stereotyped character; part of the plot twist may depend on those predictable reactions. If video fiction allocated enough time to develop fully each character, a story would be excessively long, incoherent, or be forced to focus around only a handful of characters. From the earliest records, theater, ritual dance, and literature have relied upon particular types of characters. As discussed in Chapter 3, stereotypic portrayals aid in storytelling. What probably merits attention is the cumulative effect of exclusively stereotypic portrayals, as opposed to the effects of occasionally providing nonstereotypic counterpoints: beautiful blonde women who are intelligent without being cold fish; Asians and Asian Americans not constantly tinkering with computers; scientists who are basically good—but not necessarily boring; and large black women in serious business positions and whose sole purpose is not forcefully nurturing people.

Portrayals of women and minorities assuredly have changed over the last several decades. For example, in the 1970s, the employment positions of African American television characters typically were unknown compared to those of European American characters, and the African American characters also were more likely to be of lower socioeconomic status (B. S. Greenberg & Atkin, 1982). By the 1980s, African American characters were more likely to be portrayed as professionals and in more ethnically integrated settings than they previously had been (Armstrong et al., 1992). Those earlier and more stereotypic portrayals of blacks as uneducated or poor, even when humorously intended, served to activate ethnic stereotypes. In one study (Ford, 1997), participants watched stereotypic or nonstereotypic skits with black protagonists from a popular TV program that aired during the late 1970s and early 1980s. In one such stereotypic skit, the black male character discovers that his wife used his paycheck to buy a dress. He holds up a torn dress with a large shoe print upon it and exclaims, "I ain't take it off her when I do dat neither!" In a purportedly unrelated study, participants then rated the guilt of a college student accused of physically assaulting his roommate; the accused either had a stereotypically white or black name—"Todd" or "Tyrone," respectively. Although the evidence of guilt was inconclusive, participants who rated the black student considered him more likely to be guilty if they previously had viewed stereotypic video clips.

Although such stereotypic portrayals may have subsided in recent decades, the results of this study still may have interesting implications. First, and most obviously, is that stereotypic portrayals in the media can activate stereotypes, and this activation in turn increases the likelihood that those stereotypes are used. Of course, many factors besides the media influence whether people use their stereotypes, but stereotypes obviously cannot be used if not first activated. Second, portrayals from earlier decades remain in cultural consciousness: Cable and late-night TV programming rerun older programs; video rental and cable movie channels provide easy access to older films. Conceivably, people exposed to repeated stereotypic images—who do not experience appropriate counterpoint in real life or in more recent media portrayals—may develop the strongest stereotypic associations. A final possibility that merits exploration is that exposure to older stereotypic portrayals might engender overestimates of any decline in discrimination. That is, viewers subjectively might contrast present and past portrayals, and underestimate the degree of prejudice still lingering in contemporary society.

Perhaps among the most pervasive stereotypes in society at large—and in film—is the physical attractiveness stereotype. For example, people believe that attractive individuals are independent, socially skilled, interesting, and well adjusted (Dion & Dion, 1987). Preferences for attractive individuals is evident very early in life (Langlois, Roggman, & Rieser-Danner, 1990); later in life, the work of attractive individuals is evaluated positively (Cash & Trimer, 1984) and they are more likely to benefit from blame-reducing attributions for negative outcomes and behaviors (e.g., Quigley, Johnson, & Byrne, 1995). A meta-analytic review indicates that attractive appearance is unassociated with most positive traits save those related to popularity and reduced social anxiety (Feingold, 1992). Attractive individuals thus apparently are no more intelligent, well adjusted, or morally good than their less attractive counterparts.

Film appears to echo the beauty-is-good stereotype. Animated films for children (e.g., *Beauty and the Beast*) expose viewers to this stereotype through film very early in life (Rumble & Cash, 2000). Films targeted toward adults similarly show the relation. Smith, McIntosh, and Bazzini (1999) identified the top-grossing films from 1940 to 1989, then randomly selected 100 films. They rated the main characters on physical attractiveness, moral goodness, intelligence, aggressiveness, romantic activity, apparent socioeconomic status, and final outcome. Physical attractiveness most reliably predicted moral goodness and favorable outcomes. In more recent films, physical attractiveness also predicted intelligence. To examine the possibility that exposure to stereotype-confirming films can bolster stereotype use, Smith et al. (1999) selected from their pool of films one drama and one musical that were high in the beauty-is-good relation (*The Pride of the Yankees; Road to Utopia*) and one drama and one musical that were low in that relation (*Up the Down Staircase; Rhapsody in Blue*). After exposure to one of the films, participants rated applications of potential college students whose pictures were appended to the application. The physical attractiveness stereotype was evident among all groups of participants, but it was accentuated if participants previously had been exposed to a film that upheld the beauty-is-good stereotype. Thus, films may both reflect and perpetuate the physical attractiveness stereotype.

Implicit in the beautiful-is-good stereotype is that beauty requires youth, although that requirement is more important for women than for men. For instances when film characters are older females, these older characters are often less attractive, sociable, and intelligent than their male counterparts. Older women also appear less frequently in film than do men (Bazzini, McIntosh, Smith, & Cook, 1997), although these relative frequencies on television have reversed in recent decades (Robinson & Skill, 1995). Interestingly, some older TV viewers are unperturbed by portrayals of their age cohort. One metropolitan sample showed that older viewers perceived their cohort to be portrayed neutrally or favorably on television (Hofstetter, Schultze, Mahoney, & Buss, 1993). Conceivably, this perception stems in part from preferences among older TV viewers for programs such as "Matlock" and "The Golden Girls," in which older characters are portrayed as active, powerful, and attractive (Bell, 1992).

Archetypal Themes and Myths

Fictional literature, at least in Western society, is replete with a number of recurring themes. These themes include the self-illumination of a novice who journeys into an alien culture or wasteland, a tremendous sacrifice made for love, and the tragedy that befalls the character who attempts to avoid an inevitable fate. Stories with these themes also have a clear cast of characters: the messiah figure of mysterious birth, the wise person of color (traditionally called "man's darker brother"), the female whose absolute power corrupts her absolutely, and the knight errant who saves the day but never settles down. These themes are evident in Greek theatre and mythology, in Judeo-Christian lore, the Arthurian legends and heroic poems, and in the novels of the 18th and 19th century, as well as in modern-day Westerns, science fiction, and fantasy. Although empirical work addressing them is indirect at best, the themes and characters who reflect these continued cultural prejudices are worth brief mention, particularly those that reflect gender and interracial relations.

Two female character types in particular recur throughout Western literature and seem to capture a fundamental ambivalence about the role of women in society. One character is morally good, subservient to her husband and family, and passive except in defending her honor. Without her love, the male character is incomplete and lost. She is the patient wife Penelope of The Odyssey, the damsel in distress in legends, fairy tales, and modern fantasy, and the idealized young woman in several of Charles Dickens's novels whose love potentially saves the male protagonist from moral decline and despair. Depending on her marital status and age, she is alternatively the virgin or the madonna figure. Such characters embody the contemporary notion of benevolent sexism, which reflects an idealization of women as morally superior creatures but also as requiring protection (Glick & Fiske, 1996). The other main female character embodies the notion of hostile sexism, which reflects a view of gender relations as conflictual and also expresses anger and disgust at women's attempts to obtain or wield power. This character uses her resources, often sexual or magical, to bend men to her selfish whims. She is the sorceress Circe in The Odys-

sey, and the witch and evil fairy of legend. More contemporarily, her power may derive from financial or political resources. These resources may be inherited from a late husband or acquired by "sleeping her way" to the top; still, she attempts to bend others to her will. If things ultimately end well for powerful women, it is because they are tamed by the love of a man, surrendering their power for his sake or sharing the burden of ruling political or financial empires. The contemporary lesson is that powerful women can serve "the greater good" if they accept male guidance. (Even the benevolent sister witches of the WB network's "Charmed" have a male guide and are constrained against using power for personal gain.)

Male "heroic" archetypes also recur throughout Western literature, and particularly reinforce the relation among agency, understanding of the greater good, and male gender. These are the mighty heroes of classical myth, the knights errant, the Western gunslingers, the vigilante cops, and the roguish private detectives. Cast as warrior saviors, aspects of their parentage often is mysterious or even magical (e.g., Hercules, Percival, Luke Skywalker, Fox Mulder). They burst onto the scene with intellect, strength, and moral obligation, save the day and get the girl, then return in the next episode, film, or tale to do it all over again. Real men come to the rescue. And, indeed, empirical gender differences in helping behavior are understandable in terms of the chivalry norm: men help more than women when the task is dangerous, when an audience is present, when help is needed but not explicitly requested, and when the person in distress is a young woman (Eagly & Crowley, 1986). Moreover, both his need for adventure and the greater good requires that the lone hero sacrifice simpler pleasures like a beautiful wife and a white picket fence: a sequel or subsequent episode requires that this character not be tied down to one woman. The solitary character either is avoidantly attached, seeking physical but not psychological intimacy with women (see Brennan & Shaver, 1995), or conveniently is bereft of his beloved through death or kidnapping before the sequel progresses. The other primary male archetype—the wise hermit—is too old to save the day alone, so he trains the hero and spurs him to agency. But the hermit shares a number of features with the hero: the hermit also is solitary, especially with respect to female companionship, and has an acute understanding of the greater good.

With respect to interracial relations, an enduring archetype is the wise person of color, more commonly called "man's darker brother." This character derives his wisdom from his alien perspective, largely from an allegedly close connection with the natural world. Although he is a source of wisdom, he ultimately understands that his white companion possesses a higher wisdom; he even may adopt white culture or, at the least, he lives within it rather than within his own. These characters include indigenous people such as Tonto of "The Lone Ranger" and Queequeg of *Moby Dick,* but also African American sidekicks such as Jim in *Huckleberry Finn* and Red in *The Shawshank Redemption* (a 1994 film for which Morgan Freeman was nominated for an Academy Award as best actor). In science fiction, the wise person of color may be nonhuman or even female, such as Guinan of "Star Trek: The Next Generation" or Delenn of "Babylon 5." Although this type of character possesses dignity and wisdom and is a far cry from the stereotypic ethnic sidekick of cop shows and comedy, the character remains a testimony to ethnocentrism. Members of another race, culture, or species seem to be portrayed as most laudable when they essentially accept and are absorbed into the dominant culture. (If female and not too alien in appearance, they even may have an enduring romantic relationship with a man from the dominant culture.) More recently, some of these characters have been allowed to retain practices important to their cultural identity, without the story lampooning those practices, holding them up as a bizarre curiosity, or using them as a foil for the superiority of the dominant culture. If life and art mutually imitate each other, this recent trend in film may reflect—and perhaps foster—a growing appreciation of multiculturalism.

Summary

A primary goal of fiction in film or television is to entertain, which in part requires the telling of a good story. Stereotypic and archetypal characters can be helpful in that regard. Such characters are functional in that they are easily and quickly understood. The handsome lone hero and the beautiful imperiled heroine are aesthetically pleasing to watch and encourage the audience's sympathy and identification, but they also are reflections of the physical attractiveness stereotype and prescriptive gender roles. Some contemporary TV programs attempt to turn those stereotypes on their side. The popular "Xena: Warrior Princess," for example, casts a woman in the role of the wandering hero of semimysterious birth. In direct contrast, other contemporary programs revel in the stereotypes. The characters in "South Park," for example, include a wise but oversexed and musically gifted black man, a maladjusted fat kid with delusions of grandeur, and a lisping—and entirely unbalanced—male grade school teacher who denies being gay. Characters on "The Simpsons" include a fat, stupid police officer, several pathetically frail elderly characters, and a Hindu proprietor of a convenience store. How much these images contribute to the development and perpetuation of stereotypes remains to be seen. They are, of course, intended to make people laugh and even delightedly poke fun at the overzealous politically correct movement. How successful making fun of stereotypes is in breaking them down—and with which audiences—remains to be seen.

GROUP-TARGETED HUMOR

Nine blondes and a brunette go mountain climbing, using a single rope.
    After a time, the rope weakens and clearly will not hold everyone.
    The brunette indicates that at least one of the women will need to let go of the rope in order for the others to be saved. Silence. After about 10 minutes, the brunette speaks up again: "In order to save the rest, I will release the rope and plummet to my death."
    All of the blondes applauded.
(forwarded to the author via electronic mail)

Why Is Something Funny?

According to Wyer and Collins (1992), humor is something that is perceived as amusing. What provokes the humor may be intentional or unintentional, social or nonsocial, and laughter provoking or prompting no discernible public reaction. A person may be amused by a slapstick chase scene in a comedy film, by the disheveled appearance of a colleague (e.g., a bad toupee, the accidental exposure of usually covered undergarments), the antics of a beloved pet, or a Gary Larson cartoon. Alternatively, a person may be amused by someone's exaggerated mimicry of another person's mannerisms, by a joke, or by a humorous story. The humor-eliciting stimulus may be consensually humorous to everyone present or only humorous to a few persons. For example, although many men and women continue to find dumb blonde jokes amusing, one seriously doubts that individuals with blonde hair—especially women—are as likely to share that perception.

Three major types of theories provide explanations why something is perceived as funny (Wyer & Collins, 1992). *Arousal/arousal-reduction theories* posit that humor derives from the sudden release of suppressed emotions. For example, someone high in sexism who feels hostility toward women may not feel at liberty to express his or her prejudices openly or in most public situations. Arousal builds up, until it reaches an unpleasant level. Someone tells a joke that releases the excess arousal and brings the arousal back to an optimal level. From this account, amusement at the dumb blonde joke presumably derives from suppressed hostility toward women, in particular women who apparently succeed in life by relying on physical beauty rather than by intelligence, hard work, or moral qualities. The foibles of the dumb blonde are sufficiently outrageous that the listener is amused and, according to these theories, some of the pent up arousal is released. But, as Wyer and Collins note, there is little evidence that reduction in physiological arousal is a necessary or sufficient condition for humor. Moreover, this approach cannot easily explain the experience of humor when the prior suppression of emotions is unlikely (e.g., amusement at a colleague's bad toupee may not depend on repressed negative feelings toward him).

Another relatively motivational account derives from *superiority/ disparagement theories*, which posit that humor involves a sudden realization that one is superior to someone else. The joke or event highlights some inadequacy of the person from the targeted group, so this type of communication functions as an opportunity to bolster the ego. With respect to the mountain-climbing joke above, this explanation allows the hearer to feel superior to the blonde women, who are not noble enough to sacrifice themselves, not clever enough to find a solution to the dilemma, and sufficiently stupid to be tricked into releasing the rope. Because no one could be that stupid, the joke potentially allows any hearer to feel superior. Wyer and Collins (1992) agree that these theories are particularly good at explaining group-targeted humor. However, the recognition of superiority may produce other feelings such as pride or *schadenfrude* (i.e., satisfaction at the failures of disliked others), so it is not a necessary condition for humor.

The more cognitive accounts are *incongruity resolution theories*: "Laughter arises from the view of two or more inconsistent, unsuitable, or incongruent parts of circumstances, considered as united in one complex object" (James Beattie, quoted in Manring, 1998). An initial situation or problem is presented in light of a particular set of expectations. The new information—often the punch line—cannot be understood in terms of those initial expectations. The person then finds another schema or set of expectations that explain the entire event, reinterpreting the original information in terms of the newly identified schema. Again with respect to the mountain-climbing joke above, the initial expectancy is that no one who values her own life willingly would jeopardize it and that the dilemma needs to be solved through an act of heroism or intellect. Reinterpreting the story in terms of the dumb blondes ultimately elicits the humor: dumb blondes are so dumb that they can be tricked into releasing the rope. From this perspective, then, getting the joke requires cultural knowledge of the stereotype.

Humor about Outgroups

Cataloging jokes about outgroups easily could fill several volumes. Although understudied, humor that targets outgroups may represent the largest repository of cultural knowledge of stereotypes. For example, humor often focuses on groups who are stereotypically lacking in intelligence (e.g., blondes, people of Polish descent), self-serving (e.g., lawyers, Jewish American Princesses), forgetful (e.g., drunk Irishmen or elderly people), or inordinately polite (e.g., British or Japanese individuals). The reasons for sharing a humorous episode among fellow ingroup members include sheer entertainment, engendering ingroup camaraderie, and expressing shared values and beliefs. Presumably, the transmitter also wishes to foster the impression that she or he is witty and possesses a good sense of humor. Prejudiced humor therefore has the capacity to serve a number of functions. But most people appreciate that not all potential audiences find humor in the lampooning of an outgroup. Some audience members may be amused but simultaneously will recognize that displaying their amusement will appear prejudiced. Other audience members may turn away in disgust or rise up in anger. Given implicit impression management goals, the transmitter needs to weigh the potential costs and gains of lampooning the outgroup. If the audience's reaction is highly predictable (e.g., they share one's prejudices), the costs of transmitting the joke are minimal. In contrast, because outgroup humor may involve a degree of hostility, transmitters who are uncertain of audience reactions need to minimize the association between themselves and the message. For example, in interpersonal settings, the transmitter may preface the joke by indicating from whom he or she initially heard it, hoping that people do not confuse the message with the messenger; forwarding and reforwarding jokes over electronic mail also may eventually obfuscate the source.

Most costly is incurring the wrath of a higher-status individual. Lower-status individuals joke less frequently than do higher-status individuals (Smeltzer & Leap, 1988), because the former potentially have more to lose. If offended by the joking of a lower-status person, the higher-status person typically possesses greater resources for retaliation. On the other hand, a joke may be interpreted more negatively by observers when the source is a higher-status person and the target is a lower-status person. If the joke includes sexual content, for example, people are more likely to construe the joke as sexual harassment if the source is a supervisor (Hemmasi, Graf, & Russ, 1994). Women, in particular, often fail to find humor in such jokes (Hemmasi et al., 1994; LaFrance & Woodzicky, 1998). Conceivably due their implicit lower status, many women may not feel comfortable directly confronting the source of sexual humor. They instead may feel a threat of retaliation, either because the transmitter holds more power or simply because confrontation fails to adhere to the prescriptive stereotype of women being polite and passive. For instance, women's most common response to sexist remarks, albeit nonhumorous ones, is to ask questions such as "What did you say?" (Swim & Hyers, 1999), which indirectly suggests to the speaker that he needs to rethink both the remark and the audience. Thus, not only may lower-status individuals be careful about using humor as an expression of hostility, but they also may be careful in how they react as targets of such humor.

Some humor that targets an outgroup is directed to the outgroup members themselves, or at least is intended to be overheard. To be hurtful and to incite anger, some individuals tell prejudiced jokes directly to outgroup members or exaggeratingly mimic their mannerisms. Most likely, these events occur when retaliation from the outgroup member is unlikely: The outgroup member is alone or outnumbered, or is in a relatively unpowerful position. Imagine, for example, two non-Jews at a coffee shop who observe a Jewish acquaintance preparing to pay for coffee. One non-Jew loudly might relate a joke conveying the stereotype of Jews as stingy (Question: "What is the difference between a canoe and a Jew?" Answer: "A canoe tips!"; cited in Wyer & Collins, 1992, p. 688). But as the potential cost of direct transmission increases, the transmitter might adopt a less direct approach. Irony, for example, is perceived as less aggressive than using a more literal approach like the joke, and as less damaging to the relationship (Dews, Kaplan, & Winner, 1995). In this case, the non-Jew might say to a companion, "Yep. In 200 years keeping a nickel change will pay for college." Alternatively, the non-Jew might use the opportunity to tease the acquaintance: "Aren't you going to keep the change for a phone call?" As with irony, victims perceive teasing as more hurtful than do the perpetrators (Kowalski, 2000), so these attempts at humor are not necessarily harmless. The teasing or irony even might be more hurtful when it carries a stereotypic connotation or is couched in terms of the person's group membership. In any case, irony and teasing comments can be disparaging but are less direct than a nonhumorous comment or even an ethnic joke.

Humor about Ingroups

Not all group-focused humor targets an outgroup. On occasion, individuals intentionally lampoon their own ingroup; some comedians may make a career out of doing so. Nevo (1985) proposes that ingroup humor potentially derives from three different causes:

First, the speakers may not identify with their ingroup or, at least, with the group that the audience infers is the ingroup. Humor may distinguish people with the speaker's characteristics from group members with undesirable qualities, accentuating group heterogeneity (Doosje, Ellemers, & Spears, 1995; Marques, Yzerbyt, & Leyens, 1988). For example, a professional woman in a predominantly male organization may poke fun of the gender-stereotypic qualities of homemakers or "pink-collar" workers. The potential association with devalued groups of women is threatening, so the humorous comments simultaneously function to enhance personal self-esteem while differentiating oneself from those groups.

A second reason may be hatred of one's own group or of oneself. That is, the speaker may have internalized the values of the dominant culture, which devalue the speaker's group, and ingroup-directed humor is a symptom of this internalization. Consistent with this reasoning, self-deprecation is more prevalent in lower-status rather than higher-status individuals. However, though there is little or no evidence of a direct link between self-deprecating humor and low self-esteem (or self-hatred).

The third reason, examined in depth by Nevo (1985), is that the speaker does not view the humor as disparaging. He specifically focuses on the example of Jewish humor, which involves the caricaturing of certain stereotypes (e.g., the Jewish American Princess, Jewish mothers) and jokes about various cultural practices. This sort of humor makes the ingroup the butt of the joke but is not necessarily viewed as a put-down of the group. Nevo presented Arab and Jewish residents of Israel with cartoons in which one character experienced a frustrating event. Participants completed the bubbles that indicated what the characters said. For instance, in one cartoon, an Arab drives by, splashes a Jewish person at the curb, and says, "Excuse me, sir, for splashing you with mud." The participant then wrote in the blank bubble the splashed person's response. Both groups of participants typically produced humorous responses that made the frustrator the butt of the joke if he was an Arab (e.g., "You're always dirty; that's why you want me to be dirty"). The generation of humorous retorts that ridicule the minority is consistent with previous findings: Both majorities and minorities prefer jokes about minorities (Cantor, 1976). Perhaps more interesting is that, across the various cartoons, Jews produced more self-directed humorous responses than did Arabs, but those responses typically included a positive slant on the situation (e.g., "That's OK. I need a shower anyway"). Jews, at least in this Israeli sample, may produce self-directed humor that is not disparaging.

Humor directed at the ingroup may, at least on occasion, carry some costs. If the humor is stereotypic or contains global generalizations, the humorous comment or behavior may activate stereotypes. Although people typically may accord little weight to the words of outgroup members, outgroup members who are speaking about their own group may be viewed as experts (Duval et al., 2000). Moreover, if outgroup members are speaking against the best interests of their own group (e.g., stereotyping their own group), the question of a hidden agenda is minimized. Thus, if a man high in sexism hears a woman say, "Women are gossipy," he initially may reason that (1) she, as a woman, should know and (2) it must be true if she is willing to say it. Consistent with this reasoning, Cralley and Ruscher (2000) found that men high in modern sexism applied their stereotypes when female speakers made global comments about women; men low in sexism, in contrast, did not apply their stereotypes.

But even nonprejudiced individuals might, however briefly, succumb to applying their stereotypes. Presumably, nonprejudiced individuals actively suppress their activated stereotypes when they hear prejudiced or stereotypic comments being made. But if the comment is humorously intended, stereotype suppression would be unlikely. Getting the joke essentially requires allowing the stereotype to remain accessible and, if so, the stereotype also is more likely to be applied than it otherwise would be. Investigating this possibility in a second study, Cralley and Ruscher (2000) attributed global stereotypic comments (e.g., "Women are gossipy") to women or men on TV comedy programs or TV news magazines. The male participants then wrote short stories about a woman depicted in a variety of neutral settings (e.g., drinking coffee). Low sexist men produced relatively nonstereotypic stories when the women's comments were seriously intended, as in the initial study. When these comments were humorously intended, however, they produced stories that were similar in stereotypicness to those produced by high sexist men. Receivers presumably *can* subtract out humorous intent (Wyer & Gruenfeld, 1995) but may be reluctant to suppress the stereotype and lose out on the joke. And, after all, the joking person from the stereotyped group apparently wanted them to apply the stereotype in order to get the joke. But, ironically, the joke backfires.

Summary

Group-targeted humor is a unique form of prejudiced communication. Not only does it clearly convey extant stereotypes, but it conveys them in a way that may increase their likelihood of subsequent transmission. Producing laughter in other people, when one intends to be humorous,

can be reinforcing. It is a self-esteem boost, as the teller receives validation of his or her good sense of humor, cleverness, social skills, and social standing. Like most behaviors, transmitted humor that fails to be
reinforced presumably extinguishes over time ... or at least becomes
restricted to situations in which it will remain reinforced. Group-
targeted humor also may be unique because the transmission of the
stereotype often has an indirect quality. The teller does not say directly
that "Germans are rule-oriented," "Blondes are dumb," or that "Men
think only about sex." Instead, the teller illustrates the point, and the
receiver really only gets the joke if the stereotype is applied. Finally, the
indirect format in verbally transmitted humor can obfuscate the source
who, if no one is amused, can claim simply that she was just relaying
the joke. The role of humor in perpetuating stereotypes, the functions it
plays for the prejudiced person and for ingroup solidarity are, it would
seem, vastly understudied.

HATE SPEECH

"Hate speech" currently has no consensually agreed-upon definition.
Definitions range from speech attacks based on race, religion, or sexual
orientation to any form of offensive expression directed toward women,
discrete minorities, and ethnic, religious, and racial groups. In this context, speech has come to be understood as including oral and written
communication as well as the use of symbols, parades, and other visual or nonverbal forms of expression. Termed "group libel" in the
1940s, protected groups originally included only racial, religious, and
ethnic groups; more recent definitions include groups identified by
sexual orientation, gender, or disability (for further discussion see
Walker, 1994).

An Abbreviated History

Legislation regarding hate speech continues to be a sticky issue in the
United States, as it is metaphorically stuck between two portions of the
Constitution: the First and Fourteenth Amendments. The First Amendment provides for freedom of speech, whereas the Fourteenth Amendment provides for equal protection for all citizens of the United States.
The U.S. Supreme Court recognizes several exceptions to the protection of free speech, including "fighting words" and perjury, disrup-
tions to government function (e.g., a demonstration that blocks traffic),
and creating a hostile work environment.

Fighting words are those that incite an immediate breach of peace and are intended to inflict injury; typically, the audience must be hostile to the utterance of those words and somehow be forced to hear them. The fighting words exemption dates to the 1942 case of *Chaplinsky v. New Hampshire* in which Chaplinsky was distributing antireligious literature. He reportedly harassed a police officer, by calling him a "damned Fascist" and a "God-damned racketeer." The U.S. Supreme Court held that these epithets were designed to be hurtful, were likely to break the peace in a public place, would provoke the average person to retaliation, and would prevent the recipient from pursuing his lawful occupation. Note that in the fighting words exemption, derogatory statements are face to face, impossible to ignore, and clearly intended to hurt the recipient. Unlikely to fall under the fighting words category is the mere encounter of material that insults a group or the accidentally overheard derogation of another person or group. For example, the U.S. Supreme Court upheld the right of a white citizen's group to publish an inflammatory pamphlet aimed at black Chicago residents (*Beauharnais v. Illinois*, 1952). The hostile audience was not forced to read the pamphlet, nor was it a direct face-to-face insult. This does not mean that written material and overhead comments are not prejudiced speech intended to bolster the ingroup, differentiate and belittle the outgroup, and protect the power of the ingroup. But such communications are likely to be protected under the First Amendment.

What about symbols? In 1990, several Minnesota teenagers placed a burning cross in the yard of a black family and were convicted of a misdemeanor. The city of St. Paul had made it a misdemeanor to place on public or private property any symbols and graffiti such as burning crosses or Nazi swastikas, which people reasonably know arouse anger or alarm on the basis of race, color, creed, religion, or gender. Following the cross-burning incident, the ordinance was challenged as unconstitutional (*R.A.P. v. City of St. Paul*). The U.S. Supreme Court agreed and overturned the conviction. The Court ruled that the ordinance was too broadly defined, and specifically did not require that the symbol be intended to incite breach of the peace, be directed at a particular individual, or intend to be hurtful (i.e., fighting words). The Court further indicated that the city had other means to regulate such behavior, without dragging the First Amendment into the mix. For example, the behavior involved trespassing and a risk to the destruction of private property (for additional examples and discussion see Walker, 1994).

Colleges and universities often have adopted codes of speech and conduct, but even these sometimes have been ruled as unconstitutional. For example, the University of Wisconsin code prohibited discriminatory comments or expressions directed at individuals, creating a hostile environment for education and other university-related activities. The courts ruled that the Wisconsin code was unconstitutional, given that it was not limited to words likely to incite immediate breach of the peace. Moreover, the court ruled that the prohibition against creating hostile work environment did not apply. To be considered a hostile work environment, there must be sufficient pervasive and severe harassment to alter the person's employment or educational environment. The Civil Rights Act protects employees (Title VII) and students (Title IX) from being subjected to discriminatory speech and conduct that creates an abusive environment. The court indicated that a university is not liable for the behavior of students in the same way that a company is for its employees. (Note: This does not mean that university employees are necessarily unaccountable for creating a hostile environment for students and other employees.) Finally, the Wisconsin code was ruled to be too vague. For example, the words needed to be proven to be demeaning and as actually changing the environment into a hostile one (for additional examples see Heumann & Church, 1997).

Regulating hate speech therefore remains an extremely touchy issue. In its decision to uphold the rights of the American Nazi party to march in Skokie, Illinois, in the 1970s (a town with a substantial number of World War II concentration camp survivors), the U.S. Supreme Court ruled that the right to free speech for all citizens must be protected, even of "those whose ideals it [society] quite justifiably rejects and despises" (*Collin v. Smith*, reported in Heumann & Church, 1997, p. 108). Whereas other industrialized nations have adopted hate speech legislation, the United States has a long history of scrupulously guarding First Amendment rights. On the other hand, more than 65% of minority college students report having experienced some type of race-based harassment (reported in Matsuda, Lawrence, Delgado, & Crenshaw, 1993). Some First Amendment scholars have criticized the courts for allowing First Amendment rights to take precedence over the protections of the Fourteenth Amendment (for essays see Matsuda et al., 1993). This entire dialogue is well beyond the scope of this book, but the debate provides an interesting backdrop against which to consider the effects of hate speech. For social psychologists, these effects are the most pertinent question.

Empirical Research on Hate Speech

Empirical work on hate speech is relatively limited. Experimentally examining the effects of hate speech on recipients themselves obviously would violate most researchers' codes of ethics. Retrospective reports indicate that many individuals have felt themselves the targets of group-related hate speech. For example, in a sample of college students ($N = 212$) and community residents ($N = 53$) in California, 40% of white and 26% of nonwhite women reported having been victims of gender-based hate speech; among the ethnic minorities, nearly 68% of the men and 46% of the women reported having been victims of racially based hate speech (Cowan & Hodge, 1996). These percentages are relatively in line with those reported by Matsuda et al. (1993). This California sample also considered racially based hate speech more offensive than gender-based hate speech or speech that targeted homosexual individuals, perhaps because racist speech has received greater sociopolitical attention.

To be exempt from protection under the First Amendment, the fighting words heuristic needs to apply: The derogation must be face to face, intentional, and produce an uncontrollable urge for the recipient to retaliate (i.e., disrupting the peace). Matsuda et al. (1993) note that for many recipients of hate speech, the dominant response may be withdrawal from the situation rather than immediate retaliation. When relatively low-power individuals are provoked by a higher-power person, retaliation is unlikely for fear that the attempted retaliation will escalate the degree of harm that they incur (O'Neal & Taylor, 1989). Alternatively, the recipient may be in a numerical minority when the insult occurs and so not feel safe to retort or act. A man in a group of women engaged in male bashing or a white person in a primarily black neighborhood may be unlikely to retort or retaliate, despite membership in historically powerful groups. The urge to retaliate may be squelched immediately, or may be superseded by the urge to flee. The recipient indeed may be angry, alarmed, or hurt, but the failure to retaliate maintains the peace. Moreover, indirect forms of hate speech may be as hurtful as direct face-to-face hate speech. Matsuda provides an example of a caricature of an ethnic minority with a red line drawn through it, posted on an ethnic minority student's dormitory room door. The assault is not face to face—indeed, it is anonymous—though it is manifestly intentional. If the student does experience the urge to retaliate (rather than to move from that dorm or university), against whom the student would retaliate is unclear. The anonymity of the act may disturb the student even more than a face-to-face assault, because the student cannot be certain who among the residents—and how many—are prejudiced against her or his ethnic group. Such anonymous harassments may function not only to maintain the power of the dominant group but, through fear, may accenuate that power.

Whether or not one belongs to the targeted group also affects which comments are perceived as offensive. Leets and Giles (1997) examined how perceptions of offensiveness varied as a function of group membership and the directness of the comment. Direct speech acts are those in which the literal meaning of the sentence and the speaker's intended message are identical. With indirect speech acts, the sentence may convey multiple meanings, and which meaning was the speaker's intention is ambiguous. Leets and Giles used superb examples of direct and indirect speech directed toward a person of Asian descent. Drawing from an actual court case, they note that a white clerk calling a person of Asian descent a "slanty-eyed pain in the ass" for requesting a refund is direct. In contrast, a white mother calmly telling her son's new Asian girlfriend that the mother's business associates will not accept an interracial relationship is indirect. The latter statement alternatively may be construed as racism on the speaker's part or as a statement that people outside the family are prejudiced. The ambiguity allows the speaker to deny racist intentions if necessary.

In two experiments, Leets and Giles (1997) also found that participants of Asian descent actually considered indirect messages to be more offensive than direct messages; given that only (some) direct verbal assaults are exempt from First Amendment protection, this effect is interesting. The pattern reversed for white participants. The authors suggest several distinct explanations for this pattern. First, an Asian cultural heritage that encourages the interdependent self simultaneously may engender an avoidance of conflict; the conflictual direct comment may have encouraged Asian participants to suppress their anger. To the extent that this explanation has merit, the pattern should fail to replicate with members of less interdependent ethnic groups. Second, Leets and Giles suggest that the indirect insults are "microinequities," for which a grievance or lawsuit is an unlikely recourse. Especially as an isolated incident, the indirect statement is hard to interpret as necessarily prejudiced. Finally, in considering the judgments of the white participants, the authors suggest that the black sheep effect (Marques et al., 1988) may be operating, which is an extreme negative evaluation of an ingroup member who performs negative behavior. From this perspective, white participants may have found the direct messages offensive because those messages cast whites as a whole in an unfavorable light. Data from additional white participants supported this possibility.

In addition to being offensive, hate speech and related phenomena have the capacity to activate negative stereotypes. For example, in one study, white participants overheard an ethnic slur about the skill of a black student at a debate (J. Greenberg & Pyszczynski, 1985). Compared to participants who overhead no comment or a slur unrelated to race, participants who heard the ethnic slur produced more negative ratings of the black student's skill. A later study (Kirkland, Greenberg, & Pyszczynski, 1987) not only replicated this effect when the target was a black defense attorney but also negatively affected ratings of the attorney's white client. Participants were more punitive toward the white defendant when his black attorney had been described with a derogatory ethnic label. Thus, overhearing derogatory group epithets (J. Greenberg & Pyszczynski, 1985; Kirkland et al., 1987), reading group derogatory graffiti (J. Greenberg, Kirkland, & Pyszczynski, 1988), or hearing peers condone racist attitudes (Blanchard, Crandall, Brigham, & Vaughn, 1994; Blanchard, Lilly, & Vaughn, 1991) all can activate stereotypes. As with stereotypes activated through humor or TV programming, stereotypes activated by hate speech are more likely to be used in subsequent judgments.

Summary

Hate speech involves speech attacks based on group characteristics such as race, ethnicity, gender, religion, and sexual orientation. Attacks that are face to face, that prompt an immediate breach of the peace, that disrupt government functioning, or that produce a pervasive hostile work environment are exempt from First Amendment protection. Indirect speech acts (Leets & Giles, 1997), overheard derogatory comments (e.g., J. Greenberg & Psyzczynski, 1985), overheard racist pronouncements (e.g., Blanchard et al., 1994), and prejudiced graffiti (J. Greenberg et al., 1988) are not so protected, but they still may affect both targets and observers.

In defense of the First Amendment, President Nadine Strossen of the American Civil Liberties Union (ACLU) argued that prohibiting prejudiced speech would focus on a symptom rather than an underlying problem (cited in Walker, 1994, p. 147). Indeed, prejudiced speech presumably serves functions for those who express it, including protecting the ingroup's self-esteem, outgroup simplification, and outgroup delegitimization. These will not simply vanish with a change in speech. Repressed prejudice simply goes underground, slipping out when situations are sufficiently ambiguous to allow its expression. Moreover, what exactly would be regulated is problematic. Nazis may tout the swastika as a symbol of ingroup pride, although it also is recognized as symbolizing hatred for outgroups such as Jews, blacks, and homosexuals. Similarly, some whites consider that blacks who wear a baseball cap with an X upon it as expressing hostility toward whites, although many blacks may consider this symbol a reflection of ingroup pride and respect for a great leader (Malcolm X).

The prohibition of "fighting words" notwithstanding, indirect comments may be just as hurtful to recipients. Insinuating to a colleague that her promotion helps the company avoid criticisms of too few women at the top and calmly telling a minority student that people from his group perform poorly on a particular task are certainly not boosts to the recipients' self-esteem; moreover, instilling such beliefs in them can have measurably detrimental effects on the recipients' performance (Heilman et al., 1990; Spencer, Steele, & Quinn, 1999). As the percentage of ethnic minorities in the United States increases over the next several decades, the dialogue on hate speech regulation undoubtedly will continue. Just how social science research informs this debate will depend largely on the questions that researchers choose to ask.

CHAPTER SUMMARY

Prejudiced communication has been and remains a viable part of our culture. The easily recognized stereotypic images in advertising, film, and television quickly convey how a receiver should respond to a product or character. The well-dressed Asian symbolizes hard work and technology; the beautiful woman alternatively symbolizes the seductress or the damsel in distress; and the light-skinned African American woman performer symbolizes successful assimilation into mainstream white culture. Less blatantly, minority characters serve in background roles, peppering the scene with diversity. Clearly, images have changed over the years: Blacks are no longer portrayed primarily as servants or criminals; Asians have moved out of the laundry; women can now do more than cook dinner for their families. But what currently is viewed as nonstereotypic may be interpreted as stereotypic years from now, with the benefit of hindsight. Looking back on her role as Lieutenant Uhura in "Star Trek" during its 25th anniversary, Nichelle Nichols recalls that her role as something other than a mammy or maid was unprecedented on television. At the time, she was seen as breaking down stereotypes of blacks. But she also notes that Uhura largely was a background figure, saying little more than "Message coming through, Captain." She concludes by commenting that portrayals of women and minorities have come a long way . . . and have a long way to go. What currently is deemed acceptable may well appall our future selves and descendants.

Group-targeted comments, whether humorously or viciously intended, also remain viable. The increasing popularity of the Internet in particular has helped to circulate group-targeted humor. In addition to websites devoted to humor, jokes, and stories about ill-fated outgroups appear in one's inbox with a sizable catalog of recipients and former senders. Occasionally, they begin with a disclaimer from the current sender ("Can you believe this?" or "I know this is sexist, but ... "). They even may be totally anonymous, deriving from a listserv subscription. Humor, especially when one simply is conveying the jokes that someone else has told, provides an almost acceptable way to transmit stereotypes. In the current politically correct environment, seriously stating an opinion that links Jews with materialism, blacks with sexual prowess, women with gossip mongering, or homosexual men with a keen fashion sense is likely to produce gasps from many within earshot. In contrast, transmitting a joke—among one's known ingroup or even about one's ingroup—may be seen as relatively harmless. As the limited empirical work on hate speech suggests, many individuals are offended by direct derogatory comments about outgroup members. But while indirect comments including humor may be just as hurtful to the target, frequently neither the transmitters nor members of their group are even aware of that inflicted pain.

EIGHT

Afterword: What Is Known and What Is Unknown

For you know only
A heap of broken images
—T. S. ELIOT, *The Wasteland*

The topics examined in previous chapters run the gamut of prejudiced communication, from interpersonal communication among a handful of individuals to mass communication in television, film, and newsprint. Prejudiced communication is about outgroup members, directed toward them, and even involves prejudice concerning their communication styles. It also encompasses their representation in the media, as well as the jokes that remain in shared cultural consciousness. This final chapter briefly revisits some of the recurring themes, then considers which arenas in particular require additional consideration.

MAJOR THEMES

A Hint at Representation

Prejudiced communication provides a hint at how outgroup members are represented cognitively in the minds of individuals, as well as sociocognitively in the shared stereotypes of groups or entire cultures.

First, outgroup members seem to be viewed in stereotypic, noncomplex, or negative ways. For instance, the negative or stereotypic behaviors of outgroup members are described abstractly or in ways that generalize that behavior, helping define stable dispositional characteristics of the outgroup along those dimensions. Prejudiced whites describe a black man as "aggressive" rather than as "having pushed someone yesterday"; they even may use such terms when communication is directed to the black man. Along similar lines, the behavior of an outgroup member may reflect back upon his or her group as a whole, as seen in the work on inclusiveness and generalization. They are all alike, they are just like that, isn't that just like an X? In addition to descriptive stereotypes, the major media also provides prescriptive stereotypes: Good women should be young, beautiful, and either passive or self-sacrificing; good men should be muscular, heroic, and not tied down to women; beautiful black women should have "Caucasian" features. Finally, although dramatically understudied by social psychologists, group-targeted humor also provides a peek at underlying representation. Jokes reinforce existing notions that Germans are authority oriented, that gay men are super hairdressers, that blonde women are ditzy, and that men are obsessed with sex. That people get the joke by applying the respective stereotypes is indirect evidence that, indeed, culturally shared stereotypes do exist. What ultimately is communicated—visually, orally, or textually—is an easily understood shorthand by persons who share in that culture.

Second, there is the issue of which representations are cognitively accessible. Members of some groups seem to be relatively invisible or, at the least, the degree to which they are noticed corresponds less to their numbers and more to their economic, political, or social power. The use of "he" as the generic third person singular technically is alleged to include women but may encourage more masculine imagery than terms such as "he or she" or "they." Women are implicitly but not explicitly included. Minorities such as persons of Latino, African, or Asian descent typically play background roles in advertisements. Meanwhile, minorities occasionally win Emmys and Oscars for supporting roles but almost never for lead roles. Finally, this sense of minorities (and, to some extent, women) as "background" also is evident in work on agency. Photographs of women and blacks portray them more as objects than as agents, video and audio news clips accord more agency to whites accused of crimes than to blacks, and agency—except for negative behaviors—is reserved for members of historically advantaged groups. The failure to include members of such groups, except in stereotypical roles or terms, perpetuates the separation of groups.

Perpetuation of Stereotypes

A second recurring theme throughout this volume deals with the perpetuation and transmission of stereotypes through various forms of
communication. Most directly, several empirical studies demonstrate
how the stereotypic beliefs of one individual or group can be passed
along to other group members. These studies often focus on the discussion of behaviors provided to participants by experimenters, but as
easily they might focus on storytelling and humor in more naturally
occurring conversations. Stereotypes of and prejudices against outgroup members are transmitted in everyday interactions. Jokes are
transmitted over the Internet; colleagues tell outrageous stories about
interactions with outgroup members; children observe their parents'
disgusted facial expressions as an outgroup member passes along the
street. At a less interpersonal level, films that support the beauty-is-
good stereotype further perpetuate its use, just as TV programs that
portray black characters in a stereotypic fashion or ingroup jokes that
portray women stereotypically encourage application of those respective stereotypes. Presumably, each time a stereotype is activated and
used, its accessibility is enhanced. Prejudiced communication is all
around—in interpersonal conversations, on television, on the Internet.
These diverse modes of communication may help keep stereotypes
and prejudices alive, kicking, and in the cultural consciousness.

Maintenance of Status Differences

Finally, one of the most pervasive themes is that prejudiced communication may help maintain existing status differences. According to the
general group dominance perspective, most societies are hierarchical,
and groups that enjoy the greatest privileges implicitly and explicitly
take pains to protect the hierarchy. Theoretically, this approach could
explain the stereotypic portrayals and underrepresentation of historically disadvantaged groups in the news, in advertising, and in television or film. Again, theoretically, this approach also might inform how
legislation on hate speech has proceeded in the United States. The
Fourteenth Amendment's assurance of equality continually is trumped
by the First Amendment's assurance of free speech. Hateful speech,
even indirect comments, can negatively affect recipients and observers
alike. Unfortunately, low-power recipients may have little recourse or
social support for retribution.

Status differences also are maintained by preferred cultural patterns for speech and nonverbal behavior. Members of the dominant
culture prefer speakers of the standard dialect and are prejudiced

against individuals whose nonverbal behaviors fail to mimic those of the dominant culture. Although empirical studies are limited in number, members of nondominant cultures seem more accepting of diversity in interaction patterns, perhaps because they often are pressured to become multidialectal and multicultural. Finally, higher-status individuals have touching privileges, have rights to larger and more idiosyncratic territories, have greater license to tell jokes, and can control the flow of conversation. They may patronize others with secondary baby talk or by using overly controlling talk. Outgroup members who attempt to assert their status are the most likely recipients of rude or negatively controlling speech, whereas outgroup members who "stay in their place" or are unable to assert themselves sweetly are treated like children. Like "man's darker brother," good outgroup members assimilate the customs of the ingroup but stay in their place.

WHAT NEXT?

Reducing Prejudiced Communication

There is little doubt that prejudiced communication can be hurtful. Many people are the recipients of presumptuous and patronizing speech, the recipients of hostile, ambiguous, or unhelpful feedback, and are ridiculed and assaulted by group-targeted humor and hate speech. Such individuals see their groups lampooned, ignored, and misrepresented by the major media. Diversity in nonverbal or speech patterns is not well tolerated and in some cases pressures to abandon the nonstandard language, dialect, nonverbal pattern, or manners of dress may be resented. Not everyone wishes to abandon his or her own culture in order to succeed within the dominant culture.

Because prejudice in communication largely involves behavior, some solutions may target changing the behavior itself; these solutions vary in the extent to which they treat the underlying causes of prejudiced communication. For example, hate speech legislation, such as campus speech codes or local ordinances, may reduce the use of prejudiced language in those locations. Ideally, the creation of speech codes raises consciousness about diversity, engenders dialogue about prejudice in society, and encourages people to examine their own personal prejudices. That is, at least for some individuals, such codes may help develop internal motivations to control prejudiced responding. Over time, individuals who become internally motivated to control prejudice— because it has become part of their self-concept to be nonprejudiced— spontaneously may speak in a nonprejudiced fashion. Both the symptom and the underlying cause are addressed.

But if a code or ordinance merely is an external motivator, the underlying cause of prejudiced communication remains untreated. Suppressing stereotypes of disliked groups, ironically, sometimes can increase the accessibility of those stereotypes (for a recent review see Monteith, Sherman, & Devine, 1998). In like fashion, constantly guarding against the use of prejudiced speech (e.g., hate speech, derogatory group epithets, group-targeted humor, or expressing a stereotypic belief), may increase the accessibility of stereotypes and increase the likelihood that such speech may be used. That is, when individuals are busy with the stressors and decisions of daily life, the ordinarily suppressed derogatory labels, group-targeted humor, and hateful symbols may rebound with a hurtful fury.

Along the same lines, simply teaching individuals to reduce their use of prejudiced language may not reduce the underlying beliefs. Language may provide a peek into cognitive representation, and language may even color or determine thought processes and concepts (e.g., Whorf's linguistic relativity hypothesis, 1957; for a review see Hardin & Banaji, 1993). But changing language does not necessarily change cognitive representation. Prentice (1994), for instance, conducted an experiment to examine whether teaching students to use gender-neutral language affected underlying gender imagery. On seven written reports submitted throughout the semester, the teaching assistant corrected half of the students whenever they used "he" as a generic singular. The assistant wrote a note about avoiding sexist language, and corrected the usage with "he or she." Over the course of the semester, corrected students' use of sexist language declined in the written assignments, and the use of sexist language even was attenuated on an unrelated sentence completion task. Whether the change affected their imagery, however, varied as a function of gender. When writing a short story on various themes (e.g., experiencing a travel delay during the holidays), women whose pronoun usage had been corrected generated less male imagery than women whose pronoun usage had not been corrected. But correction had little affect on men's imagery. For individuals whose ingroups benefit from a change in the language, and perhaps for individuals who are motivated to reduce their own prejudices, language change may be able to effect change in thought.

Given the possibility that changing language may not necessarily change underlying representations for everyone, to what extent have the more recent politically correct terms actually altered the ways that people think about members of historically disadvantaged groups? A person "presents with symptoms of schizophrenia," rather than being identified as "a schizophrenic"; another person is "visually impaired," rather than "blind"; and yet another "possesses a physical challenge," rather than being called "a paraplegic" or "a cripple." A black U.S. citizen alternatively might prefer to be called black, an African American, or a person of African descent. A Hispanic person might prefer to be called a Latino or Latina or may prefer reference to a specific nation. At least some of these expressions reflect efforts to be more precise or to make clear that what could be used as a overarching category label is instead one of many attributes. That is, the lengthy terms used in the contemporary politically correct climate may be intended to individuate the person. Whether they actually serve this function, especially if used without additional attributes, remains to be seen. Again, it may be that these terms change the perceptions of people who already are internally motivated to reduce their prejudices and have little affect of persons motivated only externally or who are not motivated at all.

Targeting nonverbal leakage also may not be particularly effective. Devine et al. (1996) suggest that, in the process of trying to "act normal," individuals low in prejudice may exacerbate the awkwardness of an interaction. For example, people who are worried about seeming prejudiced when talking to an outgroup member begin to worry about the right amount of eye contact, about selecting the right words, and what the outgroup member's failure to match their forward lean implies. As a result, people might display nonverbal behaviors that suggest low immediacy and produce speech that is rife with nonverbal vocalizations. The recipient may interpret the awkward behavior as reflecting underlying prejudice, rather than as a well-intended albeit botched effort to avoid prejudice. Popular and intuitively appealing programs such as diversity training need to include not only information as to the cultures of diverse groups and historical challenges faced by them; such programs also should include direct experience with individuals who display different interaction patterns, and should provide insight into what those patterns do and do not mean.

And then there is the issue of censorship. If descriptive and prescriptive stereotypic representations can elicit stereotypes, one solution sometimes proposed is censorship. In its most minimal form, censorship could involve pressure to avoid blatant stereotypic representations in the media, and pressure to include accurate and diverse representations. To some extent, economic and social pressure to influence media representations already exists (e.g., pressure to change the images of Aunt Jemima and Betty Crocker). In its more moderate form, some person or persons provide warnings of content that is potentially offensive to certain groups (adding yet another layer to the TV/movie warning lists!). And, in its extreme form, some official person or persons would ban stereotypic and prejudiced content from the mainstream media. Given that censorship largely treats symptoms of underlying prejudices and stereotypic beliefs, the disturbing task of identifying just who decides what content is acceptable, a task compounded by the fact that stereotypic and prejudiced communication is not limited to the major media, extreme censorship does not seem to be an ideal solution.

Filling Holes in the Research Picture

A re-examination of this volume finds a number of empirical "holes" that need filling.

First, and most simply, certain paradigms focus almost exclusively on specific target groups, without sufficient consideration of alternate groups. With the exception of foreigners, for example, verbal communication addressed toward ethnic outgroups is limited; the work on communication to elderly adults, however, is extensive. Whites may display nonverbal discomfort when speaking with blacks, but use of secondary baby talk or presumptuous speech toward blacks barely has been considered. Work on the news media and television, in contrast, focuses considerably on portrayals of blacks and only minimally on other groups. As the work of Fiske and colleagues (1999) indicates, outgroups are not simply interchangeable; some outgroups are disliked but considered competent whereas others are better liked but considered less competent, and perceiver judgments and treatments of such groups vary considerably. A broader sampling within paradigms, especially with a mind toward identifying underlying mechanisms such as threats to status, would help fill these gaps.

Second, a balance between naturalistic research in the field and experimental work is needed. The work on the development of shared stereotypes, including that of the present author, largely has been laboratory based. Other methods, such as sampling daily interactions, certainly need to be explored. Other work, especially on the news media, has oversampled archival and correlational techniques. And in Chapter 7 the analysis of archetypal themes largely reflects the present author's personal interpretations and inductive reasoning; to what extent these archetypes exist, their possible effects, and *why* they exist should be examined with accepted empirical methodologies.

Third, reading these diverse literatures, one largely has the impression of various disciplines and laboratories working on related problems but with only minimal awareness of each other's work. Mainstream social psychologists may not be particularly acquainted with the work on advertising; researchers examining the news media may be unaware of the general group dominance perspective; and some social cognition researchers may be unaware of the literatures on the preference for one's own accent and nonverbal patterns. This volume may provide some initial introductions to these different perspectives and encourage cross-disciplinary approaches.

Most pressing, however, is the need for theory building. Scholars (e.g., Maass, 1999) recognize that theories of prejudiced communication are sorely lacking. Even though some existing theories can be invoked to understand pieces of the puzzle, their foci of convenience may be too broad to stimulate empirical research on prejudiced communication per se. The general group dominance perspective, for example, may provide insight into why people from powerful groups limit lower-status groups' access to working within the major media, allow hate speech, or are neglectful mentors to members of lower-status groups. Similarly, speech accommodation theory predicts that people overaccomodate (e.g., use baby talk) or underaccomodate (e.g., insufficiently engage) based on their expectations, but the theory does not focus uniquely on stereotypic expectations or prejudices against the target group.

To be truly useful, a theory of prejudiced communication would need to consider the functions that prejudiced communication serves (e.g., social dominance, ego defensiveness), the mechanisms by which it operates (e.g., overaccommodation, nonverbal behavior, shared stereotype development, derogatory group epithets, transmission), as well as its effects on both targets and communicators. For example, certain functions may be best served by particular mechanisms: The social function of maintaining social barriers may encourage the development of shared stereotypes and group epithets, but not necessarily hate speech; ego-defensive functions may encourage group-targeted humor and hate speech, but not necessarily secondary baby talk. A theory would need to specify why and under what circumstances these relations hold. Alternatively, prejudiced communication may be too broad to allow for a single unified theory; even the development of several more specific theories (e.g., a theory concerned with nonverbal, verbal, and feedback-oriented communication addressed toward outgroup members; a theory concerned with the development of shared stereotypes) would be welcome. Continued interest in prejudiced communication foreshadows the development of such theories.

CONCLUSION

The main purpose of this volume was to pull together the diverse literatures that comprise prejudiced communication. Some clear themes emerge in these literatures, not only a heap of broken images. But the empirical and, more importantly, the theoretical gaps that remain suggest that researchers interested in prejudiced communication have their work cut out for them.

References

Academy of Motion Picture Arts & Sciences. (2000). Website available at: *ww3.oscars.org*

Academy of Television Arts & Sciences. (2000). Website available at: *www.emmys.org*

Alali, A. O. (1991). College newspaper editors' perceptions of how gay and lesbian issues are covered on their campus. *College Student Journal, 30,* 17–23.

Albas, D. C., McCluskey, K. W., & Albas, C. A. (1976). Perception of the emotional content of speech: A comparison of two Canadian groups. *Journal of Cross-Cultural Psychology, 7,* 481–489.

Alicke, M. D., LoSchiavo, F. M., Zerbst, J., & Zhang, S. (1997). The person who outperforms me is a genius: Maintaining perceived competence in upward social comparison. *Journal of Personality and Social Psychology, 73,* 781–789.

Allen, I. L. (1983). *The language of ethnic conflict: Social organization and lexical culture.* New York: Columbia University Press.

Allen, I. L. (1990). *Unkind words: Ethnic labeling from redskin to WASP.* New York: Bergin & Garvey.

Allport, G. W. (1989). *The nature of prejudice.* Reading, MA: Addison-Wesley. (Original work published 1954)

American Psychological Association. (1994). *Publication manual of the American Psychological Association* (4th ed.). Washington, DC: Author.

Andersen, S. M., Reznik, I., & Manzella, L. M. (1996). Eliciting facial affect, motivation, and expectancies in transference: Significant-other representations in social relations. *Journal of Personality and Social Psychology, 71,* 1108–1129.

Archer, D., Iritani, B., Kimes, D. D., & Barrios, M. (1983). Face-ism: Five studies of sex differences in facial prominence. *Journal of Personality and Social Psychology, 45,* 725–735.

Armstrong, G. B., Neuendorf, K. A., & Brentar, J. E. (1992). TV entertainment, news, and racial perceptions of college students. *Journal of Communication, 42*, 153–176.

Aron, A., Melinat, E., Aron, E. N., Vallone, R. D., & Bator, R. J. (1997). The experimental generation of interpersonal closeness: A procedure and some preliminary findings. *Personality and Social Psychology Bulletin, 23*, 363–377.

Babad, E., Bernieri, F., & Rosenthal, R. (1989). Nonverbal communication and leakage in the behavior of biased and unbiased teachers. *Journal of Personality and Social Psychology, 56*, 89–94.

Bailey, J. M., Bobrow, D., Wolfe, M., & Mikach, S. (1995). Sexual orientation of adult sons of gay fathers. *Developmental Psychology, 31*, 124–129.

Baron, R. A. (1988). Negative effects of destructive criticism: Impact on conflict, self-efficacy, and task performance. *Journal of Applied Psychology, 73*, 199–207.

Baron, R. A. (1990). Countering the effects of destructive criticism: The relative efficacy of four interventions. *Journal of Applied Psychology, 75*, 235–245.

Bar-Tal, D. (1989). Delegitimization: The extreme case of stereotyping and prejudice. In D. Bar-Tal, C. F. Graumann, A. W. Kruglanski, & W. Stroebe (Eds.), *Stereotyping and prejudice: Changing conceptions* (pp. 169–182). New York: Springer-Verlag.

Baynes, N. H. (Ed.). (1942). *The speeches of Adolf Hitler* (Vol. 1). Oxford, UK: Oxford University Press.

Bazzini, D. G., McIntosh, W. D., Smith, S. M., & Cook, S. (1997). The aging woman in popular film: Underrepresented, unattractive, unfriendly, and unintelligent. *Sex Roles, 36*, 531–543.

Beal, D. J., Ruscher, J. B., & Schnake, S. B. (in press). No benefit of the doubt: Intergroup bias and conversational convention. *British Journal of Social Psychology.*

Becker, T. E., & Klimoski, R. J. (1989). A field study of the relationship between the organizational feedback environment and performance. *Personnel Psychology, 42*, 343–358.

Bell, J. (1992). In search of a discourse on aging: The elderly on television. *Gerontologist, 32*, 305–311.

Ben-Ari, R., Schwarzwald, J., & Horiner-Levi, E. (1994). The effects of prevalent social stereotypes on intergroup attribution. *Journal of Cross-Cultural Psychology, 25*, 489–500.

Berger, J., Wagner, D. G., & Zelditch, M. Jr. (1985). Introduction: Expectation states theory—Review and assessment. In J. Berger & M. Zelditch, Jr. (Eds.), *Status, rewards, and influence: How expectations organize behavior* (pp. 1–72). San Francisco: Jossey-Bass.

Biernat, M., & Kobrynowicz, D. (1997). Gender- and race-based standards of competence: Lower minimum standards but higher ability standards for devalued groups. *Journal of Personality and Social Psychology, 72*, 544–557.

Bishop, G. D. (1979). Perceived similarity in interracial attitudes and behaviors: The effects of belief and dialect style. *Journal of Applied Social Psychology, 9*, 446–465.

Blanchard, F. A., Crandall, C. S., Brigham, J. C., & Vaughn, L. A. (1994). Condemning and condoning racism: A social context approach to interracial settings. *Journal of Applied Psychology, 79,* 993–997.

Blanchard, F. A., Lilly, T., & Vaughn, L. A. (1991). Reducing the expression of racial prejudice. *Psychological Science, 2,* 101–105.

Blascovich, J., Wyer, N., Swart, L. A., & Kibler, J. L. (1997). Racism and racial categorization. *Journal of Personality and Social Psychology, 72,* 1364–1372.

Bodenhausen, G. V., & Wyer, R. S. (1985). Effects of stereotypes on decision making and information-processing strategies. *Journal of Personality and Social Psychology, 48,* 267–282.

Bourhis, R. Y., Giles, H., Leyens, J.-P., & Tajfel, H. (1979). Psycholinguistic distinctiveness: Language divergence in Belgium. In H. Giles & R. St. Clair (Eds.), *Language and social psychology* (pp. 158–185). Oxford, UK: Blackwell.

Bourhis, R. Y., Giles, H., & Tajfel, H. (1973). Language as a determinant of Welsh identity. *European Journal of Social Psychology, 3,* 447–460.

Bradac, J. J. (1990). Language attitudes and impression formation. In H. Giles & W. P. Robinson (Eds.), *The handbook of language and social psychology* (pp. 387–412). New York: Wiley.

Brennan, K. A., & Shaver, P. R. (1995). Dimensions of adult attachment, affect regulation, and romantic relationship functioning. *Personality and Social Psychology Bulletin, 21,* 267–283.

Brewer, M. B., & Brown, R. J. (1998). Intergroup relations. In D. T. Gilbert, S. T. Fiske, & G. Lindzey (Eds.), *The handbook of social psychology* (4th ed., pp. 554–594). New York: Oxford University Press.

Brewer, M. B., Dull, V., & Lui, L. (1981). Perceptions of the elderly: Stereotypes as prototypes. *Journal of Personality and Social Psychology, 41,* 656–670.

Brewer, M. B., & Harasty, A. S. (1996). Seeing groups as entities: The role of perceiver intent. In R. M. Sorrentino & E. T. Higgins (Eds.), *Handbook of motivation and cognition: Vol. 3. The interpersonal context* (pp. 347–370). New York: Guilford Press.

Brewer, N., Socha, L., & Potter, R. (1996). Gender differences in supervisors' use of performance feedback. *Journal of Applied Psychology, 26,* 786–803.

Brigham, J. C. (1971). Ethnic stereotypes. *Psychological Bulletin, 76,* 15–38.

Brown, C. E., Dovidio, J. F., & Ellyson, S. L. (1990). Reducing sex differences in visual displays of dominance: Knowledge is power. *Personality and Social Psychology Bulletin, 16,* 358–368.

Brown, J. D., Schmidt, G. W., & Collins, R. L. (1988). Personal involvement and the evaluation of group products. *European Journal of Social Psychology, 18,* 177–179.

Brown, R., & Fish, D. (1983). The psychological causality implicit in language. *Cognition, 14,* 237–273.

Burgoon, J. K. (1991). Relational message interpretations of touch, conversational distance, and posture. *Journal of Nonverbal Behavior, 15,* 233–259.

Butler, M., & Paisley, W. (1978). Magazine coverage of women's rights. *Journal of Communication, 28,* 183–186.

Byrne, D. (1971). *The attraction paradigm.* New York: Academic Press.

Cansler, D. C., & Stiles, W. B. (1981). Relative status and interpersonal presumptuousness. *Journal of Experimental Social Psychology, 17,* 459–471.

Cantor, J. R. (1976). What is funny to whom. *Journal of Communication, 26,* 164–172.

Caplan, L. S., Wells, B. L., & Haynes, S. (1992). Breast cancer screening among older racial/ethnic minorities and whites: Barriers to early detection. *Journal of Gerontology, 47,* 101–110.

Caporael, L. R. (1981). The paralanguage of caregiving: Baby talk to the institutionalized aged. *Journal of Personality and Social Psychology, 40,* 876–884.

Caporael, L. R., Lukaszewski, M. P., & Culbertson, G. H. (1983). Secondary baby talk: Judgments by institutionalized elderly and their caregivers. *Journal of Personality and Social Psychology, 44,* 746–754.

Cargile, A. C. (1997). Attitudes toward Chinese-accented speech: An investigation in two contexts. *Journal of Language and Social Psychology, 16,* 434–443.

Cash, T. F., & Trimer, C. A. (1984). Sexism and beautyism in women's evaluation of peer performance. *Sex Roles, 10,* 87–98.

Chafe, W. L. (1979). The flow of thought and the flow of language. In T. Givon (Ed.), *Syntax and semantics: Vol. 12. Discourse and syntax* (pp. 159–181). New York: Academic Press.

Cheney, D. L., & Seyfarth, R. M. (1982). How vervet monkeys perceive their grunts: Field playback experiments. *Animal Behavior, 30,* 739–751.

Cheyne, W. (1970). Stereotyped reactions to speakers with Scottish and English regional accents. *British Journal of Social and Clinical Psychology, 9,* 77–79.

Christenfeld, N. J. S. (1995). Does it hurt to say um? *Journal of Nonverbal Behavior, 19,* 171–186.

Christenfeld, N. J. S., & Creager, B. (1996). Anxiety, alcohol, aphasia, and *ums. Journal of Personality and Social Psychology, 70,* 451–460.

Cialdini, R. B., Borden, R. J., Thorne, A., Walker, M. R., Freeman, S., & Sloan, L. R. (1976). Basking in reflected glory: Three (football) field studies. *Journal of Personality and Social Psychology, 34,* 366–375.

Clark, H. H., & Brennan, S. E. (1991). Grounding in communication. In L. B. Resnick, J. M. Levine, & S. D. Teasley (Eds.), *Perspectives on socially shared cognition* (pp. 127–149). Washington, DC: American Psychological Association.

Cole, C. M., Hill, F. A., & Dayley, L. J. (1983). Do masculine pronouns used generically lead to thoughts of men. *Sex Roles, 9,* 737–750.

Cole, T., & Leets, L. (1998). Linguistic masking devices and intergroup behavior: Further evidence of an intergroup linguistic bias. *Journal of Language and Social Psychology, 17,* 348–371.

Conway, L. G., & Schaller, M. (1998). Methods for the measurement of consensual beliefs within groups. *Group Dynamics: Theory, Research, and Practice, 2,* 1–12.

Coovert, M. D., & Reeder, G. D. (1990). Negativity effects in impression formation: The role of unit formation and schematic expectations. *Journal of Experimental Social Psychology, 26,* 49–62.

Cowan, G., & Hodge, C. (1996). Judgments of hate speech: The effects of target group, publicness, and behavioral responses of the target. *Journal of Applied Social Psychology, 26,* 355–374.

Craig, R. S. (1992). The effect of television day part on gender portrayals in television commercials: A content analysis. *Sex Roles, 26,* 197–211.

Cralley, E. L., & Ruscher, J. B. (2000). *The joke backfires: "Harmless" assertions about the ingroup may lead to increased stereotyping by the outgroup.* Unpublished manuscript, Tulane University, New Orleans, LA.

Crocker, J., & Luhtanen, R. (1990). Collective self-esteem and ingroup bias. *Journal of Personality and Social Psychology, 58,* 60–67.

Crocker, J., Voelkl, K., Testa, M., & Major, B. (1991). Social stigma: The affective consequences of attributional ambiguity. *Journal of Personality and Social Psychology, 60,* 218–228.

Cummings, L. P., & Ruscher, J. B. (1994). Resolving internal discrepancies impairs communicators' recognition memory: A linguistic perspective. *Social Cognition, 12,* 205–222.

Daniel, J. L., & Allen, A. L. (1988). Newsmagazines, public policy, and the black agenda. In G. Smitherman-Donaldson & T. A. van Dijk (Eds.), *Discourse and discrimination* (pp. 23–45). Detroit, MI: Wayne State University Press.

Darke, P. R., Chaiken, S., Bohner, G., Einwiller, S., Erb, H. P., & Hazlewood, J. D. (1998). Accuracy motivation, consensus information, and the law of large numbers: Effects on attitude judgment in the absence of argumentation. *Personality and Social Psychology Bulletin, 24,* 1205–1215.

Darling-Wolf, F. (1997). Framing the breast implant controversy: A feminist critique. *Journal of Communication Inquiry, 21,* 77–97.

de la Zerda, N., & Hopper, R. (1979). Employment interviewers' reactions to Mexican American speech. *Communication Monographs, 46,* 126–134.

DePaulo, B. M. (1998). Nonverbal communication. In D. T. Gilbert, S. T. Fiske, & G. Lindzey (Eds.), *The handbook of social psychology* (4th ed., pp. 3–40). New York: Oxford University Press.

DePaulo, B. M., & Coleman, L. M. (1986). Talking to children, foreigners, and retarded adults. *Journal of Personality and Social Psychology, 51,* 945–959.

DePaulo, B. M., & Coleman, L. M. (1987). Verbal and nonverbal communication of warmth to children, foreigners, and retarded adults. *Journal of Nonverbal Behavior, 11,* 73–88.

DePaulo, B. M., Zuckerman, M., & Rosenthal, R. (1980). Humans as lie-detectors. *Journal of Communication, 30,* 129–139.

Devine, P. G. (1989). Stereotypes and prejudice: Their automatic and controlled components. *Journal of Personality and Social Psychology, 56,* 5–18.

Devine, P. G., Evett, S. R., & Vasquez-Suson, K. A. (1996). Exploring the interpersonal dynamics of intergroup contact. In R. M. Sorrentino & E. T. Higgins (Eds.), *Handbook of motivation and cognition: Vol 3. The interpersonal context* (pp. 423–464). New York: Guilford Press.

Dew, A., & Ward, C. (1993). The effects of ethnicity and culturally congruent and incongruent nonverbal behaviors on interpersonal attraction. *Journal of Applied Social Psychology, 23,* 1376–1389.

Dews, S., Kaplan, J., & Winner, E. (1995). Why not say it directly?: The social functions of irony. *Discourse Processes, 19,* 347–367.

Dijker, A. J. M. (1987). Emotional reactions to ethnic minorities. *European Journal of Social Psychology, 17,* 305–325.

Dion, K. L., & Dion, K. K. (1987). Belief in a just world and physical attractiveness stereotyping. *Journal of Personality and Social Psychology, 52,* 775–780.

Doise, W., Sinclair, A., & Bourhis, R. Y. (1976). Evaluation of accent convergence and divergence in cooperative and competitive intergroup situations. *British Journal of Social and Clinical Psychology, 15,* 247–252.

Doosje, B., Ellemers, N., & Spears, R. (1995). Perceived intragroup variability as a function of group status and identification. *Journal of Experimental Social Psychology, 31,* 410–436.

Dovidio, J. F., Ellyson, S. L., Keating, C. F., Heltman, K., & Brown, C. E. (1988). The relationship of social power to visual displays of dominance between men and women. *Journal of Personality and Social Psychology, 54,* 233–242.

Dovidio, J. F., Smith, J. K., Donnella, A. G., & Gaertner, S. L. (1997). Racial attitudes and the death penalty. *Journal of Applied Social Psychology, 27,* 1468–1487.

Dreher, G. F., & Cox, T. H. (1996). Race, gender, and opportunity: A study of compensation attainment and the establishment of mentoring relationships. *Journal of Applied Psychology, 81,* 297–308.

Dreyer, A. S., Dreyer, C. A., & Davis, J. E. (1987). Individuality and mutuality in the language of families of field-dependent and field-independent children. *Journal of Genetic Psychology, 148,* 105–117.

Dunton, B. C., & Fazio, R. H. (1997). An individual difference measure of motivation to control prejudiced reactions. *Personality and Social Psychology Bulletin, 23,* 316–326.

Duval, L. L., & Ruscher, J. B. (1994, July). *Men use more detail to explain a gender-neutral task to women.* Poster presented at the annual meeting of the American Psychological Society, Washington, DC.

Duval, L. L., Ruscher, J. B., Welsh, K., & Catanese, S. P. (2000). Bolstering and undercutting use of the elderly stereotype through communication of stereotypic and counterstereotypic exemplars: The role of speaker age. *Basic and Applied Social Psychology, 22,* 137–146.

Eagly, A. H., & Crowley, M. (1986). Gender and helping behavior: A meta-analytic review of the social psychological literature. *Psychological Bulletin, 100,* 283–308.

Ekman, P., & Friesen, W. V. (1978). *Facial action coding system: A technique for the measurement of facial movement.* Palo Alto, CA: Consulting Psychologists Press.

Ekman, P., & O'Sullivan, M. (1991). Facial expression: Method, means, and moues. In R. S. Feldman & B. Rimé (Eds.), *Fundamentals of nonverbal behavior* (pp. 163–199). New York: Cambridge University Press.

Entman, R. M. (1992). Blacks in the news: Television, modern racism, and cultural change. *Journalism Quarterly, 69,* 341–361.

Entman, R. M. (1994). Representation and reality in the portrayal of blacks on network television news. *Journalism Quarterly, 71,* 509–520.

Fajardo, L. L., Saint-Germain, M., Meakem, T. J., Rose, C., & Hillman, B. J. (1992). Factors influencing women to undergo screening mammography. *Radiology, 184,* 59–63.

Fang, C. Y., Sidanius, J., & Pratto, F. (1998). Romance across the social status continuum: Interracial marriage and the ideological asymmetry effect. *Journal of Cross Cultural Psychology, 29,* 290–305.

Fazio, R. H. (1986). How do attitudes guide behavior? In R. M. Sorrentino & E.

T. Higgins (Eds.), *Handbook of motivation and cognition: Foundations of social behavior* (Vol. 1, pp. 204–243). New York: Guilford Press.

Fazio, R. H. (1990). Multiple processes by which attitudes guide behavior: The MODE model as an integrative framework. In M. P. Zanna (Ed.), *Advances in experimental social psychology* (Vol. 23, pp. 75–110). San Diego, CA: Academic Press.

Feingold, A. (1992). Good-looking people are not what we think. *Psychological Bulletin, 111,* 304–341.

Feldman, R. S. (1985). Nonverbal behavior, race, and the classroom teacher. *Theory into Practice, 24,* 45–49.

Feldman, R. S., & Donahoe, L. F. (1978). Nonverbal communication of affect in interracial dyads. *Journal of Educational Psychology, 70,* 979–987.

Feldman, R. S., & Orchowsky, S. (1979). Race and performance of student as determinants of teacher nonverbal behavior. *Contemporary Educational Psychology, 4,* 324–333.

Ferguson, C. A. (1979). Baby talk as a simplified register. In C. E. Snow & C. A. Ferguson (Eds.), *Talking to children: Language input and acquisition* (pp. 209–235). Cambridge, UK: Cambridge University Press.

Festinger, L. (1954). A theory of social comparison processes. *Human Relations, 7,* 117–140.

Finkelstein, L. M., Burke, M. J., & Raju, N. S. (1995). Age discrimination in simulated employment contexts: An integrative analysis. *Journal of Applied Psychology, 80,* 652–663.

Fischer, G. (1997). Gender effects on individual verdicts and on mock jury verdicts in a simulated acquaintance rape trial. *Sex Roles, 36,* 491–501.

Fiske, S. T. (1980). Attention and weight in person perception: The impact of negative and extreme behavior. *Journal of Personality and Social Psychology, 38,* 889–906.

Fiske, S. T. (1989). Examining the role of intent: Toward understanding its role in stereotyping and prejudice. In J. S. Uleman & J. A. Bargh (Eds.), *Unintended thought* (pp. 253–283). New York: Guilford Press.

Fiske, S. T. (1998). Stereotyping, prejudice, and discrimination. In D. T. Gilbert, S. T. Fiske, & G. Lindzey (Eds.), *The handbook of social psychology* (4th ed., pp. 357–411). New York: Oxford University Press.

Fiske, S. T., Bersoff, D., Borgida, E., Deaux, K., & Heilman, M. (1991). Social science research on trial: Use of sex stereotyping research in *Price Waterhouse v. Hopkins. American Psychologist, 46,* 1049–1060.

Fiske, S. T., & Neuberg, S. L. (1990). A continuum model of impression formation from category-based to individuating processes: Influence of information and motivation on attention and interpretation. In M. P. Zanna (Ed.), *Advances in experimental social psychology* (Vol. 23, pp. 1–74). New York: Academic Press.

Fiske, S. T., & Ruscher, J. B. (1993). Negative interdependence and prejudice: Whence the affect? In D. M. Mackie & D. L. Hamilton (Eds.), *Affect, cognition, and stereotyping: Interactive processes in group perception* (pp. 239–268). San Diego, CA: Academic Press.

Fiske, S. T., & Stevens, L. E. (1993). What's so special about sex?: Gender stereotyping and discrimination. In S. Oskamp & M. Costanzo (Eds.), *Claremont symposium on applied social psychology: Vol. 6. Gender issues in contemporary society* (pp. 173–196). Newbury Park, CA: Sage.

Fiske, S. T., & Taylor, S. E. (1991). *Social cognition* (2nd ed.). New York: McGraw-Hill.

Fiske, S. T., & Von Hendy, H. H. M. (1992). Personality feedback and situational norms can control stereotyping processes. *Journal of Personality and Social Psychology, 62,* 577–596.

Fiske, S. T., Xu, J., Cuddy, A. C., & Glick, P. S. (1999). (Dis)respecting versus (dis)liking: Status and interdependence predict ambivalent stereotypes of competence and warmth. *Journal of Social Issues, 55,* 473–489.

Fleming, J. H. (1994). Multiple-audience problems, tactical communication, and social interaction: A relational-regulation perspective. In M. P. Zanna (Ed.), *Advances in experimental social psychology* (Vol. 26, pp. 215–292). San Diego, CA: Academic Press.

Foertsch, J., & Gernsbacher, M. A. (1997). In search of gender neutrality: Is singular *they* a cognitively efficient substitute for generic *he*? *Psychological Science, 8,* 106–111.

Ford, T. E. (1997). Effects of stereotypical television portrayals of African-Americans on person perception. *Social Psychology Quarterly, 60,* 267–278.

Franco, F. M., & Maass, A. (1996). Implicit versus explicit strategies of out-group discrimination: The role of intentional control in biased language use and reward allocation. *Journal of Language and Social Psychology, 15,* 335–359.

Frey, D. L., & Gaertner, S. L. (1986). Helping and the avoidance of inappropriate interracial behavior: A strategy that perpetuates a non-prejudiced self-image. *Journal of Personality and Social Psychology, 50,* 1083–1090.

Fromkin, V., & Rodman, R. (1988). *An introduction to language* (4th ed.). New York: Holt.

Funder, D. C. (1987). Errors and mistakes: Evaluating the accuracy of social judgment. *Psychological Bulletin, 101,* 75–90.

Gaertner, S. L. (1973). Helping behavior and racial discrimination among liberals and conservatives. *Journal of Personality and Social Psychology, 25,* 335–341.

Gaertner, S. L., & Bickman, L. (1971). The effects of race on the elicitation of helping behavior: The wrong number technique. *Journal of Personality and Social Psychology, 20,* 218–222.

Galliker, M. (1996). Delegitimization of migrants in media discourse. Co-occurence analysis of three years of a daily paper with CD–ROMs as a data source. *Koelner Zeitschrift fuer Soziologie und Sozialpsychologie, 48,* 704–727.

Gandy, O. H. (1996). If it weren't for bad luck: Framing stories of racially comparative risk. In V. T. Berry & C. L. Manning-Miller (Eds.), *Mediated messages and African-American culture* (pp. 55–75). Thousand Oaks, CA: Sage.

Gandy, O. H., & Baron, J. (1998). Inequality: It's all in the way you look at it. *Communication Research, 25,* 505–527.

Gandy, O. H., Kopp, K., Hands, T., Frazer, K., & Phillips, D. (1997). Race and risk: Factors affecting the framing of stories about inequality, discrimination, and just plain bad luck. *Public Opinion Quarterly, 61,* 158–182.

Gardner, R. C. (1994). Stereotypes as consensual beliefs. In M. P. Zanna & J. M. Olson (Eds.), *The Ontario symposium: Vol. 7. The psychology of prejudice* (pp. 1–31). Hillsdale, NJ: Erlbaum.

Gardner, R. C., Kirby, D. M., & Finlay, J. C. (1973). Ethnic stereotypes: The significance of consensus. *Canadian Journal of Behavioural Science, 5,* 4–12.

Georgesen, J. C., & Harris, M. J. (1998). Why's my boss always holding me down?: A meta-analysis of power effects on performance evaluations. *Personality and Social Psychology Review, 2,* 184–195.

Gibbons, F. X., & McCoy, S. B. (1991). Self-esteem, similarity, and reactions to active versus passive downward comparison. *Journal of Personality and Social Psychology, 60,* 414–424.

Gilbert, D. T. (1991). How mental systems believe. *American Psychologist, 46,* 107–119.

Gilbert, G. M. (1951). Stereotype persistence and change among college students. *Journal of Abnormal and Social Psychology, 46,* 245–254.

Gilens, M. (1996). Race and poverty in America: Public misperceptions and the American news media. *Public Opinion Quarterly, 60,* 515–541.

Giles, H., Coupland, N., & Coupland, J. (1991). Accommodation theory: Communication, context, and consequence. In H. Giles, J. Coupland, & N. Coupland (Eds.), *Contexts of accommodation: Developments in applied sociolinguistics* (pp. 1–68). New York: Cambridge University Press.

Giles, H., & Williams, A. (1994). Patronizing the young: Forms and evaluations. *International Journal of Aging and Human Development, 39,* 33–53.

Gilovich, T. (1987). Secondhand information and social judgment. *Journal of Experimental Social Psychology, 23,* 59–74.

Glick, P., & Fiske, S. T. (1996). The ambivalent sexism inventory: Differentiating hostile and benevolent sexism. *Journal of Personality and Social Psychology, 70,* 461–512.

Goffman, E. (1976). *Gender advertisements.* New York: Harper & Row.

Graumann, C. F., & Wintermantel, M. (1989). Discriminatory speech acts: A functional approach. In D. Bar-Tal, C. F. Graumann, A. W. Kruglanski, & W. Stroebe (Eds.), *Stereotyping and prejudice: Changing conceptions* (pp. 183–204). New York: Springer-Verlag.

Greenbaum, P. E. (1985). Nonverbal differences in communication style between American Indian and Anglo elementary classrooms. *American Educational Research Journal, 22,* 101–115.

Greenberg, B. S., & Atkin, C. K. (1982). Learning about minorities from television: A research agenda. In G. J. Berry and C. Mitchell-Kernan (Eds.), *Television and the socialization of the minority child* (pp. 215–243). Los Angeles: Academic Press.

Greenberg, B. S., & Baptista-Fernandez, P. (1980). Hispanic-Americans: The new minority on television. In B. S. Greenberg, *Life on television: Content analyses of U.S. TV drama* (pp. 3–12). Norwood, NJ: Ablex.

Greenberg, J., Kirkland, S. L., & Pyszczynski, T. (1988). Some theoretical notions and preliminary research concerning derogatory ethnic labels. In G.

Smitherman-Donaldson & T. A. van Dijk (Eds.), *Discourse and discrimination* (pp. 74–92). Detroit, MI: Wayne State University Press.

Greenberg, J., & Pyszczynski, T. (1985). The effects of an overheard ethnic slur on evaluations of the target: How to spread a social disease. *Journal of Experimental Social Psychology, 21*, 61–72.

Greenberg, J., Pyszczynski, T., Solomon, S., Rosenblatt, A., Veeder, M., Kirkland, S., & Lyon, D. (1990). Evidence for terror management theory: II. The effects of mortality salience on reactions to those who threaten or bolster the cultural worldview. *Journal of Personality and Social Psychology, 58*, 308–318.

Gresham, F. M. (1984). Misguided mainstreaming: The case for social skills training with handicapped children. *Exceptional Children, 51*, 253–261.

Grice, H. P. (1975). Logic and conversation. In P. Cole & J. L. Morgan (Eds.), *Syntax and semantics: Speech acts* (Vol. 3, pp. 225–242). New York: Seminar Press.

Griffin, D., & Gonzalez, R. (1995). Correlational analysis of dyad-level data in the exchangeable case. *Psychological Bulletin, 118*, 430–439.

Guglielmi, R. S. (1999). Psychophysiological assessment of prejudice: Past research, current status, and future directions. *Personality and Social Psychology Review, 3*, 123–157.

Guimond, S. (2000). Group socialization and prejudice: The social transmission of intergroup attitudes and beliefs. *European Journal of Social Psychology, 30*, 335–354.

Guimond, S., & Palmer, D. L. (1996). The political socialization of commerce and social science students: Epistemic authority and attitude change. *Journal of Applied Social Psychology, 26*, 1985–2013.

Gunther, A. C. (1998). The persuasive press inference: Effects of mass media on perceived public opinion. *Communication Research, 25*, 486–504.

Hall, J. A. (1996). Touch, status, and gender at professional meetings. *Journal of Nonverbal Behavior, 20*, 23–44.

Hamilton, E. L., & Gifford, R. K. (1976). Illusory correlation in interpersonal perception: A cognitive basis of stereotypic judgments. *Journal of Experimental Social Psychology, 12*, 392–407.

Hamilton, M. C. (1988). Masculine generic terms and misperception of AIDS risk. *Journal of Applied Social Psychology, 18*, 1222–1240.

Hammer, E. D. (1996, July). *Low-prejudiced perceivers need cognitive capacity to moderate initial stereotypic dispositional attributions.* Poster presented at the annual meeting of the American Psychological Society, San Francisco, CA.

Hammer, E. D., & Ruscher, J. B. (1997). Conversing dyads explain the unexpected: Narrative and situational explanations for unexpected outcomes. *British Journal of Social Psychology, 36*, 347–360.

Hanna, J. L. (1984). Black/white nonverbal differences, dance, and dissonance: Implications for desegregation. In A. Wolfgang (Ed.), *Nonverbal behavior* (pp. 373–409). Toronto, Ontario, Canada: Hogrefe.

Harasty, A. S. (1997). The interpersonal nature of social stereotypes: Differential discussion patterns about in-groups and out-groups. *Personality and Social Psychology Bulletin, 23*, 270–284.

Harber, K. D. (1998): Feedback to minorities: Evidence of a positive bias. *Journal of Personality and Social Psychology, 74,* 622–628.

Hardin, C. D., & Higgins, E. T. (1996). Shared reality: How social verification makes the subjective objective. In R. M. Sorrentino & E. T. Higgins (Eds.), *Handbook of motivation and cognition: Vol. 3. The interpersonal context* (pp. 28–84). New York: Guilford Press.

Hardin, D. D., & Banaji, M. (1993). The influence of language on thought. *Social Cognition, 11,* 277–308.

Harrigan, J. A., & Lucic, K. S. (1988). Attitudes about gender bias in language: A reevaluation. *Sex Roles, 19,* 129–140.

Harris, M. J., Moniz, A. J., Sowards, B. A., & Krane, K. (1994). Mediation of interpersonal expectancy effects: Expectancies about the elderly. *Social Psychology Quarterly, 57,* 36–48.

Harris, R. J., & Monaco, G. E.(1978). Psychology of pragmatic implication: Information processing between the lines. *Journal of Experimental Psychology: General, 107,* 1–27.

Harrison-Speake, K., & Willis, F. N. (1995). Ratings of the appropriateness of touch among family members. *Journal of Nonverbal Behavior, 19,* 85–100.

Haslam, S. A., Turner, J. C., Oakes, P. J., McGarty, C., & Reynolds, K. J. (1998). The group as a basis for emergent stereotype consensus. In W. Stroebe & M. Hewstone (Eds.), *European review of social psychology* (Vol. 8, pp. 203–239). Chichester, West Sussex, UK: Wiley.

Hastorf, A. H., & Cantril, H. (1990). They saw a game: A case study. In A. G. Halberstadt & S. L. Ellyson (Eds.), *Social psychology readings: A century of research* (pp. 89–95). New York: McGraw-Hill. (Original work published 1954)

Hecht, M. A., & LaFrance, M. (1998). License or obligation to smile: The effect of power and sex on amount and type of smiling. *Personality and Social Psychology Bulletin, 24,* 1332–1342.

Heilman, M. E., Lucas, J. A., & Kaplow, S. R. (1990). Self-derogating consequences of preferential selection: The moderating role of initial confidence. *Organizational Behavior and Human Decision Processes, 46,* 202–216.

Hemmasi, M., Graf, L. A., & Russ, G. S. (1994). Gender-related jokes in the workplace: Sexual humor or sexual harassment. *Journal of Applied Social Psychology, 24,* 1114–1128.

Henderson-King, E. I., & Nisbett, R. E. (1996). Anti-black prejudice as a function of exposure to the negative behavior of a single black person. *Journal of Personality and Social Psychology, 71,* 654–664.

Henley, N. M. (1973). *Body politics: Power, sex, and nonverbal communication.* Englewood Cliffs, NJ: Prentice-Hall.

Henley, N. M. (1995). Body politics revisited: What do we know today? In P. J. Kalbfleisch & M. J. Cody (Eds.), *Gender, power, and communication in human relationships* (pp. 27–61). Hillsdale, NJ: Erlbaum.

Henley, N. M., & Harmons, S. (1985). The nonverbal semantics of power and gender: A perceptual study. In S. L. Ellyson & J. F. Dovidio (Eds.), *Power, dominance, and nonverbal behavior* (pp. 151–164). New York: Springer-Verlag.

Henley, N. M., Miller, M., & Beazley, J. A. (1995). Syntax, semantics, and sexual violence: Agency and the passive voice. *Journal of Language and Social Psychology, 14,* 6–84.

Henley, N. M., Miller, M. D., Beazley, J. A., Nguyen, D. N., & Kaminsky, D. (1997). *More studies in the discourse of violence: Noun usage and sexual orientation*. Paper presented at the International Conference on Language and Social Psychology, Ottawa, Canada.

Heumann, M., & Church, T. W. (1997). *Hate speech on campus: Cases, case studies, and commentary*. Boston: Northeastern University Press.

Hewstone, M., Gale, L., & Purkhardt, N. (1990). Intergroup attributions for success and failure: Group-serving bias and group-serving causal schemata. *European Bulletin of Cognitive Psychology, 10,* 23–44.

Hewstone, M., Jaspars, J., & Lalljee, M. (1982). Social representation, social attribution and social identity: Intergroup images of "public" and "comprehensive" schools. *European Journal of Social Psychology, 18,* 241–269.

Higgins, E. T. (1981). The "communication game": Implications for social cognition and persuasion. In E. T. Higgins, C. P. Herman, & M. P. Zanna (Eds.), *The Ontario Symposium: Vol. 1. Social cognition* (pp. 343–392). Hillsdale, NJ: Erlbaum.

Higgins, E. T., & Rholes, W. S. (1978). "Saying is believing": Effects of message modification on memory and liking for the person described. *Journal of Experimental Social Psychology, 14,* 363–378.

Hoffstetter, C. R., Schultze, W. A., Mahoney, S. M., & Buss, T. F. (1993). The elderly's perception of TV ageist stereotyping: TV or contextual aging? *Communication Reports, 6,* 92–100.

Hogben, M., & Waterman, C. K. (1997). Are all of your students represented in their textbooks?: A content analysis of coverage of diversity issues in introductory psychology textbooks. *Teaching of Psychology, 24,* 95–100.

Hogg, M. A., & Hains, S. C. (1998). Friendship and group identification: A new look at the role of cohesiveness in groupthink. *European Journal of Social Psychology, 28,* 323–341.

Howard, J., & Rothbart, M. (1980). Social categorization and memory for ingroup and outgroup behavior. *Journal of Personality and Social Psychology, 57,* 165–188.

Huffcutt, A. I., & Roth, P. L. (1998). Racial group differences in employment interview evaluations. *Journal of Applied Psychology, 83,* 179–189.

Hummert, M. L. (1994). Physiognomic cues to age and the activation of stereotypes of the elderly in interaction. *International Journal of Aging and Human Development, 39,* 5–19.

Hummert, M. L., Garstka, T. A., Shaner, J. L., & Strahm, S. (1995). Judgments about stereotypes of the elderly: Attitudes, age associations, and typicality ratings of young, middle-aged, and elderly adults. *Research on Aging, 17,* 168–189.

Hummert, M. L., & Ryan, E. B. (1996). Toward understanding variations in patronizing talk addressed to older adults: Psycholinguistic features of care and control. *International Journal of Psycholinguistics, 12,* 149–169.

Hyde, J. S. (1984). Children's understanding of sexist language. *Developmental Psychology, 20,* 697–706.

Ilgen, D. R., Peterson, R. B., Martin, B. A., & Boeschen, D. A. (1981). Supervisor and subordinate reactions to performance appraisal sessions. *Organizational Behavior and Human Decision Processes, 28,* 311–330.

Jackson, L. A., Sullivan, L. A., & Hodge, C. N. (1993). Stereotype effects of attributions, predictions, and evaluations: No two social judgments are quite alike. *Journal of Personality and Social Psychology, 65,* 69–84.

Jennings-Walstedt, J., Geis, F. L., & Brown, V. (1980). Influence of television commercials on women's self-confidence and independent judgment. *Journal of Personality and Social Psychology, 38,* 203–210.

Jensen, R. (1996). The politics and ethics of lesbian and gay "wedding" announcements in newspapers. *Howard Journal of Communications, 7,* 13–28.

Jetten, J., Spears, R., & Manstead, A. S. R. (1996). Intergroup norms and intergroup discrimination: Distinctive self-categorization and social identity effects. *Journal of Personality and Social Psychology, 71,* 1222–1233.

Johnson, D. W., Johnson, R. T., & Maruyama, G. (1984). Goal interdependence and interpersonal attraction in heterogeneous classrooms: A meta-analysis. In N. Miller & M. B. Brewer (Eds.), *Groups in contact: The psychology of desegregation* (pp. 187–212). London: Academic Press.

Jones, E. E., & Davis, K. E.(1965). From acts to dispositions: The attribution process in person perception. In L. Berkowitz (Ed.), *Advances in experimental social psychology* (Vol. 2, pp. 220–266). New York: Academic Press.

Jones, E. E., Farina, A., Hastorf, A. H., Markus, H., Miller, D. T., & Scott, R. A. (1984). *Social stigma: The psychology of marked relationships.* New York: Freeman.

Jones, M. (1997). Preventing the application of stereotypic biases in the courtroom: The role of detailed testimony. *Journal of Applied Social Psychology, 27,* 1767–1784.

Jupp, T., Roberts, C., & Cook-Gumperz, J. (1982). Language and disadvantage: The hidden process. In J. Gumperz (Ed.), *Language and social identity* (pp. 232–256). Cambridge, UK: Cambridge University Press.

Jussim, L., Eccles, J., & Madon, S. (1996). Social perception, social stereotypes, and teacher expectations: Accuracy and the quest for the powerful self-fulfilling prophecy. In M. P. Zanna (Ed.), *Advances in experimental social psychology* (Vol. 28., pp. 281–388). San Diego, CA: Academic Press.

Jussim, L., Fleming, C. J., Coleman, L., & Kohberger, C. (1996). The nature of stereotypes: II. A multiple-process model of evaluations. *Journal of Applied Social Psychology, 26,* 283–312.

Kahn, K. F., & Goldberg, E. N. (1991). Women candidates in the news: An examination of gender difference in U.S. Senate campaign coverage. *Public Opinion Quarterly, 55,* 180–199.

Kanter, R. M. (1977). *Men and women of the corporation.* New York: Basic Books.

Karlins, M., Coffman, T. L., & Walters, G. (1969). On the fading of social stereotypes: Studies in three generations of college students. *Journal of Personality and Social Psychology, 13,* 1–16.

Karpinski, A., & von Hippel, W. (1996). The role of the linguistic intergroup bias in expectancy maintenance. *Social Cognition, 14,* 141–164.

Katz, D., & Braly, K. (1933). Racial stereotypes of one hundred undergraduates. *Journal of Abnormal and Social Psychology, 28,* 280–290.

Kaufmann, G. (1999). The portrayal of men's family roles in television commercials. *Sex Roles, 41,* 439–458.

Kawakami, K., Dion, K. L., & Dovidio, J. F. (1998). Racial prejudice and stereo-type activation. *Personality and Social Psychology Bulletin, 24,* 407–416.

Keenan, K. L. (1997). Skin tones and physical features of blacks in magazine advertisements. *Journalism and Mass Communication Quarterly, 73,* 905–912.

Keith, V. M., & Herring, C. (1991). Skin tone and stratification in the black com-munity. *American Journal of Sociology, 97,* 760–778.

Kemper, S. (1994). Elderspeak: Speech accommodations to older adults. *Aging and Cognition, 1,* 17–28.

Kemper, S., Finter-Urczyk, A., Ferrell, P., Harden, T., & Billington, C. (1998). Using elderspeak with older adults. *Discourse Processes, 25,* 55–73.

Kenny, D. A., & La Voie, L. (1984). The social relations model. In L. Berkowitz (Ed.), *Advances in experimental social psychology* (Vol. 18, pp. 141–182). San Diego, CA: Academic Press.

Kerwin, J., & Shaffer, D. R. (1994). Mock jurors versus mock juries: The role of deliberations in reactions to inadmissible testimony. *Personality and Social Psychology Bulletin, 20,* 153–162.

Kintsch, W. (1994). The psychology of discourse processing. In M. A. Gerns-bacher (Ed.), *Handbook of psycholinguistics* (pp. 721–739). San Diego, CA: Academic Press.

Kirkland, S. L., Greenberg, J., & Pyszczynski, T. (1987). Further evidence of the deleterious effects of overheard derogatory ethnic labels: Derogation be-yond the target. *Personality and Social Psychology Bulletin, 13,* 216–227.

Kochman, T. (1981). *Black and white: Styles in conflict.* Chicago: University of Chicago Press.

Kowalski, R. M. (2000). "I was only kidding!": Victims' and perpetrators' per-ceptions of teasing. *Personality and Social Psychology Bulletin, 26,* 231–241.

Kram, K. E. (1985). *Mentoring at work: Developmental relationships in organiza-tional life.* Glenview, IL: Scott, Foresman.

Krauss, R. M., & Chiu, C. (1998). Language and social behavior. In D. T. Gilbert, S. T. Fiske, & G. Lindzey (Eds.), *The handbook of social psychology* (Vol. 2, 4th ed., pp. 41–88). New York: Oxford University Press.

Krauss, R. M., & Fussell, S. R. (1991). Constructing shared communicative en-vironments. In L. B. Resnick, J. M. Levine, & S. D. Teasley (Eds.), *Perspec-tives on socially shared cognition* (pp. 172–200). Washington, DC: American Psychological Association.

Krosnick, J. A., Li, F., & Lehman, D. R. (1990). Conversational conventions, or-der of information acquisition, and the effect of base rates and individuat-ing information on social judgments. *Journal of Personality and Social Psy-chology, 59,* 1140–1152.

Kunda, Z., & Oleson, K. C. (1995). Maintaining stereotypes in the face of disconfirmation: Constructing grounds for subtyping deviants. *Journal of Personality and Social Psychology, 68,* 565–579.

Kunda, Z., & Oleson, K. C. (1997). When exceptions prove the rule: How ex-tremity of deviance determines the impact of deviant examples on stereo-types. *Journal of Personality and Social Psychology, 72,* 965–979.

Kurtz, P. D., Harrison, M., Neisworth, J. T., & Jones, R. T. (1977). Influence of "mentally retarded" label on teachers' nonverbal behavior toward preschool children. *American Journal of Mental Deficiency, 82,* 204–206.

Lafky, S., Duffy, M., Steinmaus, M., & Berkowitz, D. (1996). Looking through gendered lenses: Female stereotyping in advertisements and gender role expectations. *Journalism and Mass Communication Quarterly, 73,* 379–388.

LaFrance, M., & Woodzicky, J. A. (1998). No laughing matter: Women's verbal and nonverbal reactions to sexist humor. In J. K. Swim & C. Stangor (Eds.), *Prejudice: The target's perspective* (pp. 61–80). San Diego, CA: Academic Press.

Laks, D. R., Beckwith, L., & Cohen, S. E. (1990). Mothers' use of personal pronouns when talking with toddlers. *Journal of Genetic Psychology, 151,* 25–32.

Lamb, S., & Keon, S. (1995). Blaming the perpetrator: Language that distorts reality in newspaper articles on men battering women. *Psychology of Women Quarterly, 19,* 209–220.

Langlois, J. H., Roggman, L.A., & Rieser-Danner, L. A. (1990). Differential social responses to attractive and unattractive faces. *Developmental Psychology, 26,* 153–159.

Larson, J. R. (1986). Supervisor's performance feedback to subordinates: The impact of subordinate performance valence and outcome dependence. *Organizational Behavior and Human Decision Processes, 37,* 391–408.

Lass, N. J., Ruscello, D. M., Harkins, K. E., & Blankenship, B. L. (1993). A comparative study of adolescents' perceptions of normal-speaking and dysarthic children. *Journal of Communication Disorders, 26,* 3–12.

Latané, B., & L'Herrou, T. (1996). Spatial clustering in the conformity game: Dynamic social impact in electronic groups. *Journal of Personality and Social Psychology, 70,* 1218–1230.

Lavine, H., Sweeney, D., & Wagner, S. H. (1999). Depicting women as sex objects in television advertising: Effects on body dissatisfaction. *Personality and Social Psychology Bulletin, 25,* 1049–1058.

Leets, L., & Giles, H. (1997). Words as weapons—When do they wound?: Investigations of harmful speech. *Human Communication Research, 24,* 260–301.

Leyens, J. P., & Yzerbyt, V. Y. (1992). The ingroup overexclusion effect: Impact of valence and confirmation on stereotypic information search. *European Journal of Social Psychology, 22,* 549–569.

Liberman, A., & Chaiken, S. (1992). Defensive processing of personally relevant health messages. *Personality and Social Psychology Bulletin, 18,* 669–679.

Linville, P. W. (1982). The complexity–extremity effect and age-based stereotyping. *Journal of Personality and Social Psychology, 42,* 193–211.

Maass, A. (1999). Linguistic intergroup bias: Stereotype perpetuation through language. In M. P. Zanna (Ed.), *Advances in experimental social psychology* (Vol. 31, pp. 79–121). San Diego, CA: Academic Press.

Maass, A., Ceccarelli, R., & Rudin, S. (1996). Linguistic intergroup bias: Evidence for in-group-protective motivation. *Journal of Personality and Social Psychology, 71,* 512–526.

Maass, A., Corvino, P., & Arcuri, L. (1994). Linguistic intergroup bias and the mass media. *Revue Internationale de Psychologie Sociale, 1,* 31–43.

Maass, A., Milesi, A., Zabbini, S., & Stahlberg, D. (1995). Linguistic intergroup bias: Differential expectancies or in-group protection? *Journal of Personality and Social Psychology, 68,* 116–126.

Maass, A., Montalcini, F., & Biciotti, E. (1998). On the (dis-)confirmability of stereotypic attributes. *European Journal of Social Psychology, 28,* 383–402.

Maass, A., Salvi, D., Arcuri, L., & Semin, G. (1989). Language use in intergroup contexts: The linguistic intergroup bias. *Journal of Personality and Social Psychology, 57,* 981–993.

MacCoun, R. J. (1990). The emergence of extralegal bias during jury deliberation. *Criminal Justice and Behavior, 17,* 303–314.

Macrae, C. N., Milne, A. B., & Bodenhausen, G. V. (1994). Stereotypes as energy-saving devices: A peek inside the cognitive toolbox. *Journal of Personality and Social Psychology, 66,* 37–47.

Major, B. (1981). Gender patterns in touching behavior. In C. Mayo & N. M. Henley (Eds.), *Gender and nonverbal behavior* (pp. 15–37). New York: Springer-Verlag.

Major, B., Carrington, P. I., & Carnevale, P. (1984). Physical attractiveness and self-esteem: Attributions for praise from an other-sex evaluator. *Personality and Social Psychology Bulletin, 10,* 43–50.

Major, B., Schmidlin, A. M., & Williams, L. (1990). Gender patterns in social touch: The impact of setting and age. *Journal of Personality and Social Psychology, 58,* 634–643.

Majors, R. (1991). Nonverbal behaviors and communication styles among African Americans. In R. L. Jones (Ed.), *Black psychology* (3rd ed., pp. 269–294). Hampton, VA: Cobb & Henry.

Malpass, R. S., & Kravitz, J. (1969). Recognition for faces of own and other race. *Journal of Personality and Social Psychology, 13,* 330–334.

Manring, M. M. (1998). *Slave in a box: The strange career of Aunt Jemima.* Charlottesville: University Press of Virginia.

Marks, G., & Miller, N. (1987). Ten years of research on the false consensus effect: An empirical and theoretical review. *Psychological Bulletin, 102,* 72–90.

Marques, J. M., Yzerbyt, V. Y., & Leyens, J. P. (1988). The "black sheep effect": Extremity of judgments toward ingroup members as a function of group identification. *European Journal of Social Psychology, 18,* 1–16.

Martell, R. F., Lane, D. M., & Emrich, C. (1996). Male-female differences: A computer simulation. *American Psychologist, 51,* 157–158.

Martyna, W. (1978). What does "he" mean? *Journal of Communication, 28,* 131–138.

Matsuda, M. J., Lawrence, C. R., Delgado, R., & Crenshaw, K. W. (1993). *Words that wound.* Boulder, CO: Westview Press.

Matsumoto, D. (1998). *Cross-cultural psychology to a cultural psychology: The impact of culture.* Paper presented at the annual meeting of the Southeastern Psychological Society, Mobile, AL.

Mauer, K. L., Park, B., & Rothbart, M. (1995). Subtyping versus subgrouping processes in stereotype representation. *Journal of Personality and Social Psychology, 69,* 812–824.

Mazingo, S. (1988). Minorities and social control in the newsroom: Thirty years after Breed. In G. Smitherman-Donaldson & T. A. van Dijk (Eds.), *Dis-*

course and discrimination (pp. 93–130). Detroit, MI: Wayne State University Press.

McCaul, K. D., Branstetter, A. D., Schroeder, D. M., & Glasgow, R. E. (1996). What is the relationship between breast cancer risk and mammography screening?: A meta-analytic review. *Health Psychology, 15,* 423–429.

McConahay, J. B. (1986). Modern racism, ambivalence, and the modern racism scale. In J. F. Dovidio & S. L. Gaertner (Eds.), *Prejudice, discrimination, and racism* (pp. 91–125). New York: Academic Press.

McConnell, A. R., & Fazio, R. H. (1996). Women as men and people: Effects of gender-marked language. *Personality and Social Psychology Bulletin, 22,* 1004–1013.

McDaniel, E., & Andersen, P. A. (1998). International patterns of interpersonal tactile communication: A field study. *Journal of Nonverbal Behavior, 22,* 59–75.

McGinley, H., Blau, G. L., & Takai, M. (1984). Attraction effects of smiling and body position: A cultural comparison. *Perceptual and Motor Skills, 58,* 915–922.

McGuire, W. J. (1968). Theory of the structure of human thought. In R. P. Abelson, E. Aronson, W. J. McGuire, T. M. Newcomb, M. J. Rosenberg, & P. H. Tannebaum (Eds.), *Theories of cognitive consistency: A sourcebook* (pp. 140–162). Chicago: Rand McNally.

McGuire, W. J., & McGuire, C. V. (1986). Differences in conceptualizing self versus conceptualizing other people as manifested in contrasting verb types used in natural speech. *Journal of Personality and Social Psychology, 51,* 1135–1143.

McLaughlin, T. L., & Goulet, N. (1999). Gender advertisements in magazines aimed at African Americans: A comparison to their occurrence in magazines aimed at Caucasians. *Sex Roles, 40,* 61–71.

Mehrabian, A. (1968). Inference of attitudes from the posture, orientation, and distance of a communicator. *Journal of Consulting and Clinical Psychology, 32,* 296–308.

Merritt, R. D., & Kok, C. J. (1997). Implications of the people = male theory for the interpretation of the Draw-a-Person Test. *Journal of Personality Assessment, 68,* 211–214.

Milich, R., McAninch, C. B., & Harris, M. J. (1992). Effects of stigmatizing information on children's peer relations: Believing is seeing. *School Psychology Review, 21,* 400–409.

Miller, C. T., Rothblum, E. D., Felicio, D., & Brand, P. (1995). Compensating for stigma: Obese and nonobese women's reactions to being visible. *Personality and Social Psychology Bulletin, 21,* 1093–1106.

Mininni, G., & Annese, S. (1997). News discourse features and adolescent identity: A diatextual analysis. *International Journal of Psycholinguistics, 13,* 5–23.

Moghaddam, F. M., Taylor, D. M., & Wright, S. C. (1993). *Social psychology in cross-cultural perspective.* New York: Freeman.

Monteith, M. J., Sherman, J. W., & Devine, P. G. (1998). Suppression as a stereotype control strategy. *Personality and Social Psychology Review, 2,* 63–82.

Moreland, R. L., & Levine, J. M. (1982). Socialization in small groups: Temporal changes in individual–group relations. In L. Berkowitz (Ed.), *Advances in experimental social psychology* (Vol. 15, pp. 137–192). New York: Academic Press.

Mulac, A., & Giles, H. (1996). You're only as old as you sound: Perceived vocal age and social meanings. *Health Communication, 8,* 199–215.

Mullen, B. (1991). Group composition, salience, and cognitive representations: The phenomenology of being in a group. *Journal of Experimental Social Psychology, 27,* 297–323.

Mullen, B., & Hu, L. (1989). Perceptions of ingroup and outgroup variability: A meta-analytic integration. *Basic and Applied Social Psychology, 10,* 233–252.

Mullen, B., & Johnson, C. (1990). Distinctiveness-based illusory correlations and stereotyping: A meta-analytic integration. *British Journal of Social Psychology, 29,* 11–27.

Mullen, B., & Johnson, C. (1993). Cognitive representation in ethnophaulisms as a function of group size: The phenomenology of being in a group. *Personality and Social Psychology Bulletin, 19,* 296–304.

Mullen, B., Rozell, D., & Johnson, C. (1996). The phenomenology of being in a group: Complexity approaches to operationalizing cognitive representation. In J. L. Nye & A. M. Brower (Eds.), *What's social about social cognition?* (pp. 205–229). Thousand Oaks, CA: Sage.

Myrick, R. (1998). AIDS discourse: A critical reading of mainstream press surveillance of marginal identity. *Journal of Homosexuality, 35,* 75–93.

Neuberg, S. L., & Fiske, S. T. (1987). Motivational influences on impression formation: Outcome dependency, accuracy-driven attention, and individuating processes. *Journal of Personality and Social Psychology, 53,* 431–444.

Neuliep, J. W. (1997). A cross-cultural comparison of teacher immediacy in American and Japanese college classrooms. *Communication Research, 24,* 431–451.

Nevo, O. (1985). Does one ever really laugh at one's own expense?: The case of Jews and Arabs in Israel. *Journal of Personality and Social Psychology, 49,* 799–807.

Newcomb, W. T. (1961). *The acquaintance process.* New York: Holt.

Ng, S. H., Bell, D., & Brooke, M. (1993). Gaining turns and achieving high influence ranking in small conversational groups. *British Journal of Social Psychology, 32,* 265–275.

Ng, S. H., & Bradac, J. (1993). *Power in language.* Newbury Park, CA: Sage.

Ng, S. H., & Chan, K. K. (1996). Biases in the description of various age groups: A linguistic category model analysis. *Bulletin of the Hong Kong Psychological Society, 36–37,* 5–20.

Nielsen, M. E, & Miller, C. E. (1997). The transmission of norms regarding decision rules. *Personality and Social Psychology Bulletin, 23,* 516–525.

Nisbett, R. E., & Wilson, T. D. (1977). Telling more than we know: Verbal reports on mental processes. *Psychological Review, 84,* 231–259.

Nisbett, R. E., Zukier, H., & Lemley, R. E. (1981). The dilution effect: Nondiagnostic information weakens the implications of diagnostic information. *Cognitive Psychology, 13,* 248–277.

Öhlschlegel, S., & Piontkowski, U. (1997). Topic progression and social categorization. *Journal of Language and Social Psychology, 16,* 444–455.

O'Neal, E. C., Kipnis, D., & Craig, K. M. (1994). Effects on the persuader of employing a coercive influence technique. *Basic and Applied Social Psychology, 15,* 225–238.

O'Neal, E. C., & Taylor, S. L. (1989). Status of the provoker, opportunity to retaliate, and interest in video violence. *Aggressive Behavior, 15,* 171–180.

Osterhout, L., Bersick, M., & McLaughlin, J. (1997). Brain potentials reflect violations of gender stereotypes. *Memory and Cognition, 5,* 273–285.

Ostrom, T. M., & Sedikides, C. (1992). Out-group homogeneity effects in natural and minimal groups. *Psychological Bulletin, 112,* 536–552.

Park, B., & Judd, C. M. (1989). Agreement on initial impressions: Differences due to perceivers, trait dimensions, and target behaviors. *Journal of Personality and Social Psychology, 56,* 493–505.

Park, B., & Rothbart, M. (1982). Perception of out-group homogeneity and levels of social categorization: Memory for the subordinate attributes of in-group and out-group members. *Journal of Personality and Social Psychology, 42,* 1051–1068.

Patterson, C. J. (1992). Children of lesbian and gay parents. *Child Development, 63,* 1025–1042.

Patterson, M. L. (1996). Social behavior and social cognition: A parallel process approach. In J. L. Nye & A. M. Brower (Eds.), *What's social about social cognition?* (pp. 87–105). Thousand Oaks, CA: Sage.

Peirce, K., & McBride, M. (1999). Aunt Jemima isn't keeping up with the Energizer bunny: Stereotyping of animated spokes-characters in advertising. *Sex Roles, 40,* 959–968.

Pendry, L. F., & Macrae, C. N. (1994). Stereotypes and mental life: The case of the motivated but thwarted tactician. *Journal of Experimental Social Psychology, 30,* 303–325.

Pennington, N., & Hastie, R. (1992). Explaining the evidence: Tests of the Story Model for juror decision making. *Journal of Personality and Social Psychology, 62,* 189–206.

Perdue, C. W., Dovidio, J. F., Gurtman, M. B., & Tyler, R. B. (1990). Us and them: Social categorization and the process of intergroup bias. *Journal of Personality and Social Psychology, 59,* 475–486.

Pettigrew, T. F. (1979). The ultimate attribution error: Extending Allport's cognitive analysis of prejudice. *Personality and Social Psychology Bulletin, 5,* 461–476.

Petty, R. E., & Wegener, D. T. (1998). Attitude change: Multiple roles for persuasion variables. In D. T. Gilbert, S. T. Fiske, & G. Lindzey (Eds.), *The handbook of social psychology* (Vol. 2, pp. 323–390). New York: Oxford University Press.

Pingree, S., Hawkins, R. P., Butler, M., & Paisley, W. (1976). A scale of sexism. *Journal of Communication, 26,* 193–200.

Pratto, F., Sidanius, J., Stallworth, L. M., & Malle, B. E. (1994). Social dominance orientation: A personality variable predicting social and political attitudes. *Journal of Personality and Social Psychology, 67,* 741–763.

Pratto, F., Stallworth, L. M., Sidanius, J., & Siers, B. (1997). The gender gap in occupational role attainment: A social dominance approach. *Journal of Personality and Social Psychology, 72,* 37–53.

Prentice, D. A. (1994). Do language reforms change our way of thinking? *Journal of Language and Social Psychology, 13,* 3–19.

Purnell, T., Idsardi, W., & Baugh, J. (1999). Perceptual and phonetic experiments on American English dialect identification. *Journal of Language and Social Psychology, 18,* 10–30.

Qualls, W. J., & Moore, D. J. (1990). Stereotyping effects on consumers' evaluation of advertising: Impact of racial differences between actors and viewers. *Psychology and Marketing, 7,* 135–151.

Quigley, B. M., Johnson, A. B., & Bryne, D. (1995). *Mock jury sentencing decisions: A meta-analysis of the attractiveness–leniency effect.* Paper presented at the annual meeting of the American Psychological Society, New York.

Roberts, C., Davies, E., & Jupp, T. (1992). *Language and discrimination: A study of communication in multi-ethnic workplaces.* London: Longman.

Robinson, J. D., & Skill, T. (1995). The invisible generation: Portrayals of the elderly on prime-time television. *Communication Reports, 8,* 111–119.

Rogan, R. G., & Hammer, M. R. (1998). An exploratory study of message affect behavior: A comparison between African Americans and Euro-Americans. *Journal of Language and Social Psychology, 17,* 449–464.

Ross, K., & Sreberny-Mohammadi, A. (1997). Playing house: Gender, politics, and the news media in Britain. *Media, Culture, and Society, 19,* 101–109.

Ross, L., Amabile, T. M., & Steinmetz, J. L. (1977). Social roles, social control and biases in social-perception processes. *Journal of Personality and Social Psychology, 35,* 485–494.

Rothbart, M., & Hallmark, W. (1988). In-group-out-group differences in the perceived efficacy of coercion and conciliation in resolving social conflict. *Journal of Personality and Social Psychology, 55,* 248–257.

Rothbart, M., & Park, B. (1986). On the confirmability and disconfirmability of trait concepts. *Journal of Personality and Social Psychology, 50,* 131–142.

Rubovits, P. C., & Maehr, M. L. (1973). Pygmalion black and white. *Journal of Personality and Social Psychology, 25,* 210–218.

Rudolph, U. (1997). Implicit verb causality: Verbal schemas and covariation information. *Journal of Language and Social Psychology, 16,* 132–158.

Rumble, A., & Cash, T. F. (2000). *Beauty versus the beast: Images of good and evil in children's animation films.* Poster presented at the annual meeting of the Society of Personality and Social Psychology, Nashville, TN.

Ruscher, J. B. (1998). Prejudice and stereotyping in everyday communication In M. P. Zanna (Ed.), *Advances in experimental social psychology* (Vol. 30, pp. 241–307). San Diego, CA: Academic Press.

Ruscher, J. B., Beal, D. J., & Schnake, S. B. (1999). *Intergroup bias in conversational conventions as a function of modern racism.* Unpublished raw data. Tulane University, New Orleans, LA.

Ruscher, J. B., Cralley, E. L., & O'Farrell, K. J. (1999). *Interpersonal cohesion encourages shared stereotypic impressions.* Contribution to a symposium, "Stereotypes as Consensually Shared Structures," Society of Experimental Social Psychology, St. Louis, MO.

Ruscher, J. B., & Duval, L. L. (1998). Multiple communicators with unique target information transmit less stereotypical impressions. *Journal of Personality and Social Psychology, 74,* 329–344.

Ruscher, J. B., & Fiske, S. T. (1990). Interpersonal competition can cause individuating processes. *Journal of Personality and Social Psychology, 58,* 832–843.

Ruscher, J. B., & Hammer, E. D. (1994). Revising disrupted impressions through conversation. *Journal of Personality and Social Psychology, 66,* 530–541.

Ruscher, J. B., Hammer, E. Y., & Hammer, E. D. (1996). Forming shared impressions through conversation: An adaptation of the Continuum Model. *Personality and Social Psychology Bulletin, 22,* 705–720.

Ruscher, J. B., & Hurley, M. M. (2000). Off-target verbosity evokes negative stereotypes of the elderly. *Journal of Language and Social Psychology, 19,* 139–147.

Ryan, E. B., Hewstone, M., & Giles, H. (1984). Language and intergroup attitudes. In J. R. Eiser (Ed.), *Attitudinal judgment* (pp. 135–158). New York: Springer-Verlag.

Sachdev, I., & Bourhis, R. Y. (1985). Social categorization and power differentials in group relations. *European Journal of Social Psychology, 15,* 415–434.

Sachdev, I., & Bourhis, R. Y. (1990). Bilinguality and multilinguality. In H. Giles & W. P. Robinson (Eds.), *Handbook of language and social psychology* (pp. 293–308). New York: Wiley.

Sanders, J. A., & Wiseman, R. L. (1990). The effects of verbal and nonverbal teacher immediacy on perceived cognitive, affective, and behavioral learning in the multicultural classroom. *Communication Education, 39,* 341–353.

Schacter, S., Christenfeld, N. J. S., Ravina, B., & Bilous, F. (1991). Speech disfluency and the structure of knowledge. *Journal of Personality and Social Psychology, 60,* 362–367.

Schaller, M., & Conway, L. G. (1999). Influence of impression-management goals on the emerging contents of group stereotypes: Support for a social-evolutionary process. *Personality and Social Psychology Bulletin, 25,* 819–833.

Schaller, M., & Latané, B. (1996). Dynamic social impact and the evolution of social representations: A natural history of stereotypes. *Journal of Communication, 46,* 64–77.

Schimel, J., Simon, L., Greenberg, J., Pyszczynski, T., Solomon, S., Waxmonsky, J., & Arndt, J. (1999). Stereotypes and terror management: Evidence that mortality salience enhances stereotypic thinking and preferences. *Journal of Personality and Social Psychology, 77,* 905–926.

Schnake, S. B. (1998). *The subtle communication of prejudice in speech to outgroup members.* Unpublished doctoral dissertation, Tulane University, New Orleans, LA.

Schnake, S. B., & Ruscher, J. B. (1998). Modern racism as a predictor of the linguistic intergroup bias. *Journal of Language and Social Psychology, 17,* 486–493.

Schnake, S. B., Ruscher, J. B., Gratz, K. L., & O'Neal, E. C. (1997). Measure for

measure?: Male retaliation commensurate with anger depends on provo-
cateur gender and aggression covertness. *Journal of Social Behavior and Personality, 12,* 937–954.

Schneider, M. E., Major, B., Luhtanen, R., & Crocker, J. (1996). Social stigma and
the potential costs of assumptive help. *Personality and Social Psychology
Bulletin, 22,* 201–209.

Schwarz, N. (1994). Judgment in social context: Biases, shortcomings, and the
logic of conversation. In M. P. Zanna (Ed.), *Advances in experimental social
psychology* (Vol. 26, pp. 123–162). San Diego, CA: Academic Press.

Schwarz, N., & Kurz, E. (1989). What's in a picture?: The impact of face-ism on
trait attribution. *European Journal of Social Psychology, 19,* 311–319.

Semin, G. R., & Fiedler, K. (1988). The cognitive functions of linguistic categories in describing persons: Social cognition and language. *Journal of Personality and Social Psychology, 54,* 558–568.

Sidanius, J., Liu, J. H., Shaw, J. S., & Pratto, F. (1994). Social dominance orientation, hierarchy attenuators and hierarchy enhancers: Social dominance
theory and the criminal justice system. *Journal of Applied Social Psychology,
24,* 338–366.

Sidanius, J., Pratto, F., & Bobo, L. (1994). Social dominance orientation and the
political psychology of gender: A case of invariance? *Journal of Personality
and Social Psychology, 67,* 998–1011.

Sidanius, J., Pratto, F., & Bobo, L. (1996). Racism, conversativism, affirmative
action, and intellectual sophistication: A matter of principled conservatism or group dominance. *Journal of Personality and Social Psychology, 70,*
476–490.

Sidanius, J., Pratto, F., & Brief, D. (1995). Group dominance and the political
psychology of gender: A cross-cultural comparison. *Political Psychology,
16,* 381–396.

Sillars, A., Shellen, W., McIntosh, A., & Pomegranate, M. (1997). Relational
characteristics of language: Elaboration and differentiation in marital conversations. *Western Journal of Communication, 61,* 403–422.

Simpson, A. W., & Erickson, M. T. (1983). Teachers' verbal and nonverbal communication as a function of teacher race, student gender, and student
race. *American Educational Research Journal, 20,* 183–198.

Skowronski, J. J., & Carlston, D. E. (1987). Social judgment and social memory:
The role of cue diagnosticity in negativity, positivity, and extremity biases. *Journal of Personality and Social Psychology, 52,* 689–699.

Smeltzer, L. R., & Leap, T. L. (1988). An analysis of individual reactions to potentially offensive jokes in work settings. *Human Relations, 41,* 295–304.

Smith, S. M., McIntosh, W. D., & Bazzini, D. G. (1999). Are the beautiful good
in Hollywood?: An investigation of the beauty-and-goodness stereotype
on film. *Basic and Applied Social Psychology, 21,* 69–80.

Smitherman-Donaldson, G. (1988). Discriminatory discourse on Afro-Ameri-
can speech. In G. Smitherman-Donaldson & T. A. van Dijk (Eds.), *Discourse and discrimination* (pp. 144–175). Detroit, MI: Wayne State University Press.

Snow, C. E., van Eeden, R., & Muysken, P. (1981). The interactional origins of foreigner talk: Municipal employees and foreign workers. *International Journal of the Sociology of Language, 28,* 81–91.

Snyder, M., & Haugen, J. A. (1995). Why does behavioral confirmation occur?: A functional perspective on the role of the target. *Personality and Social Psychology Bulletin, 21,* 963–974.

Snyder, M., & Miene, P. (1994). On the functions of stereotypes and prejudice. In M. P. Zanna & J. M. Olson (Eds.), *The Ontario Symposium: Vol. 7. The psychology of prejudice.* (pp. 33–54). Hillsdale, NJ: Erlbaum.

Spencer, S. J., Steele, C. M., & Quinn, D. M. (1999). Stereotype threat and women's math performance. *Journal of Experimental Social Psychology, 35,* 4–28.

Spender, D. (1980). *Man made language.* London: Routledge & Kegan Paul.

St. John, E. (1998). Newsroom power shortage. *Black Issues in Higher Education, 38,* 38–40.

Stangor, C., Sechrist, G. B., & Jost, J. T. (in press). Changing racial beliefs by providing consensus motivation. *Personality and Social Psychology Bulletin.*

Stasser, G., Taylor, L. A., & Hanna, C. (1989). Information sampling in structured and unstructured discussions of three- and six-person groups. *Journal of Personality and Social Psychology, 57,* 67–78.

Steele, C. (1992). Race and the schooling of Black Americans. *The Atlantic, 260,* 68–78.

Stewart, M. A., Ryan, E. B., & Giles, H. (1985). Accent and social class effects on status and solidarity evaluations. *Personality and Social Psychology Bulletin, 11,* 98–105.

Stier, D. S., & Hall, J. A. (1984). Gender differences in touch: An empirical and theoretical review. *Journal of Personality and Social Psychology, 47,* 440–459.

Storrs, D., & Kleinke, C. L. (1990). Evaluation of high and equal status male touchers. *Journal of Nonverbal Behavior, 14,* 87–95.

Street, R. L. (1990). The communicative function of paralanguage and prosody. In H. Giles & W. P. Robinson (Eds.), *Handbook of language and social psychology* (pp. 121–140). Chichester, West Sussex, UK: Wiley.

Swann, W. B., Jr. (1990). To be adored or to be known?: The interplay of self-enhancement and self-verification. In R. M. Sorrentino & E. T. Higgins (Eds.), *Handbook of motivation and cognition: Foundations of social behavior* (Vol. 2, pp. 408–448). New York: Guilford Press.

Swim, J. K., & Hyers, L. L. (1999). Excuse me—What did you just say?!: Women's public and private responses to sexist remarks. *Journal of Experimental Social Psychology, 35,* 68–88.

Tajfel, H., & Turner, J. C. (1979). An integrative theory of intergroup conflict. In W. G. Austin & S. Worchel (Eds.), *The social psychology of intergroup relations* (pp. 33–50). Pacific Grove, CA: Brooks/Cole.

Taylor, C. R., & Stern, B. B. (1997). Asian-Americans: Television advertising and the "model minority" stereotype. *Journal of Advertising, 26,* 47–61.

Taylor, D. M., & Jaggi, V. (1974). Ethnocentrism and causal attribution in a South Indian context. *Journal of Cross-Cultural Psychology, 5,* 162–171.

Taylor, D. M., Wright, S. C., & Porter, L. E. (1994). Dimensions of perceived discrimination: The personal/group discrimination discrepancy. In M. P.

Zanna & J. M. Olson (Eds.), *The Ontario Symposium: Vol. 7. The psychology of prejudice* (pp. 233–256). Hillsdale, NJ: Erlbaum.

Taylor, M. C. (1979). Race, sex, and the expression of self-fulfilling prophecies in a laboratory teaching situation. *Journal of Personality and Social Psychology, 37,* 897–912.

Taylor, S. E., Brown, J. D. (1988). Illusion and well-being: A social psychological perspective on mental health. *Psychological Bulletin, 103,* 193–210.

Tetlock, P. E. (1983). Accountability and the perseverance of first impressions. *Social Psychology Quarterly, 46,* 285–292.

Tetlock, P. E., & Boettger, R. (1989). Accountability: A social magnifier of the dilution effect. *Journal of Personality and Social Psychology, 57,* 388–398.

Tetlock, P. E., & Kim, J. I. (1987). Accountability and judgment processes in a personality prediction task. *Journal of Personality and Social Psychology, 52,* 700–709.

Tetlock, P. E., Sitka, L., & Boettger, R. (1989). Social and cognitive strategies for coping with accountability: Conformity, complexity, and bolstering. *Journal of Personality and Social Psychology, 57,* 632–640.

Thomas, D. A. (1990). The impact of race on managers' experiences of developmental relationships (mentoring and sponsorship): An intra-organizational study. *Journal of Organizational Behavior, 11,* 479–492.

Thompson, L. L., & Crocker, J. (1990). Downward social comparison in the minimal intergroup situation: A test of a self-enhancement interpretation. *Journal of Applied Social Psychology, 20,* 1166–1184.

Turner, M. E., Pratkanis, A. R., Probasco, P., & Leve, C. (1992). Threat, cohesion, and group effectiveness: Testing a social identity maintenance perspective on groupthink. *Journal of Personality and Social Psychology, 63,* 781–796.

Tversky, A., & Kahneman, D. (1981). The framing of decisions and the psychology of choice. *Science, 211,* 453–458.

Valdman, A. (1981). Sociolinguistic aspects of foreigner talk. *International Journal of the Sociology of Language, 28,* 41–52.

Valencia, J., Gil de Montes, L., Arruti, I., & Carbonell, A. (1998). El sesgo lingueístico intergrupal: El efecto de la valencia de las categorías lingueísticas [The linguistic intergroup bias: The effect of valence of the linguistic categories]. *Revista de Psicología Social, 13,* 117–127.

Vallacher, R. R., & Wegner, D. M. (1987). What do people think they're doing?: Action identification and human behavior. *Psychological Review, 94,* 3–15.

Vallacher, R. R., Wegner, D. M., McMahan, S. C., Cotter, J., & Larsen, K. A. (1992). On winning friends and influencing people: Action identification and self-presentation of success. *Social Cognition, 10,* 335–355.

van Bezooijen, R., & Gooskens, C. (1999). Identification of language varieties: The contribution of different linguistic levels. *Journal of Language and Social Psychology, 18,* 31–48.

van Dijk, T. A. (1984). *Prejudice in discourse: An analysis of ethnic prejudices in cognition and conversation.* Amsterdam & Philadelophia: Benjamins.

van Dijk, T. A. (1987). *Communicating racism.* Newbury Park, CA: Sage.

van Dijk, T. A. (1988). How "they" hit the headlines: Ethnic minorities in the press. In G. Smitherman-Donaldson & T. A. van Dijk (Eds.), *Discourse and discrimination* (pp. 221–262). Detroit, MI: Wayne State University Press.

van Dijk, T. A. (1990). Social cognition and discourse. In H. Giles & W. P. Robinson (Eds.), *Handbook of language and social psychology* (pp. 163–183). Chichester, West Sussex, UK: Wiley.

Vanman, E. J., Paul, B. Y., Ito, T. A., & Miller, N. (1997). The modern face of prejudice and structural features that moderate the effect of cooperation on affect. *Journal of Personality and Social Psychology, 73,* 941–959.

Verkuyten, M. (1996). Personal self-esteem and prejudice among ethnic majority and minority youth. *Journal of Research in Personality, 30,* 248–263.

Vinokur, A., & Burnstein, E. (1974). Effects of partially shared persuasive arguments on group-induced shifts: A group problem solving approach. *Journal of Personality and Social Psychology, 29,* 305–315.

von Hippel, W., Sekaquaptewa, D., & Vargas, P. (1997). The linguistic intergroup bias as an implicit indicator of prejudice. *Journal of Experimental Social Psychology, 33,* 490–509.

Vrij, A., Dragt, A., & Koppelaar, L. (1992). Interviews with ethnic interviewees: Non-verbal communication errors in impression formation. *Journal of Community and Applied Social Psychology, 2,* 199–208.

Walker, S. (1994). *Hate speech: The history of an American controversy.* Lincoln: University of Nebraska Press.

Wann, D. L., Schrader, M. P., Allison, J. A., & McGeorge, K. K. (1998). The inequitable newspaper coverage of men's and women's athletics at small, medium, and large universities. *Journal of Sport and Social Issues, 22,* 79–87.

Webster, D. M., Kruglanski, A. W., & Pattison, D. A. (1997). Motivated language use in intergroup contexts: Need for closure effects on the linguistic intergroup bias. *Journal of Personality and Social Psychology, 72,* 1122–1131.

Wegner, D. M. (1987). Transactive memory: A contemporary analysis of the group mind. In B. Mullen & G. R. Goethals (Eds.), *Theories of group behavior* (pp. 185–208). New York: Springer-Verlag.

Wegner, D. M., Wenzlaff, R., Kerker, R. M., & Beattie, A. E. (1981). Incrimination through innuendo: Can media questions become public answers? *Journal of Personality and Social Psychology, 40,* 822–832.

Weinberg, M. (Ed.). (1970). Strivings of the negro people. In *W. E. B. DuBois: A reader.* New York: Harper & Row.

Whittler, T. E. (1991). The effects of actors' race in commercial advertising. *Journal of Advertising, 20*(1), 55–60.

Whittler, T. E., & Dimes, J. (1991). Viewers' reactions to racial cues in advertising stimuli. *Journal of Advertising Research, 31*(6), 37–46.

Whorf, B. L. (1957). *Language, thought, and reality.* Cambridge, MA: MIT Press.

Wigboldus, D. H. J., Semin, G. R., & Spears, R. (2000). How do we communicate stereotypes?: Linguistic bases and inferential consequences. *Journal of Personality and Social Psychology, 78,* 5–18.

Wilder, D. A. (1981). Perceiving persons as a group: Categorization and intergroup relations. In D. L. Hamilton (Ed.), *Cognitive processes in stereotyping and intergroup behavior* (pp. 213–258). Hillsdale, NJ: Erlbaum.

Wilkes, R. E., & Valencia, H. (1989). Hispanics and blacks in television commercials. *Journal of Advertising, 18*(1), 19–25.

Willson, A., & Lloyd, B., (1990). Gender vs. power: Self-posed behavior revisited. *Sex Roles, 23,* 91–98.

Wilson, R. G., Hart A., & Dawes, P. J. (1988). Mastectomy or conservation: The patient's choice. *British Medical Journal, 297,* 1167–1169.

Winkel, F. W. (1990). Crime reporting in the newspapers: An exploratory study of the effects of ethnic references in crime news. *Social Behaviour, 5,* 87–101.

Winkel, F. W., & Vrij, A. (1990). Interaction and impression formation in a cross-cultural dyad: Frequency and meaning of culturally determined gaze in a police interview setting. *Social Behaviour, 5,* 335–350.

Wittenbaum, G. M., Hubbell, A. P., & Zuckerman, C. (1999). Mutual enhancement: Toward an understanding of the collective preference for shared information. *Journal of Personality and Social Psychology, 77,* 967–978.

Woolfson, P. (1991). Aspects of non-verbal accommodation to language in a bilingual Montreal hospital setting. *Journal of Linguistic Anthropology, 1,* 178–188.

Word, C. O., Zanna, M. P., & Cooper, J. (1974). The nonverbal mediation of self-fulfilling prophecies in interracial interaction. *Journal of Experimental Social Psychology, 10,* 109–120.

Wyer, R. S., Jr., & Collins, J. E. (1992). A theory of humor elicitation. *Psychological Review, 99,* 663–688.

Wyer, R. S., Jr., & Gruenfeld, D. H. (1995). Information processing in social contexts: Implications for social memory and judgment. In M. P. Zanna (Ed.), *Advances in experimental social psychology* (Vol. 27, pp. 49–91). San Diego, CA: Academic Press.

Zebrowitz, L. A., Brownlow, S., & Olson, K. (1992). Baby talk to the babyfaced. *Journal of Nonverbal Behavior, 16,* 143–158.

Zuber, J. A., Crott, H. W., & Werner, J. (1992). Choice shift and group polarization: An analysis of the status of arguments and social decision schemas. *Journal of Personality and Social Psychology, 62,* 50–61.

Zuckerman, M. (1986). On the meaning and implications of facial prominence. *Journal of Nonverbal Behavior, 10,* 215–229.

Zuckerman, M., & Kieffer, S. C. (1994). Race differences in face-ism: Does facial prominence imply dominance? *Journal of Personality and Social Psychology, 66,* 86–92.

Index

237

CPSIA information can be obtained at www.ICGtesting.com
Printed in the USA
BVOW08*1114130715

407331BV00001B/1/P